AF251738

# UNDERSTANDING POLITICAL PARTICIPATION

# Understanding Political Participation

## Green Party Membership in Scotland

LYNN BENNIE
*University of Aberdeen, UK*

**ASHGATE**

© Lynn Bennie 2004

All rights reserved. No part of this publication may be reproduced, stored in a retrieval system or transmitted in any form or by any means, electronic, mechanical, photocopying, recording or otherwise without the prior permission of the publisher.

Published by
Ashgate Publishing Limited
Gower House
Croft Road
Aldershot
Hants GU11 3HR
England

Ashgate Publishing Company
Suite 420
101 Cherry Street
Burlington, VT 05401-4405
USA

Ashgate website: http://www.ashgate.com

**British Library Cataloguing in Publication Data**
Bennie, Lynn G.
Understanding political participation : Green Party membership in Scotland
1. Green Party. Scottish Green Party 2. Party affiliation - Scotland 3. Political participation - Scotland 4. Green movement - Scotland - History
I. Title
324.2'411087

**Library of Congress Cataloging-in-Publication Data**
Bennie, Lynn G.
Understanding political participation : Green Party membership in Scotland / by Lynn Bennie.
p. cm.
Includes bibliographical references and index.
ISBN 0-7546-1723-8
1. Scottish Green Party--Membership. 2. Political parties--Scotland. 3. Political participation--Scotland. 4. Scotland--Politics and government--20th century. I. Title.

JN1371.S37B46 2004
324.241'0987'09411--dc22

2004015069

ISBN 0 7546 1723 8

Printed and bound in Great Britain by MPG Books Ltd, Bodmin, Cornwall

# Contents

# List of Tables

# List of Figures

# Acknowledgements

I would like to take this opportunity to thank some of the people who have supported me over the years. First, Wolfgang Rüdig for giving me my first academic post as Research Assistant on a study of the British Greens and for developing my understanding of green parties. Without him, this book would not exist. Second, Gavin Corbett and others in the Scottish Green Party for their invaluable help with the surveys and documenting the party's history. Third, my friends and colleagues at Aberdeen University who have helped in so many ways. Finally, those nearest and dearest to me; namely my partner Fraser, my mother Ellen, my brother David, and my late father William. Last but definitely not least Cathryn, who entered the world as the final manuscript made its way to Ashgate, and who to me is proof that nature is wonderful.

# List of Abbreviations

| | |
|---|---|
| AMS | Additional Member System |
| BBC | British Broadcasting Corporation |
| BSA | British Social Attitudes |
| CND | Campaign for Nuclear Disarmament |
| DMR | Direct Marketing Recruit |
| ESRC | Economic and Social Research Council |
| EU | European Union |
| FoE | Friends of the Earth |
| GDP | Gross Domestic Product |
| GM | Genetic Modification |
| MORI | Market and Opinion Research International |
| MP | Member of Parliament |
| MSP | Member of the Scottish Parliament |
| NAMBI | Not Affecting My Best Interests |
| NATO | North Atlantic Treaty Organisation |
| NGO | Non-Governmental Organisation |
| NHS | National Health Service |
| NIMBY | Not In My Back Yard |
| NSM | New Social Movement |
| NSPCC | National Society for the Prevention of Cruelty to Children |
| OFFTB | Organic Food and Farming Targets Bill |
| PEB | Party Election Broadcast |
| POS | Political Opportunity Structure |
| PPC | Prospective Parliamentary Candidate |
| PPP | Public Private Partnership |
| PR | Proportional Representation |
| RMT | Resource Mobilisation Theory |
| RSPB | Royal Society for the Protection of Birds |
| RSPCA | Royal Society for the Prevention of Cruelty to Animals |
| SANE | Scotland Against Nuclear Expansion |
| SCRAM | Scottish Campaign to Resist the Atomic Menace |
| SCUP | Scottish Conservative and Unionist Party |
| SDP | Social Democratic Party |
| SGP | Scottish Green Party |
| SLD | Social and Liberal Democrats |
| SMO | Social Movement Organisation |
| SNP | Scottish National Party |
| SNR | Social Network Recruit |
| SSA | Scottish Socialist Alliance |
| SSP | Scottish Socialist Party |

| | |
|---|---|
| STV | Single Transferable Vote |
| TAGS | Towards a Green Scotland |
| UK | United Kingdom |
| USA/US | United States of America |
| WWF | World Wildlife Fund |

# Chapter 1

# Introduction

Green parties are becoming increasingly prominent in modern western democracies. Consequently, much has been written on the green party phenomenon, most studies concentrating on explaining the electoral fortunes of such parties, either in case study form or through comparative analysis of green parties (Franklin and Rüdig 1992, 1995; Kitschelt 1988; Müller-Rommel 1982, 1989, 1998; O'Neill 1997; Parkin 1989; Richardson and Rootes 1995; Rüdig 1985, 1992; Rüdig and Franklin 1992). More recent accounts, however, have focused on the challenges faced by green parties in government and opposition (Bomberg 2002; Burchell 2001, 2002; Doherty 2002; Mair 2001; Müller-Rommel and Poguntke 2002; Rüdig 2002; Talshir 2002). A small number of studies have examined membership and activism in green parties (Kitschelt and Hellemans 1990; Poguntke 1990; Prendiville and Chafer 1990; Rüdig *et al.* 1991, 1993, 1996). However, very little attention has been given to the question of why individuals are recruited into and devote time and energy to green parties. The following pages form such an analysis of green party membership in Scotland, in an attempt to shed greater theoretical and empirical light on the processes influencing membership of a green party.

The end of the 1980s was a quite extraordinary period in the history of green politics in Britain. Green ideas suddenly became salient and 'fashionable' and there was a dramatic increase in all forms of environmental behaviour, including voting green (Bennie and Rüdig 1993; Curtice 1989; Franklin and Rüdig 1992; Franklin and Rüdig 1995; Pattie *et al.* 1991; Rüdig and Franklin 1992; Rüdig *et al.* 1996). Furthermore, the Greens across the UK recorded a remarkable increase in membership levels. The Scottish Greens, who formally voted to become independent of the other green parties of the UK in 1989, did not attract the same level of electoral support or membership as Greens in the South of England (Rüdig *et al.* 1991: 19). Nevertheless, the rise in membership was quite exceptional. The Greens in Scotland had never before managed to recruit more than a few hundred members, but at the end of the 1980s they experienced an unprecedented influx of members, reaching a peak of over 1,200.[1] Almost as dramatic was the rapid decline in party membership during the early 1990s. Unfortunately for the party the new members left almost as quickly as they had arrived, and the party was unable to attract new members to replace them. The realisation of a Scottish Parliament in 1999 changed the political landscape and created a more promising set of opportunities for the Greens. Membership rose as a response – from 350 in 1999

---

[1] All membership figures provided by the Scottish Green Party.

to 780 by the end of 2003 – however membership levels did not begin to challenge those of 1989/1990.

This book attempts to explain these developments. While electoral support will be explored, the principal objective is to develop an understanding of motivations behind Scottish Green Party (SGP) membership.[2] The party was able to convince, by its standards, a large number of supporters to fill out a membership form and join the party at the end of the 1980s. By 1993, most of these members had allowed their membership to lapse. This research is an attempt to understand the fluctuation in membership support. What factors explain membership of this small and rather marginalised political party? Traditionally, participation of this kind, when the immediate returns for membership are less than obvious, has been treated as paradoxical. The terms used to describe this process vary; it can be referred to as the paradox of social movement, the collective action problem, or the collective action dilemma. Nevertheless, precisely how groups mobilise for political action and overcome this problem has been the subject of a great deal of research by both political scientists and sociologists in the last three decades. Baumgartner and Leech (1998: 8, 169), for example, identify the area as one of major advance.

A number of established theories on why the individual participates in collective action provide a theoretical framework (these are reviewed extensively in chapter 3). Many observers of political participation focus on *who* actually participates (see Parry *et al.* 1992). In other words they examine the individual's socio-economic characteristics and point to the resources and political skills of individuals who participate. This book does explore the socio-economic background of Scottish Green Party members. However, it will be argued that examination of the individuals with the capacity and skills to participate does not fully illuminate *how* and *why* they become involved.

'How' participants become involved, or the routes into membership, are also investigated in this study. Drawing on the organisational perspective in political science and resource mobilisation approaches in sociology, it will be suggested that a party, group or organisation can draw potential participants into membership but sometimes the joining process is explained by rather higher levels of self-initiative on the part of the member. As for motivations behind membership – the 'why' of joining – a useful body of literature is rational choice theory, which explores the costs and benefits of participation to the individual. Inspired by the work of Olson (1965), an extensive range of ideas has been generated to explore incentives behind membership, including selective material incentives, solidary incentives, and collective purposive incentives (see Clarke and Wilson 1961). This book explores incentives behind membership of the Scottish Greens. In the case of a small green party which can offer very little in the way of selective returns for membership we would *expect* collective incentives to be most important. While recognising the limitations of strict economics-based analyses of membership, in that it is very difficult to measure rationality, it will be argued, in line with Wilson (1995: 26),

---

[2]The study examines membership which is formally recognised by the party. This is not a study of activism.

that 'people join associations for a variety of reasons and that they are more or less rational about action taken on behalf of these reasons'.

Other models to be explored include interactionist or network theories (see della Porta and Diani 1999; Diani 2003a, 2003b). Experience of movement involvement, and interaction with other participants in 'solidarity networks', is said to increase the probability of mobilisation into other groups. These experiences may be important in a green party which is likely to have links with other environmental organisations.

Another important group of theories are 'political opportunity structure' approaches. These suggest that collective behaviour is the result of interaction between the individual and a wide political environment. While 'political opportunity structure' is a rather all-embracing term which can include political, economic and social factors it may be useful in developing an understanding of green party development.[3] These approaches predict that movement activists will channel their activities to take advantage of the opportunities that are presented to them by the political system (Kitschelt 1986, 1989; Kreisi 1995; McAdam *et al.* 1996; Tarrow 1996). It is possible that increases in membership of the Scottish Greens may be the result of environmental movement supporters turning to the party at times when it is viewed as a credible political force. Conversely, there may be periods when membership of the party may not have been viewed as such a good 'opportunity'. In other words, these theories may offer some useful insights into the *timing* of joining.

Garner (1996: 43) makes the point that a number of 'why' questions are addressed by different theories: Why do some individuals join movements? Why do some movements successfully accomplish their goals while others do not? Why do some societies have higher rates of movement activity than others? This study addresses the question of why people become involved as members in the Scottish Green Party. However, it will be suggested that, in order to fully understand *why* people join, one must also consider *who* joins, *how* they join and *when* they join. The study examines individual level data i.e. it involves a mainly micro level of analysis, rather than exploring the wider issues of state/movement relations, or the impact of social movements. However, it will be argued that the structural setting of collective action and available political opportunities are important because they influence the expectations and attitudes of individuals who are potential party participants.

The study of party membership has recently experienced a revival amongst political scientists, marking a deeper appreciation of the value of party members (Bennie *et al.* 1996; Katz and Mair 1992, 1994; Scarrow 1996; Seyd and Whiteley 1992, 1999, 2002; Whiteley and Seyd 1998, 2002; Whiteley *et al.* 1994). While an interest in party membership amongst political scientists is not new (Blondel 1973; Duverger 1954, 1964; May 1973; McKenzie 1964; McKitterick 1960; Michels 1962; Minkin 1978), traditional studies were primarily interested in the implications for party democracy i.e. the distribution of power in the parties. The

---

[3]It has previously been argued that support for the Greens in Britain was related to economic cycles, political cycles, and issue-attention cycles (Rüdig *et al.* 1993: 5).

new wave of studies – of the Labour, Conservative and Liberal Democrat parties – have employed surveys to examine ordinary party members and have provided a wealth of information on what makes the party member 'tick'. However, the small parties in British politics have been sadly neglected in this respect. Only the Greens have been examined in such detail, providing valuable information on all aspects of the membership experience (see Rüdig *et al.* 1991, 1993, 1996). All of these studies however have been British level studies. Indeed very little attention has been paid to the party member in Scotland. Small scale, localised studies do exist (for example Bond 1999) but very little is known about the experiences of party members in Scotland. This study of the Scottish Greens makes some contribution to expanding our knowledge of the Scottish party member, although we would expect a member of a green party to be driven by different motivations from those which influence a traditional party member. For example, a Labour member in Scotland is likely to feel that their party can 'make a difference' in policy terms. The Scottish Green Party, until very recently, has appeared almost completely ineffective in this regard.

The study of members of environmental groups, peace and human rights organisations has been quite extensive, largely within the social movement tradition. Parkin (1968) conducted a postal survey of CND marchers and members in 1965.[4] Taylor and Pritchard (1980) conducted a postal survey in 1979 of people who had been members between 1958 and 1965.[5] In 1978, Cotgrove (1982) surveyed a group of 'New Environmentalists' (Conservation Society and Friends of the Earth), and in 1980 a group of 'Nature Conservationists' (World Wildlife Fund).[6] Byrne (1988) conducted a 1985 postal survey of CND members.[7] Finally, the political scientists Jordan and Maloney (1997) conducted postal surveys of Friends of the Earth and Amnesty International in 1993.[8] However, as in the work on parties, the Scottish dimension of membership has been seriously under-researched. Any studies of environmental groups in Scotland have tended to focus on the *group* (its internal dynamics, relations with policy-makers and so on) rather than the individual member (for example McDowell 1993). Clearly, there is a major gap in our information on Scottish green participation.

As well as contributing to our understanding of political participation, and 'filling a gap' in academic research, this study of a green party allows us to address some wider theoretical questions regarding the place of such parties in traditional party systems. Much has been written about the decline of traditional, class-based,

---

[4]Survey of marchers N=445 (81% response rate). Postal survey of CND members N 358 (61% response rate).

[5]N=403 (self-selected participants who responded to advertisement). Also interviewed leading figures.

[6]New environmentalists N=441 (79% response rate). Nature conservationists N 313 (64% response rate).

[7]N=620 (61% response rate).

[8]FoE survey N 681 (68.1% response rate). Amnesty International survey N=376 (75.2% response rate). Jordan and Maloney also conducted a survey of lapsed, new and veteran FoE members.

political parties, the argument being that parties are experiencing a decline in membership, attachment and support (see Dalton and Wattenberg 2002; Katz and Mair 1992, 1994; LeDuc *et al.* 1996, 2002; Webb 1996, 2000; Widfeldt 1997). Moreover, it has been suggested that green and left-libertarian parties may be in a position to threaten the traditional parties (Fisher 1980; Müller-Rommel 1989; Müller-Rommel and Poguntke 1995). However, the decline of party thesis is not universally accepted. Webb (1996, 2000) for one argues that the traditional parties are still 'legitimate' and have merely been adapting to a changing political environment. Furthermore, there is little evidence to suggest that green parties are *replacing* traditional parties. The signs are that green voters are exceptionally volatile, and this is particularly true in Britain (see Franklin and Rüdig 1995; Rüdig and Franklin 1992). More important in the context of this discussion, green parties also appear to have problems building up a stable membership. This may be because green activists are ideologically opposed to formal organisation, or because green parties generally have little to offer in the way of material and social incentives as 'rewards' for membership.

To some extent, studying membership of a green party enables us to assess the relationship between traditional party and green party membership. For example, are increases in Scottish Green membership the result of movement of members between parties? In other words, do the Scottish Greens attract disaffected ex-members of the traditional political parties, or do they tend to mobilise individuals who have never previously been involved in party politics? Furthermore, when members leave the Greens do they turn (or return to) the other parties, do they turn to alternative green organisations, or do they turn their backs on all forms of political involvement?

These questions obviously have major implications for the Scottish Green Party itself. Until now the party has known very little about its own members. An understanding of why members join and leave helps a party to develop an effective recruitment strategy, and can contribute towards building a more stable membership base. Furthermore, members are especially important to a party like the Scottish Greens because membership subscriptions and donations are the party's main source of income.

However, understanding motivations behind party membership has wider implications for our understanding of political participation. The pluralist tradition (Dahl 1961, 1982) assumes that people will join groups to promote common or shared interests. Joining groups and parties is regarded as an important feature of a modern liberal democracy. From this point of view, it is important to study and to understand why people join political parties and groups. This book does not attempt to address the 'democratic value' of Scottish Green Party membership. However, the fluctuations in Scottish Green Party membership represent an interesting case in the history of collective action. From the point of view of political science and the study of parties, the membership dynamics of the Scottish Greens require explanation.

## The Data

The analysis of Scottish Green members is based on a number of surveys conducted between 1990 and 2002. The first survey took place in December 1990, two months after the Scottish Greens formally separated from the other green parties of the UK.[9] At the time of the survey the party in Scotland had 998 members (numbers had already begun to decline). All of these members were sent a 24-page questionnaire and covering letter, followed-up with a reminder postcard. Seven questionnaires were returned because the respondent had moved away or was not known at the address given. A total of 509 completed questionnaires were returned, a response rate of 51.4 per cent. This was regarded as very satisfactory, as the questionnaire was fairly lengthy. In addition, as membership levels had already begun to decline quite steeply this must have had an adverse effect on the rate of response.

The 1990 survey of Scottish Greens was part of an ESRC funded study of UK Greens directed by Wolfgang Rüdig, Department of Government, University of Strathclyde.[10] In this larger study, questionnaires were sent to a randomly selected sample of 8,604 members of the UK Greens (roughly half of the membership). A total of 4,357 completed questionnaires were returned, a net response rate of 51.1 per cent. This was the biggest survey of green party members ever conducted. Results of the main project of UK Greens (the English, Welsh and Northern Irish Greens) have been reported elsewhere (Rüdig *et al.* 1991, 1993, 1996), but the Scottish results have not been published until now.[11]

The 1990 Scottish Green Party questionnaire responses were later supplemented with the results of a telephone survey, conducted in 1997. The mail questionnaire had asked respondents to give their telephone number if they were willing to discuss some of the points raised in the questionnaire, on an anonymous basis. Of the 509 questionnaire respondents in 1990, 304 (60 per cent) had provided a telephone number where they could be contacted. Seven years later, 136 of these numbers were unobtainable (no longer existed). The remaining 168 numbers were called on up to four occasions. 64 of these respondents had moved on and were unreachable. 43 did not reply or were unwilling to be interviewed.[12] This left 61 respondents who were willing to participate in a fairly in-depth telephone interview which lasted between 10 and 30 minutes. Clearly, the methodological techniques employed in telephone interviews are very different from those of a mailed questionnaire. The 1997 exercise was an attempt to gather

---

[9]When the Scottish Greens set up their own organisation in 1990, this created two green parties in the UK: The Scottish Green Party and the Green Party of England, Wales and Northern Ireland. The Northern Irish Greens also broke away a number of years later.

[10]The work was funded by ESRC award number R 000 23 2404. The other member of the research team was Professor Mark N. Franklin.

[11]The UK study was able to build on the 1990 questionnaire responses with two follow-up questionnaires, in 1991 and 1992. A study of lapsed members was also carried out in 1993. See Rüdig *et al.* 1993 for full details.

[12]This included a small number of 1990 respondents who were now deceased.

qualitative interview data which would complement the 'hard' quantitative data gathered in 1990. The main purpose of the 1997 exercise was to develop an understanding of members who had stayed in the party, as compared with those who had allowed their membership to lapse.

Other qualitative research methods employed in the study included a series of face-to-face interviews with Scottish Green Party founders and activists. Over a period of ten years or so it has been possible to speak to a number of prominent figures in the party. These discussions were particularly important in understanding the historical development of the party. In addition, information was gained through observing party conferences and meetings, and through reading the party's membership newsletters.

Finally, a new survey of Scottish Greens was able to investigate the characteristics and motivations of members in 2002. This survey was part of a British Academy funded study of European green party members, led by Dr. Wolfgang Rüdig at the University of Strathclyde. In September 2002, 517 20-page questionnaires were sent to the membership of the Scottish Green Party, ten of which did not reach the members because the addressee had moved away. A total of 260 usable questionnaires were returned, producing an overall response rate of 51.3 per cent.

The study of the Scottish Green Party and its members over a twelve year period was not without its problems. Owing to a very informal and decentralised membership registration system in the early years, the party was only able to make rather rough estimates about membership levels at this time. Furthermore, computer problems following the 1990 membership peak meant that the party lost important membership details from its records, and it subsequently lost touch with many of its members. This also had consequences for the project. While the UK study developed into a panel study of members, this was not possible in Scotland.

Furthermore, attempts to trace the historical development of the party had a number of obstacles. For example, party documents relating to the early years of the Scottish Greens were very difficult to track down, having never been archived by the party. The lack of written documentation combined with the fact that only a very small number of activists have been with the party since its foundation. Although these party figures were very co-operative and happy to provide interviews, as is often the case with qualitative approaches, these interviews often produced contradictory information. For example, there was some variation in accounts of the year in which the Scottish Greens were actually founded.

The nature and timing of the surveys also meant that some groups in the party, for example lapsed members, were probably under-represented in the questionnaire responses. For example, in 1990 membership numbers were declining quite steeply at the time of the survey and it is inevitable that those leaving the party would be least motivated to reply. Conversely, activists were probably over-represented. The 1997 telephone interviews also had some problems with representativeness. Those members who were contacted in 1997 were the least mobile of the 1990 members. In other words they were significantly older, more likely to be employed, more likely to own their own house and so on. Furthermore, as the following discussion is based on individual-level accounts of why the members joined, the data-sets do not give variances between joiners and non-joiners. As Johnson (1995: 3) argues, it would be better if we had a sample of members and non-members to fully understand differences between the two.

The lack of data on membership of other Scottish parties and groups also presents some complications. Where possible, the book attempts to compare the characteristics of Scottish Greens with other political participants – members of political parties, environmental and peace groups. However, these other studies have all examined *British* members which perhaps suggests that they are not directly comparable. While recognising the weakness in Scottish-British comparisons, it was felt that any information on participants in other movements was worth noting, in order to assess the distinctiveness of green party members.

Overall, the problems encountered in the researching and writing of the book are rather typical of other behavioural science type studies of political participation.[13] None of the problems outlined negate the overall value of the findings. It is hoped that the combination of qualitative and quantitative methodological techniques employed has produced a detailed and robust account of Scottish Green Party membership.


**Scotland and the Environment**

One of the themes of this book is that it is important to consider the time period and political setting if we are to fully understand the decision to join a party. Indeed, it is a well established tradition in the study of European green parties to examine contextual features of political systems to explain variations in the development of such parties (for example, Richardson and Rootes 1995). Factors considered include levels of environmental consciousness, the impact of institutional structures, and the dynamics of party competition (Rootes 1995). Therefore, before the analysis turns to assessing membership of the Scottish Greens, this section considers the relationship between Scottish politics and the development of environmentalism. This involves examining the three areas of environmental awareness of the population, political system effects, and the nature of party competition in Scotland.

---

[13]Behavioural science is commonly regarded as an empirical attempt to understand political behaviour at the individual or aggregate level. Sanders (1995: 58) explains: 'The behavioural approach to social and political analysis concentrates on a single, deceptively simple, question: Why do people behave in the way they do? What differentiates behaviouralists from other social scientists is their insistence (a) that *observable* behaviour, whether it is at the level of the individual or the social aggregate, should be the focus of analysis; and (b) that any explanation of that behaviour should be susceptible to empirical testing'. Behavioural science approaches were developed from the 1950s onwards and broadened the scope of political science (Kavanagh 1983: 2; Stoker 1995: 4), moving beyond political philosophy and the study of institutions to that of diverse forms of observable political behaviour (individual and group actors), with an emphasis on quantitative research.

Economic cycles are widely recognised to have an influence on political agendas as well as the fortunes of government and opposition parties. For example, far-right parties are expected to rise at times of economic crisis. Green parties, on the other hand, are expected to do best during times of economic prosperity, on the grounds that economic well-being probably ranks higher than environmental protection in the 'hierarchy of needs' (Inglehart 1977, 1990; Maslow 1954).[14] Or, as Lowe and Goyder (1983: 25) suggest, environmental concern is linked to a prosperous economy because people then 'count the mounting external costs of unbridled economic growth'. These theories appear to fit the green experience in Britain quite well. The rise in popularity of these issues came at the end of a period of economic growth, Worcester's (1997: 164-165) MORI evidence pointing to an increase in concern for the environment as unemployment declined.

Scotland however has experienced some unique patterns in its social and economic development and these have not encouraged the rise of environmentalism. The work of Rokkan and his colleagues (Rokkan and Urwin 1983; Rokkan *et al.* 1987) on centre-periphery state relationships suggested that Scotland and Wales had experienced a decline in economic security and living standards, relative to the 'core' regions of the South East of England. And others have noted that the decline of the traditional industries contributed to rising unemployment across Britain but the effects were most deeply felt in Scotland and in the northern regions of England (see McCrone 1980, 1992). In these circumstances one might expect the populations of periphery states to be more concerned about traditional economic issues, in other words be more materialistic.[15]

While recent economic statistics suggest a converging of the Scottish and British economies, election studies over the years have pointed to a distinctiveness in Scottish political culture. The perception of an economic North-South divide was particularly evident during the 1980s, one view being that Scotland was becoming less well off because the government of the day did not protect Scottish

---

[14]Theories of post-material value change rest on two central hypothesis: a scarcity hypothesis and a socialisation hypothesis. The scarcity hypothesis suggests that short-term economic changes can increase or decrease post-materialism (period effects). This idea is based on the work of Maslow (1954) who argued that economic security is a primary need of human beings and that higher level concerns, including self-esteem and psychological rewards gained from our environment, only come into play when basic economic needs have been satisfied. Inglehart's socialisation hypothesis points to long-term cohort effects: particular age groups will be influenced by the prevailing economic conditions during their formative years. In this way, Inglehart argues that generations since the war have become increasingly post-material because of increasing economic prosperity, despite short-term fluctuations during times of economic recession.

[15]Scotland still relies a little more on manufacturing and the primary sector than the UK as a whole (Peat and Boyle 1999: 14), and the public sector is relatively more significant in Scotland. Peat and Boyle (1999: 16) estimate that, in 1996, the public sector made up 22 per cent of GDP in Scotland, and 18 per cent in the UK overall. Moreover, during the last few decades Scots have experienced a lower GDP per head than the rest of the UK.

interests (see Bennie *et al.* 1997; Brown *et al.* 1998, 1999; Curtice 1992).  Since that time, some studies have suggested that Scotland is more socialist and a little more liberal than other parts of Britain, although differences can be exaggerated (Bennie *et al.* 1997; Brown *et al.* 1999: 77; Milller *et al.* 1996).  Certainly, Scotland has displayed relatively high levels of (working) class identity, regardless of actual occupational structures, with more than seven in every ten Scots describing themselves as working class (when forced to choose between the classes) compared to around 60 per cent in England and Wales (see Brand *et al.* 1993, 1995; Brown *et al.* 1999: 64; Paterson *et al.* 2001: 109; Surridge 2003: 141). This is combined with high levels of national identity; around three quarters of Scots describe themselves as Scottish rather than British, with these feelings of national identity becoming more intense over the years (Rosie and Bond 2003: 118).

The evidence suggests that values in Scotland remain materialist in character.  They revolve around questions of wealth distribution and economic prosperity, leading Brown *et al.* (1999: 91) to refer to a 'dominant discourse of nationalist and socialist values'. Furthermore, support for the creation of a Scottish parliament was based on the belief that a parliament would improve the economic conditions of Scotland (Brown *et al.* 1999; Paterson *et al.* 2001: 95), and post-devolution election studies confirm such attitudes, although expectations of the Scottish Parliament have declined somewhat (Bromley *et al.* 2003; Curtice *et al.* 2002).  Unfortunately for the Greens in Scotland, economic materialism has not encouraged the spread of 'new politics' ideas.

Against the background described above we might expect the environment to be an issue of low priority in Scotland.  Is there any evidence to suggest that Scottish voters have been less concerned about environmental issues than voters in other parts of Britain? Unfortunately, research on Scottish environmental attitudes and behaviour has been very limited in scope, making it exceptionally difficult to reach any definitive conclusions on patterns of opinion or activity. A small number of studies have examined Scottish public opinion and behaviour in relation to the environment and the evidence produced has been largely contradictory.

The rise of British environmental consciousness during the 1980s has been well documented (Bennie and Rüdig 1993; Rüdig *et al.* 1993; Yearley 1991). Jacobs and Worcester (1990: 16) reveal that in December 1988 5 per cent identified environmental issues as among the most important.  However, by July 1989 environmental issues came top of the public's list of priorities, nominated by 35 per cent, leading Jacobs and Worcester (1990: 35) to remark that 'a new, green plasma is pumping through Britain's veins'.[16]  There can be little doubt that

---

[16]The British Social Attitudes (BSA) series also documents the increase in concern for the environment at this time (Young 1991).  For example, it illustrates that the global issues of great concern in 1990 were the greenhouse effect and the thinning of the ozone layer: 87% of BSA respondents in 1990 claimed they were concerned about ozone depletion, and 82% were concerned about the build up of greenhouse gases (Young 1991: 114).  The BSA surveys also confirm the popularity of green consumerism e.g. 77% said they bought

environmentalism was *fashionable* at the end of the 1980s, and green consumerism was a particularly potent motivation amongst young people (see Bennie and Rüdig 1993: 13-14). Clearly, some sectors of the population pick up 'the environment' as a fashion statement.

In all, at the end of the 1980s global environmental issues appeared to enter the up-swing period of the Downs 'issue attention cycle', what he calls 'alarmed discovery and euphoric enthusiasm', with exceptionally high levels of concern being expressed by the general public (Downs 1972, 1973). The rise in concern for the environment was not sustained however. While more than a third of MORI respondents pointed to the environment as one of the most important issues facing the country in July 1989, by November 1990 the figure had dropped to below 9 per cent, and to only 4 per cent by the end of 1991, remaining under 10 per cent until the 1997 General Election and beyond (Worcester 1997: 163). Traditional issues (unemployment, health, law and order, and education) regained their place at the top of the list of the nation's priorities.[17]

Can we assume that public opinion in Scotland followed exactly the same path as opinion elsewhere in the UK? An analysis of Green voting in 1989 by Pattie *et al.* (1991: 288, 294) suggested a rather low level of concern for environmental issues in Scotland. They argued that voters resident in Scotland, Wales and Northern England were more concerned about traditional political issues – jobs, housing and so on – and less concerned about the environment than people living in the Midlands and the South. In the study the Scots showed less concern for global environmental issues and pollution; people in the South of England were most concerned. Scots appeared less concerned even after differences in employment, earnings, and social class had been considered.

However, a 1991 study of attitudes towards environmental issues commissioned by the Scottish Office Environment Department provides evidence that environmental issues *had* emerged as important in Scotland (Wilkinson and Waterton 1991). According to this survey, the Scottish public were most concerned about the pollution of rivers, lochs and seas and raw sewage put into the sea, followed by the quality of drinking water, nuclear waste and damage to the ozone layer (Wilkinson and Waterton 1991: 1). A comparison of Scottish attitudes with those in England and Wales in 1989 revealed broadly similar attitudes, the top two issues of concern being identical, but Scottish respondents indicated that they were more likely to 'act green' by using ozone friendly aerosols, picking up litter and so on (Wilkinson and Waterton 1991: 69).

---

environment friendly aerosols, and 58% toiletries or cosmetics not tested on animals (Young 1991: 122).

[17]Environmental pressure groups also reported a sharp rise in their membership and income levels at the end of the 1980s, followed by a decline after 1990 (McCormick 1991: 152; Rüdig *et al.* 1993: 17; Young 1993: 17). However, since 1995 membership has begun to rise again (Rawcliffe 1998: 74).

McCormick and McDowell (1999) report the results of a survey conducted in March 1998 on environmental beliefs and behaviour.[18] They point to a number of indicators which suggest that Scots were indeed concerned about environmental issues and, more significantly, that they were willing to bear some costs of protecting the environment. Two thirds of respondents in the study agreed that 'Scotland should develop alternative sources of energy such as wind and water power, and reduce its use of North Sea oil and nuclear power, even if it costs more in the short-term' (McCormick and McDowell 1999: 47).

Based on this evidence, the East of Scotland appeared more environmentally aware than the West (McCormick and McDowell 1999: 55). The biggest difference was in support for cycle routes as a way of reducing car use: support for this proposal in the East was 15 per cent above that in the West. However, the East of the country was consistently more in favour of green measures (more are in favour of 'sustainable development', more likely to believe that the countryside is at risk, and less likely to favour jobs at the expense of green belt areas) (McCormick and McDowell 1999: 55). Measurements of green activities revealed a similar pattern. Residents in the East were more likely to buy organic foods, more likely to recycle paper, and more likely to indicate reduced car use. However, respondents living in the West were more likely to buy environmentally/ozone friendly goods (McCormick and McDowell 1999: 61).

It appears safe to conclude that a rise in concern for the environment, followed by a decline in interest in these issues, took place in all parts of Britain at the end of the 1980s. In other words, an issue attention cycle effect was evident in Scotland also. Moreover, it can be argued that some environmental issues are likely to raise *more* concern in Scotland, in particular nuclear issues. Nuclear military sites at Rosyth, Holy Loch and Faslane, and nuclear power stations at Dounreay, Hunterston and Torness, result in a higher public profile for these issues in Scotland. Election studies do suggest that Scots tend to be more in favour of unilateral nuclear disarmament (Brown *et al.* 1998: 164), and at the end of the 1980s, the future of nuclear power was a highly salient issue in Scotland, with the planned privatisation of the electricity industry being widely debated (see Saville 1990). However, it is worth noting that attitudes towards nuclear issues are often human-centred, and form a separate dimension from attitudes towards other environmental issues (see Pattie *et al.* 1991). As Pattie *et al.* (1991: 292) explain, 'to be anti-nuclear does not also necessarily mean that one is against expansion of housing, industry and modern farming into the countryside'.

British traditions in political decision-making and systems used to elect representatives have presented other problems for the development of green parties across Britain. Britain's traditional political system has been described as one of 'bureaucratic accommodation' (Jordan and Richardson 1997). The policy-making system was regarded as centralised and secretive, based on consultation between interested parties (McCormick 1991; Rootes 1997; Rüdig 1994). The existence of

---

[18]The questions were included in the Scottish Population Omnibus, and conducted by Market Research Scotland. A total of 1013 household interviews were conducted in March 1998.

a Scottish political system was acknowledged (Kellas 1989, 1990), but the features of the policy-making process applied throughout Britain. To an extent, this style of decision-making encouraged the success of environmental groups. By offering the prize of consultation the policy process provided an incentive for groups to behave in a non-confrontational and 'responsible' manner. Environmental groups in Britain have on the whole taken the bait of consultation when offered and have thus developed a reputation for 'reform environmentalism' (Rüdig 1994:2). As Rüdig (1994) describes, environmental groups in Britain have been regarded as successful, moderate and professional (also see McCormick 1991).

In Britain environmental groups and green parties developed quite separately (Rootes 1995: 80). This contrasts with the relationship between green groups and parties in some other European countries. For example, in Germany, the Greens evolved from the New Left social movements of the 1960s and 1970s (Frankland and Shoonmaker 1992).[19] Evidence on environmental activists in Scotland supports the suggestion that environmental groups tended to function independently of the party. McDowell's (1993: 259) study of the Scottish environmental movement revealed that very few of Scotland's main environmental groups had direct contact with the party. To an extent, then, marginalisation of the Greens can be viewed as a product of the political system. The closed, centralised nature of the policy process, which offered environmental groups the opportunity to contribute, encouraged the splintering of the environmental movement. The result was that groups appeared to be most effective, and the Greens tended to be 'left out in the cold'.

In addition to this the Greens throughout Britain were forced to fight elections under a first-past-the-post electoral system which discriminated against small parties with low levels of widespread support. Under this system the Greens found it impossible to achieve electoral representation at Westminster, leading them to consistently argue that they would have performed better under a system of proportional representation (for example, McCabe 1994: 1). Clearly, for most of their history, the Greens in Scotland and the rest of Britain have functioned within a rather inhospitable institutional setting, and with no public funding of political parties the cost of contesting elections has at times been crippling. What Frankland (1990: 25) calls 'legal/institutional barriers' have been very difficult for the Greens to surmount.

However, these kinds of constraints are not permanent or unchanging. The Scottish Parliamentary Elections provide evidence that some proportionality in electoral systems can produce Green representation. The Additional Member System used to elect Members of the Scottish Parliament (MSPs), which emerged from the Scottish Constitutional Convention agreement, resulted in the voter being given two votes, and introduced an element of proportionality to elections in Scotland. The Scottish Parliament consists of 129 members, 73 of whom are elected from traditional constituencies under first-past-the-post rules. The other 56 MSPs are elected from regional (closed) party lists; on the second ballot voters

---

[19]Although this relationship only really applied at the party formation stage. Once the party was created, the overlaps became less apparent.

choose a party and, taking into account the constituency candidates already elected, seats are allocated so that a party's total number of elected candidates roughly reflects its share of the second ballot vote.[20] In Scotland, on average, a party has to achieve over 6 per cent of the vote to gain representation. For a party like the Greens this represents a realistic objective, unlike the winner-takes-all approach of Westminster elections. Standing in all the regional lists costs the party only £4,000, compared to over £30,000 for a full set of Westminster General Election candidates. It is impossible to over-estimate the importance of the new electoral system to the Greens in Scotland. The Greens could never hope to achieve representation under traditional Westminster rules but the introduction of a system which was designed to increase the popular legitimacy of the Scottish Parliament presented the Scottish Green Party with new hope.

Rootes (1997: 88-89; also see Rootes 1995) describes 'the shifting balance of political competition' as the 'most unambiguously contingent factor influencing opportunities presented to social movements and social movement parties'. In the case of the Scottish Greens, the dynamics of party political competition are no less important to their development. The decline of the Conservatives since the 1950s and the strength of the SNP contribute to Scottish exceptionalism and confirm the existence of a distinct party system in Scotland (see Bennie and Clark 2003). Within the confines of a four-party system there has traditionally been little room for a small party like the Greens to make an impression. Indeed, the Greens in England do not have to contend with the extra 'nationalist dimension'.

Another important aspect of party competition is the apparent 'greening' of the other political parties over the last two decades. All the parties in Britain have flirted with the environment as an issue since the 1970s, but interest has been expressed only periodically and it was only at the end of the 1980s that this concern manifested itself in the form of a 'crescendo of interest' (see Carter 2002; Flynn and Lowe 1992: 9-10; Garner 1996, 2000; Robinson 1992). Some parties, however, are greener than others. The Conservatives have always given the impression of being reluctant environmentalists, despite Thatcher's attempts to embrace sustainability as a campaigning theme for the party (see Carter 1997: 156-157; Flynn and Lowe 1992; Frankland 1990: 13; Jacobs and Worcester 1990; Rüdig *et al.* 1993:16).[21] In Scotland, Conservative environmental proposals have always lacked detail or substance, such as the rather empty promises to pursue a 'balanced transport policy' (Scottish Conservative and Unionist Party 1997: 24-25). Even by 2003, the environment hardly featured at all in key election pledges (Scottish Conservative and Unionist Party 2003). Commitments to a major roads-building programme and to maintaining nuclear power led Friends of the Earth

---

[20]In effect, the list seats provide some compensation for the lack of proportionality at the constituency level, however, this is not a strictly proportional system.

[21]Jacobs and Worcester (1990: 17) on why the environment became such an important issue in 1989, and so quickly, put it down to Mrs. Thatcher's conversion and the intense interest this generated in the media; 'perhaps the combination of Mrs Thatcher and the media was enough to account for the whole phenomenon'.

Scotland to give the Conservatives' environment-related proposals a rating of zero out of ten (Friends of the Earth Scotland 2003).

The Labour Party in the 1980s had adopted a fairly radical environmental programme. They had been committed to unilateral nuclear disarmament and, following Chernobyl, a non-nuclear energy policy. However, the party's modernisation programme involved a watering down of many of its radical policies, including its position on unilateral nuclear disarmament. The New Labour approach to the environment has included attempts to pursue an integrated transport policy with a new rail authority and more effective regulation, and a commitment to 'environmental internationalism' which has involved strengthening co-operation with the European Union and taking the lead in reducing carbon dioxide emissions (see Jacobs 1997; Jacobs 1999; Young 2000). During the 1990s Scottish Labour promised a moratorium on road building and to stop the building of new nuclear power stations (Scottish Labour Party 1992, 1997). Since devolution, however, the party has been accused of reneging on previous commitments, for example by pursuing a large-scale road-building plan. Certainly, election manifestos have contained few clear environmental pledges beyond recycling targets, the expansion of renewable energy, and implementing international agreements and European standards (Scottish Labour 2003). For these reasons, FoE rated the 2003 manifesto four out of ten (Friends of the Earth Scotland 2003).

The Scottish National Party (SNP) at first appears quite compatible with an environmental agenda. The party had been staunchly unilateralist since the 1960s and had a long-term commitment to a non-nuclear energy policy. Indeed the party has provided a home for many anti-nuclear activists in Scotland. Mitchell (1996: 199) notes that the SNP 'drew members and ideas' from the Campaign for Nuclear Disarmament (CND). In 1990s manifestos, the party was committed to unilateral nuclear disarmament and promised to cancel immediately the Trident programme and remove Polaris. Instead, the party said it would invest £1.5m from the Trident programme into health, housing, education and jobs. The SNP promised to withdraw from membership of NATO because of the organisation's commitment to nuclear weapons. Instead the SNP supported a conventional defence strategy. The SNP was completely opposed to the depositing and reprocessing of nuclear waste in Scotland Nuclear and energy production would also be phased out. More general commitments included encouraging the developing of renewable resources and support for international initiatives, and the return of Railtrack into public ownership (Scottish National Party 1997). However, in 1999, fourteen 'key policies' included proposals to reform land laws and bring water back into public ownership but few other environment related policies. The SNP's anti-nuclear energy policy was not listed as one of the key policy areas (Scottish National Party 1999). By 2003, the SNP were anti-GM, and were promising to introduce quite ambitious climate change measures, including measures to reduce car use and increase investment in renewables (Scottish National Party 2003). However, contradictory commitments, including support for road building and a refusal to commit to congestion charging, resulted in a FoE rating of five points from ten (Friends of the Earth Scotland 2003).

Generally speaking, the SNP has remained fully committed to economic growth and environmental policies are overshadowed by the main themes of health, education, housing, jobs, social justice, and economic prosperity. Moreover, while the SNP anti-nuclear position would be compatible with an ecological agenda, as has already been suggested this issue tends to be viewed as separate from other environmental issues, by the parties and public alike. Indeed it can be argued that the nuclear issue has a special place in Scottish politics, aside from all other environmental issues (see Martin 1988).

The Liberal Party was the first British party to reject nuclear energy and in 1979 its manifesto had looked very green indeed. The party promised government support for conservation, energy saving and recycling, was opposed to nuclear power, and was committed to reducing the number of cars in cities, as well as cutting public spending on new roads (Liberal Party 1979). At the 1979 Liberal conference the party passed a motion challenging conventional approaches to economic growth, which stated that 'sustained economic growth, as conventionally measured, is neither feasible nor desirable', although the party leadership was not fully supportive (see Flynn and Lowe 1992: 14; Frankland 1990: 10).[22]

In Scotland, the Liberal Democrats have for a long time advocated the phasing out of nuclear power stations and the introduction of an energy tax. In 1991 the party spoke of a need for 'the imposition of taxation on pollution-causing and resource depleting products' and advocated an alternative to GDP as a measure of growth, 'with new indicators, measuring depletion of non-renewable resources, standards of environmental quality and indicators of life and personal fulfilment, such as literacy rates and life expectancy' (The Liberal Democrats 1991). And the party was already committed to an alternative transport policy which would include the application of energy tax to fuel and the introduction of road pricing in congested urban areas. Scottish Liberal Democrat manifestos since then have contained a detailed set of environment policies including a carbon tax on fossil fuels. In the 1999 and 2003 elections to the Scottish Parliament the Liberal Democrats emphasised the importance of integrating environmental objectives into all policy areas, and significantly more so than the other parties (Scottish Liberal Democrats 1999; Scottish Liberal Democrats 2003). It comes as no surprise that FoE have consistently rated the Scottish Liberal Democrats as the most green of the four main parties in Scotland – in 2003 eight marks out of ten, only one behind the Greens – although even the Scottish Liberal Democrats do not oppose some major road building projects like the M74 in Glasgow or Aberdeen Western bypass.[23]

So the Liberal Democrats offer a fairly radical set of policies to voters who are concerned about the environment and we would expect the Greens and Liberal

---

[22]However, alliance and formal merger with the SDP in 1988 led to a watering down of some of the Liberal Party's green and civil and military nuclear policies.

[23]The SSP manifesto of 2003 is rated five out of ten by FoE Scotland. While the party is pro-sustainable development and organic farming, and objects to the M74 development, the 2003 manifesto fails to commit to congestion charging or clear energy efficiency targets. Nor does the document rule out a future for nuclear power (FoE Scotland 2003).

Democrats to be competing for the support of these voters. The development of the Greens is therefore likely to be related to the strength of the Liberal Democrats. However, it is worth noting that Scottish Liberal Democrat policies have at times appeared less ecologically radical than those of the Federal party, mainly due to commitments to protect the rural communities of Scotland who would suffer from, for example, increased motoring costs. Working with Labour in coalition has also led to compromise on some manifesto commitments, including backing down on their opposition to the growing of GM crops (McWhirter 2004).

All in all, recent years have seen a slow but steady politicisation of the environment in Scotland. However, the other parties in Scotland have by no means prioritised the environment as an important electoral issue and green issues remain rather low-key in Scotland's party political discourse.

**Book Outline**

The central objective of the book is to explain motivations behind membership of the Scottish Green Party. To this end, a number of different aspects of the membership experience are explored. Chapter 2 begins with an account of the historical development of the Scottish Greens, illustrating the rather marginal status of this small party during most of its twenty-five year history. The chapter documents the election experiences of the Scottish Greens, including the relative highs of 1989, 1999 and 2003. It will be shown that the 1989 green wave did not have as dramatic an effect in Scotland as in some parts of Britain but since devolution the Scottish Greens have enjoyed genuine success. These contextual details are important because they influence the perceptions of party members as well as potential members. This discussion is followed by a review of the theoretical aspects of participation in chapter 3. The theoretical review reflects the fact that, to date, the most sophisticated attempts to address what influences mobilisation have come from the study of social movements. A number of different models of participation are discussed, from traditional approaches which view participation as the result of a psychological state of alienation to more contemporary approaches which emphasise the rationality of decision-making, the costs and benefits of membership, the role of movement organisers and the significance of political opportunities. Based on the literature, the chapter outlines a number of specific propositions to be tested. These relate to who joins, how they join, why they join and when they join.

Chapters 4, 5 and 6 employ the empirical data gathered in 1990 to explore these questions in detail. Chapter 4 explores the socio-demographic background of Scottish Green Party members at this time, as well as their historical involvement in traditional parties and movement politics. Chapter 5 addresses how and why these Scottish Greens joined the party. The mechanisms through which the members became involved will be explored, allowing us to assess the importance of party recruitment techniques at this time. The chapter's main focus however is on why the members joined, based on self-declared reasons for joining offered by the 1990 questionnaire respondents. This involves discussion of various different 'incentives' and influences. Chapter 6 looks at *when* the members joined and explores the suggestion that the member who joined at the end of the 1980s was a new 'type' of Green, influenced by the political context of the day, perhaps motivated by the desire to be fashionable. The chapter contains a comparison of those members who joined the party before and after Green issues reached a peak of publicity.

Chapter 7 reports on the results of the telephone interviews conducted in 1997 which attempted to identify the 1997 membership status of the original questionnaire respondents, and further explored reasons for joining as well as reasons for leaving. The interviewees were asked to restate why they had joined the Scottish Greens, on the grounds that ex post rationalisation may have changed their assessment. Reasons for leaving are also explored at length, based on a combination of the 1990 questionnaire data and the 1997 telephone responses. The key theme to emerge from the findings is the importance of organisational *effectiveness* to the respondents. The members' perceptions of party and environmental pressure group effectiveness are explored and related to the decision to stay with the party or to leave.

Chapter 8 brings the analysis up to date by reporting the results of the survey of Scottish Greens conducted in 2002 i.e. following the first elections to the Scottish Parliament in 1999 but preceding the 2003 round of elections. The focus of this chapter is the extent of variation between the members in 1990 and 2002, in terms of social characteristics, political background, and motivations for joining the party. In other words, was the party in 2002 attracting a similar kind of member to that in 1990, or is there evidence to suggest that the party is expanding its membership base? Finally, chapter 9 concludes the discussion by assessing how the empirical findings relate to the theoretical accounts of why people participate, and it considers the implications for the Scottish Green Party itself.

# Chapter 2

# The Greens in Scotland: A Record of Electoral Events

The Greens have been active in Scottish politics for two-and-a-half decades.  This chapter documents the development of the Scottish Greens, from their foundation in the late 1970s to their greatest electoral achievement in 2003.  The chapter concentrates on electoral experiences but also considers the membership development, political programme and ideological character of the party. The Scottish Greens are a good example of a green party that found it difficult to make an impact in elections dominated by a first-past-the post electoral system.  Yet, they have had some electoral successes.  These include a rise in support in the 1989 European Election and, with the introduction of a more proportional electoral system for Scottish Parliament Elections, the election of Robin Harper as a Green MSP in 1999.  Moreover, this was followed by a dramatic increase in the number of Green MSPs in the 2003 Holyrood elections.

**Green Roots in Scotland: Party Foundations**

Green party activity in England began in 1973 with the creation of 'People', Europe's first green party.[1] In Scotland, high-profile campaigns against nuclear power and nuclear weapons formed a backdrop to party activity.  SCRAM (The Scottish Campaign to Resist the Atomic Menace) was formed in 1975 in Edinburgh, and played a prominent role in protests against the building of the nuclear power station at Torness (Parkin 1989: 220; Rüdig 1990a: 182). There were undoubtedly links between the anti-nuclear campaigns of the 1970s and the roots of Scottish Green Party activity in and around Edinburgh (Rüdig 1990a: 182).  However, these groups generally preferred to distance themselves from green party politics (Parkin 1989: 219; Rootes 1995: 83-85; Rüdig 1990a: 327). Indeed, the Scottish arm of the Ecologists did not formally come into existence

---

[1]People was established in Coventry in 1973.  In the February and October 1974 General Elections People fielded 5 and 4 candidates, receiving 1.8% and 0.7% in the contested constituencies.  They became the Ecology Party in 1975, and changed their name to the Green Party in 1985.  For a history of the British Greens see Byrne 1989, 1997, pp.150-157; Frankland 1990; Garner 1996, pp.128-139;  Kemp and Wall 1990, ch 2; McCulloch 1992, 1993; O'Neill 1997; Parkin 1989, ch.13; Porritt and Winner 1988, ch. 3; Rootes 1995, ch. 4; Rüdig and Lowe 1986; Wall 2003.

until November 1978. The 'formation' of the Scottish Ecologists took place in the Edinburgh house of Leslie Spoor, a retired teacher and former long-term member of the Labour Party, who had joined the British Ecology Party in 1977 and served on its executive committee. There were around a dozen founding members, half of whom belonged to the Spoor family.

The ideology of the British Ecologists had originally been inspired by the works of Paul Ehrlich (1968; Ehrlich and Ehrlich 1972), the Club of Rome Report (Meadows *et al.* 1972) and Edward Goldsmith (1971, 1978). Most notable was Goldsmith's 'Blueprint for Survival', which was published in the *Ecologist* magazine and provided the basis for the party's first General Election manifesto. Goldsmith claimed that industrial society was threatening the survival of the planet and advocated an ecological society based on a complex mix of community decentralisation, traditional family structures and central planning. Policy recommendations included the rejection of equal rights for women, strengthening law and order and a more restrictive immigration policy. However, this 'survivalist' tradition was criticised for its authoritarian undertones, and by the end of the 1970s (by the time the Ecologists had mobilised in Scotland) the British party had developed a rather more gradualist, democratic agenda. This was combined with an increasingly professional approach to elections, at both the local and national levels (Porritt 1984: 9). Rüdig and Lowe (1986: 272) describe the rising influence of a new national leadership at the end of the 1970s, which included Jonathon Porritt and Jonathon Tyler.

> Their conception was of structural reform initiated by an ecological government which had gained a foothold through the electoral process, leading to a steady-state economy with decentralized political institutions (Rüdig and Lowe 1986: 272).

The new style of leadership involved a rejection of the survivalist ideology and the development of a more democratic, pragmatic and 'accessible' ecological vision (Kemp and Wall 1990: 26). At this time the party's key principles were established. A scepticism of industrialism, recognition that the earth's resources were finite, and a belief in self-reliance, community, democracy and 'non-exploitation' lay at the heart of party philosophy (McCulloch 1992: 428; Porritt 1984). Dobson (1992: 111; 2002:97, 229) categorises this as a 'deep green' holistic philosophy and notes the move from the 'conservative eco-survivalism' of the early 1970s towards a 'more left-influenced political programme' at the end of the 1970s. Rüdig (1996: 256-257) associates these changes with the party's attempts to improve on 'political respectability'.

The ideological motivation of green activists has always been difficult to 'pin-down', with a range of ideological ideas seen throughout the green movement (see Bennie *et al.* 1995; McCulloch 1988; Mitchell 1980). However, there is no reason to assume that the party's activists in Scotland were particularly distinct in their ideological objectives. In other words, those active in Scotland at this time fully endorsed the post-survivalist democratic ecological view. Nevertheless, interviews with leading Scottish activists also revealed a rather pragmatic explanation for the party's foundation in Scotland. They argued that the environmental movement in Scotland needed a party political wing to ensure that green issues were discussed during elections. They had no clear expectations about how well the party would perform in elections; they simply wanted the opportunity to challenge the 'grey' parties in Scotland and to raise awareness of green issues.

The first Scottish Ecology candidate stood five years after Ecologists had begun to contest elections in England. In May 1979, Spoor's son-in-law, Stuart Biggar, stood in Edinburgh South, receiving 552 votes (1.2 per cent of the vote).[2] Party offices were set up in Edinburgh, Glasgow, Inverness and Montrose, and the party claimed to have attracted 80 (mainly Edinburgh) members.[3] The environment was not an important issue during the 1979 election, in the wake of mounting economic problems, and the 1979 Referendum on Scottish Devolution. Moreover, the election of a Conservative government led by Margaret Thatcher left the small number of Ecologist activists in Scotland badly demoralised. Spoor claims that the election result was 'too much to bear' for many of them, leaving Spoor and his son Brian as the only prominent activists in 1980.[4]

During the 1980s, the Ecologists in Scotland existed as a fringe party. In the General Elections of 1983 and 1987, they presented very few candidates (eleven and twelve respectively) and attracted less than 5,000 votes.[5] In 1983, their best performance was in Edinburgh Pentlands (1.6 per cent); in 1987 Orkney and Shetland, with 1.8 per cent of the votes cast. In 1984 the Ecologists in Scotland put forward their first candidate in a European Parliamentary Election, in Lothians, and attracted 1.4 per cent of the vote. The Chernobyl accident had occurred in 1986, and this provided the Greens with some publicity, but it had little effect in the context of a national election. Throughout the 1980s Green activities were concentrated in the big cities of Edinburgh and Glasgow and in the far North. At this time, the party also began the development of some key green policy ideas. The Highland Greens, for example, produced the 'Manifesto for a Rural Economy', a 'human-scale' vision of land reform, in 1988.

Membership at this time climbed very slowly, from under 100 members in 1980 to around 250 by the middle of the decade. Generally, Ecologists throughout Britain had a very low profile during this period, leading Rüdig and Lowe (1986) to refer to the 'stillborn' character of green politics in Britain. However, the party was about to experience a dramatic upturn.

---

[2]Across Britain the Ecologists fielded 53 candidates in 1979 which led to their first five-minute television broadcast, regarded as an important development in the party's road towards respectability (Rüdig and Lowe 1986).
[3]All membership statistics provided by the party.
[4]Interview with Leslie Spoor, 1997.
[5]In 1983, this amounted to 0.87%, and in 1987 1%, of the vote in contested seats.

## The Crest of a Green Wave: 1989

The European Elections of 15 June 1989 represented an important turning point for the Greens. Party candidates stood in all eight European constituencies in Scotland. Indeed the Greens were the only small party in Scotland to put forward a full list of candidates. The party stood on a platform of traditional green issues – sustainable growth and the development of renewable energy sources – and it criticised the European Union for being centralised, bureaucratic and unresponsive. The Greens in Scotland received 115,000 votes, 7.2 per cent of the vote, considerably more than they had ever achieved in a national election. This was, nevertheless, insufficient to win electoral representation under Britain's first-past-the-post electoral system. The Greens' best result was in the Lothians region, where Robin Harper attracted 10.2 per cent of the vote; their worst performance in Strathclyde East (5.0 per cent) (Table 2.1).[6]

The vote was achieved against a background of increasing support for the SNP and rapidly declining support for Britain's traditional 'third place' party, the Social and Liberal Democrats (soon to become the Liberal Democrats). The Greens managed to 'overtake' the SLD, forcing them into fifth place. Indeed, it appears that the Greens were mainly competing with the Liberal Democrats (Rüdig *et al.* 1993: 35). Analyses of public attitudes revealed that positive feelings for the Greens correlated strongly with positive feelings for the Liberal Democrats, but were negatively related to support for the Conservatives. In Scotland, warm feelings toward the Greens also correlated positively with support for the SNP (Rüdig *et al.* 1993: 39). Indeed, Rüdig and Franklin (1992: 49) suggest that, along with Liberal Democrat voters, Scottish and Welsh nationalist voters were the most likely to consider voting Green in the future.

Opinion polls and local election results had shown little indication of a rise in Green support in Scotland, although there was a high level of dissatisfaction with the Conservative government of the day. For example, around three-quarters of Scots opposed the community charge/poll tax (McCrone 1989: 343; McCrone 1990: 285). In the May 1988 district elections in Scotland the Greens had 37 candidates who attracted an average of 136 votes each. All 'other' parties together attracted only 2 per cent of the vote (Bochel and Denver 1989: 26). In November 1988, the party stood in the Glasgow Govan by-election (won by the SNP's Jim Sillars) and received 1.1 per cent of the vote (345 votes). Given the apparent low level of interest in the Greens, the European Election result was a major surprise.

The Greens' performance in Scotland was undoubtedly less dramatic than in some other parts of Britain, leading Frankland (1990: 20) to argue that the Green vote in Scotland was 'not large enough to be relevant to the tactical considerations of the major parties'. However, with a record of very low levels of support, the result for the Greens in Scotland was quite exceptional.[7]

---

[6]Turnout was relatively healthy in Scotland; at 41% it was higher than the UK figure of 36.6% UK.

[7]In Wales the Greens finished ahead of the nationalists in three of the four Euro-

Green support in Britain overall was even more impressive, at 14.5 per cent of the total votes cast (2,292,696 votes). This was regarded by some as 'the political event of the decade' (Kemp and Wall 1990: 34). The party put forward a full slate of candidates (78 plus one in Northern Ireland), finished as the third party overall, and saved all its deposits.[8] In some Euro-constituencies in the South of England the party attracted over 20 per cent of the vote (Burgess and Lee 1990: 206; Frankland 1990: 7; Rootes 1995: 68; Rüdig *et al.* 1991: 19).[9] The local elections, which took place the month before the European poll, gave some indication that the Green vote was on the increase in England (Frankland 1990: 15-17; Rootes 1991: 41). Similarly, opinion polls pointed to a gradual increase in support in the run-up to polling day (Burgess and Lee 1990: 201). Nevertheless, the final results far exceeded both expectations and previous election performances. In 1984, the party had put forward 16 candidates (plus one in N.Ireland), attracted only 0.56 per cent of the vote (74,176 votes) and lost all deposits.

**Table 2.1  Distribution of Party Support in Euro-constituencies 1989 (%)**

|                        | Con  | Lab  | SLD | SNP  | Green |
|------------------------|------|------|-----|------|-------|
| Glasgow                | 10.7 | 55.4 | 2.0 | 25.0 | 6.3   |
| Highlands & Islands    | 16.8 | 13.9 | 8.3 | 51.6 | 9.5   |
| Lothians               | 23.7 | 41.4 | 4.2 | 20.5 | 10.2  |
| Mid-Scotland and Fife  | 21.0 | 46.1 | 4.0 | 22.6 | 6.4   |
| North East Scotland    | 26.7 | 30.7 | 6.0 | 29.4 | 7.3   |
| South of Scotland      | 32.2 | 39.8 | 5.1 | 17.2 | 5.7   |
| Strathclyde East       | 11.4 | 56.2 | 2.2 | 25.1 | 5.0   |
| Strathclyde West       | 21.8 | 42.7 | 3.9 | 23.8 | 7.8   |

*Source*: Bochel and Denver 1990: 92

Analysis of Green voters in the UK (*i.e.* including Scottish Green voters) revealed a distinct profile (Franklin and Rüdig 1995: 424-427; Rüdig and Franklin 1992: 42-43; Rüdig *et al.* 1993: 41).[10] According to these findings, Green voters were younger than the population, considerably less likely to have finished their

---

constituencies, on 11.2% of the vote.

[8]It has been estimated that, under a proportional list system of elections the Greens would have gained 11 seats (see for example Burgess and Lee 1990: 203).

[9]Two by-elections took place at the same time as the European Elections in 1989, one in Vauxhall, the other in Glasgow Central. In Vauxhall the Greens received 6.1%, making this the first saved deposit in a Westminster seat. In Glasgow the party's candidate Irene Brandt won 3.8% of the vote. She lost her deposit but finished fourth, ahead of all the other minor parties, including the newly formed Social and Liberal Democrats.

[10]The very small number of Scottish respondents prevents analysis of Scottish Green voters.

schooling at the earliest possible date, and significantly more likely to have a professional occupation. Analysis of their values suggests that Green voters were a little more post-materialist in their views, however their Left-Right orientation was similar to the rest of the population (Franklin and Rüdig 1995: 427-430). Overall, these findings do not provide a great deal of support for theories which predict that voting Green is related to post-materialist values and a concern for 'New Left' type issues (Inglehart 1977, 1990, 1997). Voting Green was, however, strongly related to concern for the environment: 53 per cent of Green voters pointed to the environment as one of the top three political issues, compared to only 30 per cent of the entire electorate. The 'greenhouse effect' was strongly related to the Green vote but anti-nuclear attitudes were not (Rüdig *et al.* 1993: 33). The data also reveals that a large influence on the decision to vote Green was the desire 'to give a warning to government' (Rüdig *et al.* 1993: 34).

In Scotland, most commentators put the Green vote down to protest. Bochel and Denver (1990: 98), for example, stated: 'We would go along with those who have interpreted the Green vote as essentially indicating disaffection from the other parties in other words, a "protest vote"'. They refer to a *Scotsman* MORI poll during the 1989 election campaign which suggested that the poll tax/community charge and the traditional issues of unemployment and the NHS were the major issues for voters in June 1989 (Bochel and Denver 1990: 96). Certainly, protest voting (over issues like the poll tax) might partly explain the lower level of support for the Greens in Scotland, given the availability of both the Liberal Democrats and the SNP as vehicles for protest. However, it is probably over-simplistic to regard the Green vote in 1989 as a simple protest against the unpopular Conservative government of the day. The same *Scotsman* MORI poll referred to by Bochel and Denver (1990: 98) revealed that 9 per cent of voters said they would 'take the environment into account when deciding how to vote'.[11]

Indeed, it can be no coincidence that environmental issues had enjoyed an unprecedented prominence in Britain in the run-up to these elections, with politicians and media commentators showing more interest in these issues than ever before. Increases in scientific evidence of environmental degradation, the occurrence of environmental accidents and events, and an economic development boom combined to provide high-profile exposure of green issues at this time (Curtice 1989; Pattie *et al.* 1991; Rootes 1991, 1995a; Rüdig *et al.* 1993, 1996).

---

[11]An opinion poll conducted by NOP/Independent found that the vast majority of UK Green voters (74%) claimed they had voted positively for the party; only 16% said they had voted against other parties (Kellner 1989).

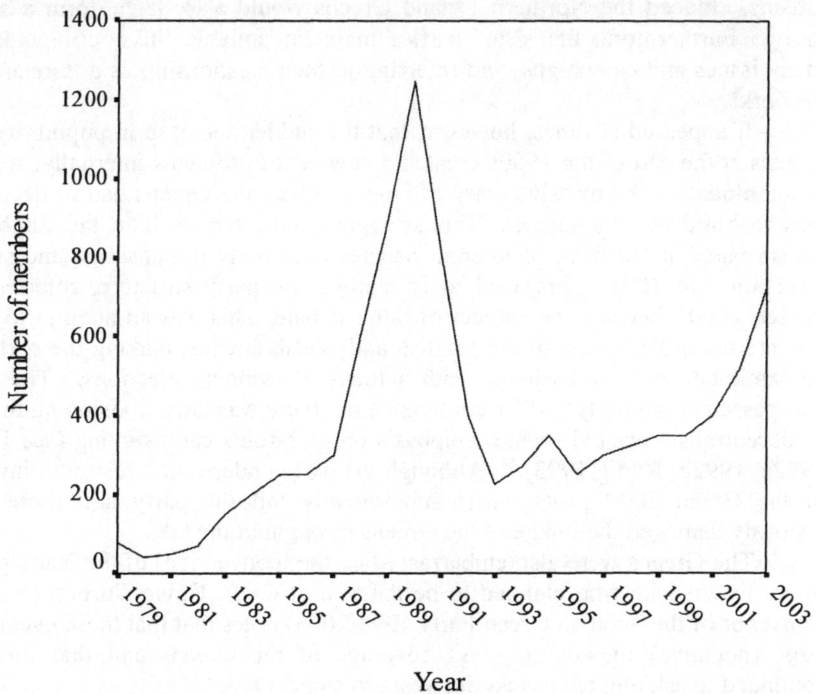


**Figure 2.1  Scottish Green Party Membership**

Following these elections, the Greens in Scotland were buoyant, the rise of Green voting coinciding with a remarkable increase in party membership (Figure 2.1).  In 1990 membership of the Scottish Greens rose to a high of 1,250.  There was also a good deal of local party activity, with branch organisations estimated at 36, although there was no formal structure for setting up local parties at this time. Instead, local branches informally emerged from small groups of local activists on the ground.[12]   This represented a quite unprecedented period of success for the Greens in Scotland. At this time, the party was also making progress in the development of its policy programme, including the publication of a green vision for Scotland 'Towards a Green Scotland', or TAGS, in 1990.  Furthermore, the Scottish Greens formally voted for their independence from the UK party in September of 1989, creating two Green parties in the UK: the Scottish Green Party and the Green Party of England, Wales and Northern Ireland.[13]   This move towards

---

[12]The down-side of this rather organic party structure was that when local activists left or became less active, local parties quickly died.
[13]Scottish Greens voted for their independence by three to one (Kemp and Wall 1990: 34).

independence for the Scottish Greens was consistent with the Green belief in decentralisation and regional autonomy, not the result of division amongst the Greens. Indeed the Northern Ireland Greens would also, later, form a separate party. Furthermore, the sister parties maintain amiable links, co-operating on many issues and campaigns, and referring to their relationship as a 'Green islands network'.

It appeared at times, however, that the sudden increase in popularity of the Greens at the end of the 1980s created a new set of problems internally. A well as accommodating the massive entry of new members the Greens had to decide how best to build on this success. This struggle manifested itself in the English and Welsh party in the form of internal debates over party organisation and strategic direction. In 1991 a proposal to streamline the party structure, referred to as 'Green 2000', became the subject of bitter debate. This was an attempt to reform the internal organisation of the English and Welsh Greens, making the party more 'streamlined' and professional, with a focus on winning elections. The motion was passed at the party's 1991 conference but there was deep division on the issue, as decentralists wanted greater emphasis on grassroots campaigning (see Doherty 1992a, 1992b; Rüdig 1993).[14] Although the party underwent a restructuring, many of the Green 2000 protagonists subsequently left the party and these events seriously damaged the image of the Greens throughout the UK.

The Greens were also embarrassed by the 'conversion' of the leading Green figure David Icke who claimed to be the Son of God. Gavin Corbett (Executive Convenor of the Scottish Green Party 1998-2003) notes that that these events had a large (negative) impact on press coverage of the Greens and that journalists continued to ask him about Icke for years to come.

The Scottish Green Party (a separate party by 1990) was less troubled by internal conflict than the Green Party of England and Wales, and it experienced less pressure to become 'professional'. The Scottish Greens resisted traditional forms of party organisation and maintained a sense of radicalism.[15] The reasons for the lack of conflict amongst Scottish Greens are less than clear. One view is that the Greens in Scotland were more realistic about the pace of change, partly because they had not experienced the same dizzy heights of success as the Greens in England in 1989, and partly due to the more competitive party system in Scotland. In short, the Greens in Scotland had lower expectations coming out of the 1989 elections and were not confronted with the immediate need to debate electoral strategy or party organisation.

Certainly, the Scottish Greens were not so troubled by the belief that some party members were hungry for personal power and media attention. While Jonathon Porritt and Sara Parkin were viewed with suspicion by many in the party South of the border, prominent figures in Scotland at this time – for example David Spaven and Lizbeth Collie – enjoyed a relatively high media profile without

---

[14]Indeed, the motion was passed against the wishes of activists, due to the mobilising of passive members' proxy votes (see Doherty 1992a; Doherty 1992b; Rüdig 1993).
[15]For example they often advocated non-violent civil disobedience as a legitimate form of protest (Cramb 1992).

generating significant levels of resentment.  Nevertheless, like their sister party, the Scottish Greens did experience a loss of talent when activists like Tony Clayton, Irene Brandt and David Spaven chose to scale-down their party involvement in 1991 and 1992.

**More Difficult Times: The 1990s**

In the 1990 regional elections the Scottish Greens put forward 109 candidates and attracted just over 35,000 votes, which was the largest number of votes ever received by a 'minor' party in a Scottish regional election (Denver 1994: 77). More importantly, Roger Winter was elected as regional councillor for the Scottish Green Party in Highland.  While Greens in England had already enjoyed some success at the local level, Winter was the Scottish party's first ever elected representative. However, Winter was soon to abandon the Greens, transferring his allegiance to the SNP.   The pattern of raised expectation followed by disappointment was characteristic of party development at the time.  While the Scottish Greens avoided the extreme internal bickering prevalent in England, they were unable to avoid a return to marginal status.

The party suffered from chronic under-funding and inefficient organisation of party business.  For a period (1990-1993) the party's internal organisation was nothing short of shambolic.  The party was unable to cope with the increase in membership in 1989/1990 and the recording of membership broke down. Members simply drifted away.  Strategically, the Greens in Scotland were accused of political naiveté.  While strongly supporting the setting up of a parliament in Scotland, the Greens withdrew from the Scottish Constitutional Convention in 1990 because of failure to agree on the principles of a multi-option referendum and a timetable for moving towards a system of proportional representation.  On the one hand, this strategy appeared to leave the party without a voice in the debate over Scotland's constitutional future. On the other hand, the Greens kept up their campaign for a Scottish Parliament by participating in broad alliances (Common Cause, Democracy for Scotland, and Scotland United) aimed at generating grassroots support for constitutional change.  The tactics employed – public demonstrations, vigils and petitions – contrasted with the elite-led Scottish Constitutional Convention's drafting of a constitutional package for change. Mitchell (1996: 242) argues that the Greens' withdrawal from the Convention was better handled than the SNP's. However, when the Greens returned to the negotiations in 1995 they had little influence (see Lynch 1996; Taylor 1999).

In the 1992 General Election the Scottish Greens fielded 19 candidates, more than in any previous General Election, but received an average of just over 1 per cent of the vote in the contested seats. The loss of all deposits once again demoralised the party. Furthermore, the party experienced a corresponding decline in membership levels and activity rates, reaching another low-point in 1993. Membership fell to only a few hundred (225) by 1993 and most party branches ceased activity.[16]  All in all, the 1992 General Election had a devastating effect on Scottish green activism, and not only because the party itself had such a poor result.  The Conservative victory came as a shock to politicians and pundits who had predicted a Labour win (Bochel and Denver 1992; MacWhirter 1992).  The issue of Scotland's constitutional future had been a prominent theme during the campaign, and Labour's defeat dashed hopes of a Scottish Parliament which had been a major motivation for many Green activists.

In the final elections to regional authorities in May 1994, prior to the creation of single tier local authorities, the party put forward a much smaller number of candidates than in 1990 (36) and received just over 6,000 votes for its efforts.  Scottish Militant Labour (SML) surpassed this total with more than 11,000 votes (see Denver and Bochel 1994).  In the June 1994 European Elections the Scottish Green Party was able to offer a full slate of candidates, in all eight constituencies, but only because of financial assistance from Greens in England. The Greens suffered from a lack of media coverage and attracted only 1.6 per cent of the vote overall.  The Green vote collapsed across Scotland, its best regional performance (2.6 per cent in the Lothians area) well down on the 1989 result (when the party had attracted over 10 per cent) (see Denver 1994; Lynch 1994). The Greens throughout the UK suffered a sharp electoral decline but the performance of the Scottish Greens was once again poor relative to other British regions. The Green vote amounted to 3.5 per cent in England and 2.0 per cent in Wales.

These were testing times for the party, with increasing support for the SNP and the recovery of the Liberal Democrats.  In 1994, one commentator argued, 'The rapid decline of the Greens since 1989 has returned them to the status of a fringe party' (Lynch 1994: 56). At a very poorly attended and demoralised 1994 annual Autumn conference the party debated the idea of withdrawing from the next General Election.  It was suggested that the Greens in Scotland faced a hopeless fight under the first-past-the-post electoral system and that to lose badly again would harm the development of the party because this would lead to another haemorrhaging of members.

During the early 1990s some prominent activists in the party (including Des Craig and Duncan McCabe) focused their attention on promoting a green democracy in Scotland.  Certainly, the party made efforts to co-operate with other groups and parties.[17]  As well as returning to the Scottish Constitutional Convention, the party stepped up its activities in support of a Scottish Parliament by participating in such forums as the Scottish Civic Assembly, the Coalition for

---

[16]At the same time, there were some signs that the party was beginning to reorganise internal structures to capitalise on the activists who remained in the party.  In Edinburgh, for example, the six constituency-based branches (which were effectively dormant) were merged into one city branch.

[17]Perhaps learning from the 'pragmatic realism' of the Greens in Wales who achieved their first taste of national electoral success through an alliance with Plaid Cymru.  Cynog Dafis, a Plaid Cymru MP, was elected in 1992 on a joint ticket with the Greens, although the agreement was later terminated (see Wall 2003: 32).

Scottish Democracy, and the Vigil for a Scottish Parliament. However, others in the party were wary of focussing entirely on promoting the Scottish Parliament, keen instead to develop the wider range of green policies.

In the 1995 Westminster by-election in Perth and Kinross the Scottish Greens received only 0.5 per cent of the votes and finished seventh, behind both the Monster Raving Loony Party and the UK Independence Party. In the 1995 Scottish Unitary Authority Elections the Scottish Greens put forward 22 candidates and attracted 4.8 per cent of the vote in these seats.

In 1997 the Scottish Greens' participation in the General Election was minimal (see Table 2.2). The party put forward five candidates.[18] It failed to attract more than 1.5 per cent of the vote in any constituency and averaged 0.84 per cent (1,721 votes). Robin Harper in Edinburgh Pentlands received only 224 votes (0.49 per cent). The Greens also faced increasing competition from other small parties. Tommy Sheridan's Scottish Socialist Alliance put forward 16 candidates in 1997 and attracted 9,508 votes, 1.8 per cent of votes cast.

**Table 2.2  Scottish Green General Election Results 1979-2001**

| Year | Candidates | Votes | Average % vote in contested seats |
|------|------------|-------|-----------------------------------|
| 1979 | 1 | 552 | 1.20 |
| 1983 | 11 | 3,854 | 0.87 |
| 1987 | 12 | 4,667 | 1.08 |
| 1992 | 19 | 8,309 | 1.09 |
| 1997 | 5 | 1,721 | 0.84 |
| 2001 | 4 | 4,551 | 3.55 |

In the 1997 devolution referendum campaign, the party continued to fully support the creation of a Scottish Parliament with a reformed electoral system but once again the Greens had a very low profile. The referendum campaign was characterised by a lack of local campaigning and the dominance of the media, factors which undermined the role of small parties like the Greens. It is fair to say that throughout the 1990s, despite their best efforts, the Scottish Greens found it very difficult to get noticed. However, the success of the devolution referendum and the imminent prospect of a Scottish Parliament ultimately provided an important motivation for many Greens.

In the approach to the year 2000 the Scottish Greens appeared to have learned some lessons from their years in Scotland's political wilderness. Organisationally, the party began to organise informally around larger geographical units, which in most cases reflected the eight European

---

[18]In Caithness, Sutherland & Easter Ross; Edinburgh Central; Edinburgh Pentlands; Inverness East, Nairn & Lochaber; and Ross, Skye & Inverness West.

constituencies, soon to become the Scottish Parliament regions.  This in effect expanded the geographical catchment of the most successful local parties, such as Glasgow and Edinburgh.  However, the restructuring was an incremental process and at the end of the 1990s some members of the party remained very isolated, without regular communication from the party.  Indeed, formal reorganisation did not take place until 2001.  Despite the period of organisational transition, membership started to rise again, slowly.

**The 1999 Scottish Parliamentary Election**

The circumstances in which the Scottish Greens found themselves in the run-up to the first Scottish Parliamentary Election provided some good reasons for optimism.  The element of proportionality in the Additional Member System of elections provided opportunities for small parties with 6 to 7 per cent of the vote. Moreover, changes in the rules governing elections made it easier for the Greens to stand in all areas of Scotland, giving every voter the opportunity to support the party.[19]

The Greens decided not to stand in the first-past-the-post constituencies where there was little hope of success.  However, this was more than a simple cost consideration.  Rather, the party was alert to the importance of concentrating the Green vote where there was a genuine possibility of election gains i.e. the regional lists.  For similar reasons they chose not to contest over 1200 local government seats.  So, the party put forward a list in each of the eight regions.  In this way, they were able to stand in all areas with a total of 41 candidates. Only three other small parties contested all regional list seats; the newly formed Scottish Socialist Party (previously Scottish Militant/Scottish Socialist Alliance), the Socialist Labour Party, and the Natural Law Party.

Another important aspect of a small party's campaign can be a Party Election Broadcast (PEB). In the Scottish Parliament Elections it was decided that a party would be permitted a broadcast if it was standing in 1/6 of the constituencies, or in at least 4 regions (with 7 or more candidates).  The latter provision was inserted only after some forthright discussion between the Scottish Green Party and the BBC's political adviser.  Ultimately, the party's strategy of

---

[19]Under the old rules, elections were an expensive business, as all candidates were required to deposit £500, to be returned only if the candidates attracted 5% of the vote. In the Scottish Parliamentary Elections, a £500 deposit was required to stand in a constituency *or* a regional list (with up to 12 names on each list).  It therefore cost a party £4,000 to field a list of candidates in every region, compared to £36,000 (72 x £500) for fielding a full slate of constituency candidates (as in a Westminster General Election).

As for the return of deposits, in both the constituency and regional seats this was 5% (1/20 of the vote), as in a British General Election.  Although in the regions this was described as '5% or if a candidate was returned because technically a candidate might be returned on less than 5%'.

standing in all regions with over 40 candidates therefore secured a broadcast, adding to the party's profile.[20]

There can be little doubt that the new electoral context galvanised the Greens in Scotland, and their campaign was both inventive and effective. The Greens adopted simple campaign slogans. Early election literature urged the electorate to 'Vote Green 2/Too'. Closer to election day, and especially prominent on lamp-post posters in the Lothians area, party campaigners' main slogan was '2nd Vote Green'. The party also used an enormous luminous green '2' as an election prop, now displayed in an Edinburgh museum. The objective was to inform all voters that they could vote Green on the regional lists. At every opportunity the Greens emphasised that 'Scottish Green Party' would appear on the peach coloured ballot paper, and they constantly referred to 'around 6 per cent' as the golden threshold beyond which they would be elected.

When the Greens launched their list in February 1999 Robin Harper urged Labour supporters who were concerned about the environment to consider giving their second vote to the Greens. At the same time, he attacked Labour for not delivering its promises on the environment. The party was also keen to illustrate that it was not a single-issue party, emphasising a range of environmental and social issues. Traditional green proposals included pollution controls, the development of renewable energy technologies, the closure of nuclear power stations, an integrated transport policy, a ban on GM crops, and a basic income scheme. Other policies included a Land Value Tax, a Scottish Community Bank to fund community businesses, abolition of student tuition fees and the reintroduction of grants for the less well off, and 'greater independence for Scotland' (Scottish Green Party 1999). In particular, the GM issue was one that the party benefited from. This had reached a high point on the political agenda in late 1998/early 1999 and the party felt that they were able to make this 'their issue'.[21]

All in all, the Green campaign was dynamic and media-friendly. It was also effectively targeted towards areas where the party was already most visible. For example, the party did not attempt to rally support in the Borders area. The decision to concentrate grassroots campaigning on the city centre streets of Edinburgh was combined with simple media stunts and press releases, designed to enhance the party's credibility. For example, on 2 April 1999 the Greens announced the results of a System Three Poll (commissioned by the party) which showed that 13 per cent of people were very or quite likely to vote Green with their second vote.[22] The structure of the party also proved very flexible, allowing the activists to respond to events.[23] Moreover, financial donations to the party (one

---

[20]However, the party itself viewed the Green PEB in 1999 as rather poor. It is assumed that the PEB did very little to improve the party's prospects on election day.

[21]This is the view of Gavin Corbett. In addition, argues Corbett, the party enjoyed positive publicity following the Electoral Commission's initial refusal to register the Scottish Green Party as a separate party. In his view, the party received a great deal of sympathetic coverage from these events, which the Scottish Greens attempted to exploit to the full.

[22]1% of the poll respondents said they were very likely to vote Green.

[23]Although there was a central Campaign Strategy Group and election leaflets were

member pledged £20,000) enabled the party to run an office in Edinburgh, with one part-time member of staff from October 1998 to June 1999.[24]

In the event, both the Greens and the SSP successfully entered the new Scottish Parliament, with one representative each, along with the Independent Dennis Canavan in Falkirk West. Robin Harper was elected for the Greens in the Lothians region on 6.91 per cent of the vote; Tommy Sheridan became the sole SSP MSP with 7.25 per cent of the vote in the Glasgow area.[25] It was perhaps no surprise that the Greens should break through in the Lothians area, as this had always been an area of relative strength for the party.[26] Their next best performance was in Glasgow, with just under 4 per cent (see Table 2.3). Overall, the Scottish Green Party averaged 3.59 per cent in the list votes, meaning that they were the most successful small party in the regions.

**Table 2.3  The Regional Green Vote in the Scottish Parliamentary Elections, 7 May 1999**

|  | Votes (N) | % |
|---|---|---|
| Highlands and Islands | 7, 560 | 3.75 |
| North East Scotland | 8, 067 | 2.83 |
| Mid Scotland and Fife | 11,821 | 3.87 |
| West of Scotland | 8,175 | 2.63 |
| Glasgow | 10,159 | 3.96 |
| Central Scotland | 5,926 | 1.79 |
| Lothian | 22,848 | 6.91 |
| South of Scotland | 9,468 | 2.97 |
| Total | 84,024 | 3.59 |

The Greens' breakthrough into Parliamentary politics represented the end of a very long campaign for Robin Harper, an Edinburgh school teacher. Harper had been a party member since 1985. Before May 1999, he had stood in two European

---

produced centrally, to keep costs down.

[24]Corbett argues that the setting up the office enhanced the central capacity of the party and provided a much-needed focus for other volunteer workers.

[25]The election pundits did not predict their success. Malcolm Dickson, for example, writing in *The Herald* (23 April 1999) argued that the System Three polls showed little sign of Green (or SSP) support but suggested that the Highlands and Islands Alliance had 'an outside chance'.

[26]The Green result was made all the more dramatic by delays at the count in Edinburgh. The Lothians Regional list result was announced more than 17 hours after the count had begun, having been suspended at 6.30am on the Friday morning when council workers reached the end of their shift. They resumed at 1pm and the result was announced at 4pm. The returning officer Tom Aitchison, the city's chief executive, argued that the logistical task of counting 750,000 ballot papers was exacerbated by the length of the ballot paper for the second vote, with 17 party lists (*Press and Journal* 08.05.99).

Elections and the 1998 North East European by-election, two UK General Elections, and in the Perth & Kinross Westminster by-election. On each occasion, he paid his own deposit (£500 for UK Parliament, £1,000 for Euros) and lost every single deposit except in the 1989 European Election.

**Signs of Sustainable Success: 1999 to 2003**

By 1999 the Scottish Greens could boast that Harper was the first nationally elected green parliamentarian in Britain, greatly enhancing the party's credibility. Unfortunately for the Greens, however, these events made little difference to membership figures. In the Autumn of 1999 the party had around 350 members, which was a small increase on the period before the election (around 300), but was very low compared to 1990 standards.

In June 1999, the Greens fought another European Election. For the first time in Britain, proportional representation was used in these elections, and Scotland was treated as one European region.[27] However, at around 10 per cent, the threshold at which representation could be achieved in Scotland was much higher than in the Scottish Parliamentary Elections, and indeed higher than in most other regions of Britain. For this reason, the Greens had little chance of being elected but they achieved 5.8 per cent of the overall vote, suggesting an increase in support across the country since the Scottish election (see Table 2.4).[28] Moreover, elsewhere in Britain, the proportional electoral system led to the election of two Greens (in London, with 7.7 per cent of the vote and in the South East with 7.4 per cent). This provided some evidence that voters would support Greens when a 'fair' electoral system gave them a realistic chance of being elected.

**Table 2.4  Scottish Green European Election Results**

|      | Candidates | Votes | % Vote |
|------|------------|---------|--------|
| 1979 | 0 | 0 | 0.0 |
| 1984 | 1 | 2,560 | 0.2 |
| 1989 | 8 | 115,028 | 7.2 |
| 1994 | 8 | 23,304 | 1.6 |
| 1999 | 8 | 57,142 | 5.8 |

Westminster General Elections, however, remained stubbornly first-past-the-post in character, providing very little incentive for the Greens to participate. The Scottish Greens, still resource-poor, thus chose to offer only four candidates in

---

[27]Therefore each party put forward one list of candidates. The deposit was £5,000 but the parties retained their deposit if they achieved more than 2.5% of the vote.

[28]All 'other parties' together attracted an unprecedented 15% of the Scottish vote.

the 2001 General Election.  The candidates stood in Glasgow Kelvin, Edinburgh Central, Stirling, and Ross, Skye & Inverness West, attracting 4,551 votes, an average of 3.55 per cent (0.2 per cent overall).  However, the party was cheered by the result in the Edinburgh constituency where, with 5.3 per cent of the vote, it retained its deposit for the first time in a British General Election.  It also came within 55 votes of retaining its deposit in Glasgow Kelvin.[29]  Moreover, the Greens regarded these constituencies as key areas of support and the decision to stand here reflected a strategic attempt to maintain a presence in territories where they might do well in 2003.

During this time, the party was also benefiting from Robin Harper's experiences as a Member of the Scottish Parliament.  As an MSP Harper demonstrated a unique personal style of politics which was based on hard work, consensus and an amiable personality.  One characteristic of his first four years in the Parliament was the amount of time he dedicated to constituency work, talking to student groups, schools, local businesses and so on.  Furthermore, Harper's MSP status brought with it certain entitlements: Members' legislation, committee work (he was a member of the Transport and the Environment Committee and of 27 cross-party groups, some of which he convened), and interventions in parliamentary debates all provided the opportunity to generate publicity and contribute to political debate (see Bennie 2002). In particular, Harper focused attention on the issue of organic farming, with the introduction of his Organic Farming Targets (Scotland) Bill.  While the Bill did not become law, Harper argues that support for the bill forced the Executive to adopt similar measures, in the form of the Scottish Executive Organic Action Plan (Harper 2003: 1).

Furthermore, Harper also developed a useful working relationship with other MSPs, particularly those not attached to the major parties.[30]  One analysis of MSP voting patterns within the chamber indicated that Harper, Sheridan and Canavan had the look of an informal voting alliance, much more likely to support the SNP than the Executive parties (Cowley 2002: 98). While ideologically different the three were at times able to work together to embarrass the major parties.  Taylor (2002: 221) refers to the three as the 'three Amigos…never a composite group, more a convenient huddle'.  This relationship meant that when parliamentary votes were close, the small parties mattered.[31]

The election of Robin Harper brought a number of other benefits to the party. Harper enjoyed the support of two full-time parliamentary employees (one researcher and one administrator) who produced detailed work on specific issues,

---

[29]Across Britain 10 Green deposits were saved. No Green candidate had ever before retained a deposit in a British General Election.

[30]Interviewed in the *Sunday Herald* (25.04.99) Robin Harper argued that if elected he would seek to forge alliances with members of other parties on individual issues: 'I have met so many people from different parties, on platforms and so on, and I find them agreeing with me.  They say, as Robin says, poverty is a major cause of ill health, or, as Robin says, public transport needs massive investment and we have common ground'.

[31]Such as when the opposition parties combined to defeat an executive attempt to introduce fire service reform in the form of an emergency motion (*The Herald* 09.01.03).

such as GM food, organic production targets, and housing policy. Furthermore, environmental NGOs which had previously kept their distance from the party began to develop a working relationship with Harper in the Parliament, providing useful back-up and informational support on issues such as organic farming. Indeed Harper came to be regarded as a specialist in many of these areas. For example, he was widely interviewed and reported by the media on problems associated with genetically modified crop trials (*The Scotsman* 16.08.02).

So, the party could look forward with some confidence to the 2003 Scottish Parliament Election, not least because the polls pointed to a likely increase in the number of Green MSPs.[32] Throughout the first four years of the Scottish Parliament, support for the Greens stood at around 3-4 per cent in the list vote. Over the year of 2002, the party was averaging 4.4 per cent of the second vote, behind the SSP who were attracting 6.7 per cent in the same period (System Three/*The Herald*). As the May 1st elections approached, however, support for the Greens began to rise, as it looked increasingly likely that Britain would go to war in Iraq. NFO System Three polling in February and March 2003 indicated that Green support stood at 6 per cent (the SSP figures were 7 and 10 per cent) (*The Herald* 08.02.03; *The Herald* 07.03.03). At the end of April, the Greens were on around 7 per cent of the list vote, and the SSP on 10 per cent (*The Herald* 29.04.03; *The Scotsman* 01.05.03). Based on these levels of support, pundits were forecasting four to six Green MSPs and up to nine for the SSP (*The Herald* 29.04.03; *The Scotsman* 01.05.03).

The 2003 Green campaign was similar to that of 1999 but also rather more ambitious, organised and strategic. Indeed, the election budget available to the party was nearly twice as large as that of 1999 (Corbett 2003a: 4). This meant that the party enjoyed the benefits of a team of staff in the months running up to the election, as opposed to the one part-timer in 1999, and was also able to invest in more polished election materials.[33] Once again, the party chose not to contest the constituency contests, but increased the total number of list candidates to 68 urging voters to support 'Team Green' in the regional seats.[34] Thus, the party maintained the 'Second Vote' strategy, emphasising that Green candidates were standing in the regions only.

In 2003 the party attempted to capitalise on Harper's record in the Parliament. Whilst attacking executive ministers for 'sitting on their hands' for four years, instead of tackling environmental issues, Harper was portrayed as the green 'conscience of the Parliament'. Harper and the other Greens emphasised the

---

[32]Note, however, that some polling companies, such as MORI, Scottish Opinion, and Yougov did not record the Green vote separately.

[33]The range of campaigning techniques was expanded, including the distribution of green pledge-cards and windmills. Moreover, the Green campaign reached more areas than in the previous election. In areas like South of Scotland and Mid Scotland and Fife party activists toured extensively. Unlike the SSP, however, the party did not have any high-profile media stars to support their campaign.

[34]Note that this figure was reduced by the day of the election. The party lost 18% of candidates between the call for nominations and election day.

party's attempts to work with others in the spirit of 'new politics' during the first four years of devolution and the need to build on this good work with a larger team of Green MSPs (*The Herald* 18.04.03). While Harper's time in the Parliament had been interpreted by some as lacking dynamism and radicalism the Greens' portrayed Harper's pragmatic and moderate approach as an asset (see Taylor 2002: 226-227). This theme continued throughout the campaign and beyond. Following her election, Eleanor Scott, now the Green group's leader in the Parliament, declared an intention to pursue 'thoughtful, co-operative politics' (*Sunday Herald* 01.06.03) and Harper stated that the Green group would work in 'consensual and effective' ways (*The Scotsman* 05.05.03).

Thus, the party image projected during the campaign was that the Greens represented a new, consensual kind of politics, very different from the confrontational style of traditional party politics. The party wanted to protect this image by avoiding confrontation with the other parties. Importantly, this involved avoiding any claims that the Greens were about to break through in massive numbers, thus threatening the position of the other parties. In other words, the Greens were aware that attacks from the other parties would be damaging, and they did not have the resources at the time to respond in like fashion. They therefore projected more sober images of a small, radical party willing to play a meaningful role in the new Parliament but not likely to be a large presence in any coalition negotiations. By and large, the tactics worked.

Media attention was also a much more significant feature of the Green campaign in 2003. Many commentators continued to talk of only four parties in Scotland, and the Greens found themselves excluded from some high-profile debates (for example, the BBC leadership debates). Nevertheless, given the apparent high levels of voter disillusionment with mainstream politics and the increased opportunities for 'other' candidates under PR, some in the media were eager to talk to the Greens. Certainly, the party received more attention than ever before, and the image projected of Harper was one of an agreeable 'nice guy', contrasting with Sheridan's more hard-edged and uncompromising, if more dynamic, persona. Moreover, the party's coalition potential was raised by the media for the first time during this campaign, and the Green manifesto discussed in some detail, although not always positively. The party itself was unhappy with the media's coverage, complaining that media analysis was either unfairly disparaging of the party, or, more typically, neglected to include the Greens at all.[35] Certainly, the media highlighted some of the party's policies perceived to be most 'wacky', including goldfish bans and dope cafes, while neglecting core Green policies. It is worth noting, however, that the so-called 'wacky' ideas of goldfish bans and dope cafes did not appear in the party's election manifesto.

The party again emphasised a mix of environmental and social justice themes, pointing to the Green pillars of environmental responsibility and social

---

[35]Following the election, some commentators argued that the Greens benefited from a lack of serious media exposure. Douglas Fraser suggests that the Greens were portrayed as outsiders by the media pundits, and this helped distance them from 'tainted' mainstream parties in what was an 'anti-politics' election (Fraser 2003: 29).

justice. The manifesto referred to the party's five key principles of 'environmental wisdom, non-violence, radical democracy, equality and social justice' (Scottish Green Party 2003: 2). The manifesto contained the traditional green policies of green taxation, a citizens income to replace most benefits, the phasing out of nuclear power, the removal of all nuclear weapons, an end to GM trials, a plastic bag tax and congestion charges. They argued for the halting of major trunk road building, including the cancellation of the M74 extension, the expansion of the Cairngorms National Park, and for a dedicated environment minister. A land value tax was also promoted as a replacement for council tax and business rates. In many of these areas, therefore, the party did not distinguish between devolved and retained powers, choosing to present a more general picture of what the Greens stood for.

In the devolved policy areas of health, education and transport the party made a range of commitments including improved pay and conditions for health professionals, free school meals for all children attending state schools, abolition of school league tables, abolition of deferred tuition fees, an end to public-private partnerships (PPPs), and the return of rail to public ownership. On most of these issues, the party is firmly positioned on the left of Scottish politics. In addition, the party campaigned against the war in Iraq, and in support of the fire-fighters. The party favoured STV for local council elections and argued that Scotland should 'work towards independence'.

The party was confident that the number of Green MSPs would rise, but the result was better than many expected (Table 2.5). On polling day Harper cautiously referred to five MSPs as the 'sheer delight' scenario, while noting that this was probably optimistic (*Sunday Herald* 04.05.03). In fact the party experienced an increase in its vote of 57.3 per cent (48,114 more votes) and was successful in six of the eight regions. Despite the existence of Margo MacDonald standing as an Independent on the Lothians list the party attracted enough support to have two candidates elected in this area. In fact, the 12.01 per cent achieved in Lothian was the party's best ever regional result. With 31,908 votes the Greens out-performed the Scottish Liberal Democrats and all other small party and independent candidates.[36] Moreover, with 6.9 per cent of the vote overall, the Greens finished as fifth largest party, ahead of the SSP both in number of seats and share of the vote (Table 2.6).[37]

---

[36]When broken down into traditional constituencies, we find that the Greens attracted over 10% of the vote in seven constituencies. The party's three best performances were in Edinburgh Central (19.7%), Edinburgh South (16.8%), and Glasgow Kelvin (13.7%).

[37]A total of 17 MSPs were elected from small parties or as Independents. Other successful list candidates who did not belong to the main parties were Margo MacDonald standing as an Independent in Lothians, and John Swinburne of the Scottish Senior Citizens Unity Party in Central Scotland. In the constituencies, small parties and others attracted 9.6% of constituency votes. Dr. Jean Turner won the Strathkelvin and Bearsden constituency campaigning to stop the closure of a local hospital, while Dennis Canavan retained his seat as an Independent in Falkirk West.

**Table 2.5  The Regional Green Vote in the Scottish Parliamentary
Elections, 1 May 2003**

|  | Votes (N) | % | MSPs |
|---|---|---|---|
| Highlands and Islands | 13,935 | 8.27 | Eleanor Scott |
| North East Scotland | 12,724 | 5.22 | Shiona Baird |
| Mid Scotland and Fyfe | 17,147 | 6.86 | Mark Russell |
| West of Scotland | 14,544 | 5.66 | - |
| Glasgow | 14,570 | 7.13 | Patrick Harvie |
| Central Scotland | 12,248 | 4.66 | - |
| Lothian | 31,908 | 12.01 | R.Harper & M.Ballard |
| South of Scotland | 15,062 | 5.72 | Chris Balance |
| Total | 132,138 | 6.90 | 7 MSPs |

**Table 2.6  Results of the Scottish Parliamentary Elections, 1 May 2003**

|  | Const MSPs | List MSPs | Total | Change | % List vote |
|---|---|---|---|---|---|
| Cons | 3 | 15 | 18 | 0 | 15.5 |
| Green | 0 | 7 | 7 | +6 | 6.9 |
| Labour | 46 | 4 | 50 | -5 | 29.3 |
| LibDem | 13 | 4 | 17 | -1 | 11.8 |
| SNP | 9 | 18 | 27 | -8 | 20.9 |
| SSP | 0 | 6 | 6 | +5 | 6.7 |
| Others | 2 | 2 | 4 | +3 | 8.9 |

Following the election, there was renewed media interest in the Greens, much of which centred on whether the party would be prepared to form part of a coalition. The Green position was that they would not want to be involved in formal coalition discussions, preferring instead to work with other parties on a policy by policy basis (*Sunday Herald* 04.05.03). In addition, the media began to be more critical of the Greens' policies, with commentators asking 'Did the voters know what they voted for?'. A media backlash took place following the success of the UK Greens in 1989 (Kemp and Wall 1990: 33) and a similar pattern was evident in Scotland in 2003. The Greens, however, took this as a sign that they were now being taken more seriously.

The impact of the election success on the Greens cannot be over-estimated. The Greens (and SSP) are now represented on the Parliament's Business Bureau, the body that decides on legislative priorities and the scheduling of debates, as well as a number of different parliamentary committees.[38] As a parliamentary group the Greens now have more power to initiate debate and to introduce members' bills.[39] Within weeks of the election, the party had already put forward proposals for a Warm Homes Bill and a Civil Partnerships Bill, and the party was also working with the SSP and SNP in attempts to increase the number of free school meals (*The Herald* 05.06.03). Moreover, the resources available to the party in Parliament have increased dramatically, each MSP receiving around £55,000 for administrative and research support. In June 2003 the party was able to advertise for a number of support staff including a Parliamentary group co-ordinator, research and policy officers, a press officer, a head of media and communications, various administrators and six constituency support workers.[40]

The party infrastructure is also being improved. At the time of the 1999 elections, only a small number of local parties were active in Scotland – Dundee, Highland, Edinburgh and Strathclyde. By 2003 the organisation had developed, with properly functioning regional parties throughout Scotland, creating a two-tier structure of local and regional parties. Legally, the party is obliged to run a more professional financial system and in some respects this means more central coordination. Membership is now centrally administered, as is the administration of candidate selection for Scottish and European elections, although the choice of candidates is entirely local. The centre also has more influence over the setting up of local parties, developing, for example, model local and regional constitutions. This reorganisation amounts to a pooling of administrative tasks centrally, to ensure that the party meets the obligations of the Political Parties, Elections and Referendum Act 2000, while leaving campaigning decisions locally. Nevertheless, in 2003 the Greens still lacked a campaign presence in some areas, such as the North East and West of Scotland, and the party continues to experience difficulties developing networks of local parties within the regions.

Membership development has also reflected the party's recent electoral success. The 1999 election had very little impact on membership, numbers remaining stubbornly low (only 350 by Autumn 1999). Writing in the party's newsletter following the 2003 election success, the party's executive convenor Gavin Corbett argued that the party in 1999 had missed an opportunity to recruit

---

[38] Greens have places on the Enterprise, Communities, Environment and Rural Development, Audit, Procedures and Equal Opportunities committees.

[39] The group decided that Eleanor Scott, the party council convenor, would lead the Green group in Parliament, and that Robin Harper would be principal speaker.

[40] As Gavin Corbett argues, this does present some potential problems for the Greens. While the seven Parliamentarians enjoy significant professional support (around 16 full-time equivalent staff), the party itself is still very small and can only afford to employ 1.6 full-time equivalent staff, meaning they still rely heavily on volunteer workers.

new members because it had not been prepared for Harper's success. He stated: 'We had not prepared fully for what it would mean for our profile as a party. Although we expected a flood of new members, it was no more than a trickle, because we had not geared up for recruitment' (Corbett 2003b: 6).

By 2001, however, the party was beginning to develop a recruitment strategy, with a new membership leaflet and a guide to members on how to recruit others. During the 2001 General Election campaign around 40 new members joined the Scottish Greens and membership eventually reached 520 by September 2002. By the 2003 Scottish elections, the party was being more proactive in its recruitment techniques, including the creation of new members' packs in an attempt to retain new entrants. During the 2003 campaign the party recorded a membership of just over 600 and this rose to 721 by the end of June. Following the election, the party rewrote its recruitment literature, incorporating the party's electoral success, and set a recruitment target of 900 members by the end of 2003. In fact, membership stood at 780 by the end of 2003, short of the stated target but a very healthy level compared to previous years.

*Conclusion*

This chapter has documented the electoral results and membership development of the Greens in Scotland. It is clear that, despite a fairly lengthy lifespan, for most of its existence the Green party in Scotland struggled to get noticed within a rather inhospitable political environment. As discussed in chapter 1, the existence of a strong working class culture and high levels of national identity has tended to work against the rise in support for environmentalism. However, levels of environmental concern are not necessarily good indicators of Green support. Other factors are more relevant in explaining the long-term difficulties faced by the Scottish Greens. In the pre-devolution years, Britain's centralised political system, the first-past-the-post electoral system, and the dynamics of four-party competition presented substantial barriers to a green electoral challenge and the building of a green movement. Competition for votes was particularly fierce in Scotland as voters concerned about nuclear issues had a natural home in the SNP.

Despite the problems faced by the Greens in Scotland, the party experienced an up-turn in its electoral fortunes at the end of the 1980s, and, with the advent of devolution, achieved its greatest electoral successes in the Scottish Parliamentary Elections of 1999 and 2003. The rise of the Green vote in 1989 appears to have been strongly related to increases in environmental awareness at the time, combined with a series of environmental 'events', widespread media attention, and an element of protest voting. However, the success of the Scottish Greens in 1999 and 2003 was inspired by devolution of power and, more importantly, the element of proportionality in the electoral system used to elect MSPs. This has made it possible for a small party like the Greens to mount a more serious challenge. It is important to note that the election of Robin Harper in 1999 and of six additional Green MSPs in 2003 was achieved against a background of rather low interest in the environment at the time. In other words, unlike 1989, the environment was not at the height of an 'issue attention cycle'. The party itself should be given credit for utilising the new institutional arrangements. It made the most of a limited amount of resources and showed it could run a dynamic and effective campaign.

Since the election of Robin Harper to the Scottish Parliament in 1999, the pattern emerging is that the Greens can make an impact in elections influenced by proportional representation. Under first-past-the-post rules, retaining deposits is the best the party can achieve. A combination of the new electoral context, increased media interest and the voters' disaffection with mainstream politics has resulted in a rise in support for the Greens. In 2003, small parties and independent candidates attracted 23 per cent of the regional list vote, suggesting that voters may be becoming increasingly disaffected with the mainstream parties. In the period before the election, it was becoming clear that Scottish voters were rather disappointed with devolution, and levels of trust in politicians were declining (Bromley *et al.* 2003; McEwen 2003).[41] Furthermore, analyses of the 2003 campaign suggest that the main parties were viewed as very similar, that party leaders were uninspiring, and that there was a general lack of policy debate (Boon and Curtice 2003; Curtice 2003; MacWhirter 2003: McEwen 2003: 62). Under these circumstances it was perhaps unsurprising that voters turned to 'other' parties and independent candidates in significant numbers.

There is some uncertainty, however, over which party or parties suffer most from the existence of small parties, and specifically the Greens. The party to suffer most from the general trend was the SNP, losing a total of 10 regional list seats, although this was partly the result of some SNP gains in first-past-the-post seats. While Labour also lost votes to these parties, the dynamics of regional list voting have less of an impact on this party because of its strength in the constituencies. As for the Green vote, there is further evidence to suggest that the Liberal Democrats may suffer most from the presence of the Scottish Greens. Denver's (2003: 50-51) analysis of the election results suggests a significant relationship between the Green and Liberal Democrat vote; the higher the Green vote, the worse the Liberal Democrat list performance relative to their constituency vote.

Furthermore, increasing familiarity with the voting system may be encouraging more voters to support different parties in the two ballots. While the precise flow of votes between first and second votes is impossible to establish, estimates of 'ticket-splitting' in 2003 range from 17.1 per cent (Denver 2003:50) to 29 per cent (Curtice 2003a: 12). Most observers accept that the incidence of ticket-splitting has increased since 1999.[42] In some areas, well over a third of

---

[41]Although the same survey evidence reveals that Scots are still very attached to the Parliament and devolution in principle, with levels of trust in the Scottish Parliament considerably higher than for the UK Parliament and support for increasing the fiscal powers of the Parliament (McEwen 2003: 58-59; Curtice *et al* 2002; Bromley *et al* 2003: 17-19). Moreover increased levels of voter cynicism in politicians are not exclusive to Scotland (see Norris 1999; Curtice 2002).

[42]Denver and MacAllister's (1999: 25) 'minimum switchers' measure suggested a figure of 11.6% in 1999. Other estimates however were much higher, with Paterson *et al.* (2002: 78) claiming that 20% of voters voted differently on the two ballots in 1999.

voters were prepared to vote differently in the second ballot. In Edinburgh Central, Denver (2003: 50) estimates that the 'minimum switcher' figure stood at 34.6 per cent.

These general trends – disaffection with the main parties and increasing familiarity with the electoral system – are advantageous to the Greens, particularly when one considers that voters are more likely to support small parties in elections to a body which is seen as less important than the UK Parliament (Curtice 2003b: 12). However, these developments should be considered with caution by the party. Greens are not guaranteed future representation at current levels. As Curtice (2003b: 13) points out, a reduction of the Green vote by only 1 per cent could significantly reduce the number of Green MSPs. Furthermore, other parties are likely to be much more confrontational towards the Greens in future elections.

These developments also have considerable implications for the development of party membership. Success in elections tends to attract waves of new members. However, in some respects small parties like the Greens are often ill-prepared for massive surges in membership. This appears to have been the case in 1989/1990. The party was simply unable to hang on to the members who joined during this period. In 1999, the election of one MSP did not lead to a massive influx of members. Rather, there was a very gradual increase in membership numbers, developing alongside the moderate increase in electoral support and more prominent media profile. This was a much more sustainable situation for the party. The 2003 election has resulted in a significant increase in members but the signs are that this resembles membership recruitment of 1999 rather than 1989/1990. Moreover, the party is being considerably more proactive and strategic in its attempts to attract members, as opposed to reacting to events as they occur.

The height of Scottish Green membership, however, occurred in 1989/1990 (see Figure 2.1). These membership dynamics, which form the main body of this book, need to be explained. Why exactly did people join the Scottish Green Party at this time? As background to answering this question, chapter three explores the diversity of academic approaches in attempts to understand motivations behind membership.

Chapter 3

# Explaining Participation: Learning From Social Movement Approaches

The view that political participation is out of the ordinary and in some way paradoxical has been a common theme of many studies, the argument being that participation involves many obvious costs but few obvious benefits. As Dahl (1961: 279) observed, 'instead of seeking to explain why citizens are not interested, concerned and active, the task is to explain why a few citizens are'. Certainly, few people become involved in 'high-cost' participation (see Parry and Moyser 1992). So, why do *some* people become involved? A number of theoretical approaches have been developed in an attempt to address this question. However, political scientists and sociologists have developed theories on participation quite independently. Social movement theory, with its analysis of the formation and development of social movements has done most to address the question of why people join movement organisations. In this chapter, both political science and social movement approaches are considered in an attempt to identify common themes and develop an understanding of motivations behind joining which will be used as a framework for analysis.

**The Study of Participation and Party Membership in Political Science**

*Political Participation*

The study of participation is a well-established tradition in political science (Almond and Verba 1963; Barnes and Kasse 1979; Butler and Stokes 1969; Dahl 1961; Parry, Moyser and Day 1992; Norris 2002; Verba and Nie 1972; Verba *et al.* 1978; Verba *et al.* 1995). Participation is viewed by some as essential to a modern liberal democracy (Barber 1984; Barnes and Kasse 1979; Dahl 1982; Held 1987), and some commentators have expressed concern over evidence of a recent decline in 'civic engagement' (Skocpol and Fiorina 1999). A 'realist' school, however, has argued that too much democracy is in fact detrimental to society (Schumpeter 1943). Aside from these normative approaches, studies have examined motivations behind a diverse range of political behaviour, including voting, political protest, contacting politicians and joining groups or parties, activities which have been described as 'conventional' and 'unconventional'.[1] Amongst other questions, scholars have explored the extent of political participation, the social profile of participants, and why people participate.

Some studies of political participation suggest that only a small minority of citizens actually participate politically. The political scientist Lester Milbrath (1965) outlined a hierarchy of political involvement where the vast majority of American citizens were inactive or engaged in 'spectator activities' including voting and engaging in political discussion, or wearing a political badge. By contrast, a very small group of citizens (between one and seven percent) were classified by Milbrath (1965: 21) as 'gladiators' because they participated in both low-cost and high-cost activities such as soliciting party funds or standing as a party candidate. In other words, participation is seen as being 'hierarchically ordered' (Kornberg *et al.* 1979: 61). Generally low levels of political participation led Dahl (1961: 279) to comment: 'Instead of seeking to explain why citizens are not interested, concerned and active, the task is to explain why a few citizens *are*'. However, if political participation is defined broadly to include all forms of contact with the political system (for example voting) the level of participation can appear much higher (see Verba and Nie 1972).

More recent studies suggest that participation is patterned around 'modes' or types of activities, that citizens gravitate towards different types of participation. For example, Parry *et al.* (1992: 416) conclude that participation is 'multi-dimensional': 'It was not a case of people doing more or less across the board. Rather, people (to the degree that they participated at all) tended to have taken one type of action – contacted a councillor or gone on a protest march'. In other words, there are different types, or 'modes', of participation, and super-activists are not responsible for all forms of participation, contrary to the Milbrath thesis. These findings confirm those of Verba and Nie (1972: 118-120) who identified a number of different modes of participation and the socio-economic groups likely to participate in these ways. They calculated that only 22 per cent of the American public were completely inactive (mainly lower socio-economic groups), and that 11 per cent were 'complete activists' who participated in all sorts of ways (higher socio-economic groups). However, the rest of the population tended to focus on one of four different categories of participation: voting (21 per cent); 'particularised contacting' (4 per cent) which entailed contacting politicians about a narrow issue affecting the individual directly; 'communalist activities' (20 per cent) where citizens attempted to deal with more general issues, but affecting specific communities; and, finally, taking part in party campaign activity (15 per cent) which is less community based but more conflictual. Verba and Nie (1972: 121) argued that 'each of the modes of participation is distinctive' in the sense that citizens tend to fall into one category. According to this view, participation is not

---

[1]Dalton (1996: 40) refers to conventional forms as 'voting, campaigns, group activities, and other methods normally associated with democratic politics'. Unconventional activities include protests and demonstrations.

necessarily cumulative because different types of participation exist, apart from others.[2]

In her review of political science approaches to political participation, Norris (2002: 15, Ch.2) argues that five factors can be used to explain levels and trends in participation in different countries: the extent of societal modernisation; state structures; mobilising agencies; the resources of individual citizens; and the motivation of individuals. The first of these approaches, modernisation theories, points to changes in Western liberal democracies that encourage a new form of citizen politics (Bell 1999; Dalton 1998; Inglehart 1990, 1997). Inglehart, for example, argues that modern societies are under-going a shift from materialist to 'post-materialist' values. His theory rests on the idea that post-war European societies have been relatively prosperous and, with basic needs satisfied, post-war cohorts have developed a different value system from earlier generations, moving away from material concerns towards 'quality of life' issues, which include a desire for participation and a rejection of traditional hierarchies. In sum, Inglehart points to a new, more active, form of political participation, brought about by structural changes in post-war societies.

The second approach described by Norris is the institutional approach, which examines how the structure of the state influences trends in participation. Important factors considered in this approach include electoral rules and constitutional frameworks which can be used, for example, to explain variations in electoral turnout (Jackman 1987). Thirdly, agency theories (for example, Rosenstone and Hansen 1993) examine the role of 'mobilizing organizations' – including campaigning groups, parties, trade unions, and social networks – in recruiting and organising participation. Norris includes Putnam's theory of social capital in this category, with its analysis of voluntary organisations (see Putnam 1995, 2000, 2002). Finally, Norris gives an account of the civic voluntarism model, as developed by Verba *et al.* (1995) which looks to the resources of individuals – socioeconomic status and education – and to motivational factors such as political interest and trust in its attempts to explain who participates. In this way Norris (2002: 20) illustrates a range of theories, moving from macro-level accounts (societal modernisation/structure of the state) to meso level influences (mobilising agencies) and finally micro-level theories (resources and motivation of individuals).[3]

However, identifying the extent and patterns of participation doesn't explain *why* people participate. In other words, only some of these approaches are useful in explaining individual level behaviour, such as the decision to join a political party. The meso-level and micro-level approaches described by Norris are most useful here. We take a closer look at some of the most influential theories below.

---

[2]Norris (2002: 195-196) confirms this 'clustering' effect around modes of participation.

[3]Micro-level factors are those correlates that function at the level of the individual, while macro-level analysis involves consideration of the wider political environment. Norris's own analysis concentrates on state structures, mobilising agencies (including organizational networks), and aggregate levels of political interest/culture (structure, agency, and culture) as key variables in understanding participation.

## Resource-Based Approaches and Civic Voluntarism

Some authors emphasise the importance of socio-economic factors as an explanation for participation: high socio-economic status leads to a distinct set of skills and attitudes, including civic duty and efficacy, thus producing higher levels of participation amongst these socio-economic 'types' (Barnes and Kasse 1979; Kornberg *et al.* 1979; Parry, Moyser and Day 1992; Verba and Nie 1972; Verba *et al.* 1978; Verba *et al.* 1995).[4]

One of the most extensive British studies of participation to adopt such an approach was by Parry, Moyser and Day (1992: 16), participation defined here as 'taking part in the process of formulation, passage and implementation of public policies'.[5] The model developed by Parry *et al.* (1992: 21) is based on a recognition of the importance of key resources as the foundation of participation: 'What conditions whether a person will participate or not is, aside from an interest which is at stake, the extent to which he or she possesses the resources to act' (Parry *et al.* 1992: 20). The inclination to participate can also be influenced by certain 'background variables' which include class, gender, age and individual values, and Parry *et al.* (1992: 20) argue that participation is often 'triggered' by contextual issues or developments which affect individual interests but which are very difficult to predict. Furthermore, Parry *et al.* (1992: 21) point to the impact of political participation on decision-makers, the implication being that participation that appears ineffective will discourage further participation. The 'educative effect' of participation is described as a 'side-product', in that the experience of participation can in some way influence the likelihood of future activity, but this is not a central feature of the model. Rather, Parry *et al.*'s (1992: 422) conclude that there are two major influences on 'the propensity to become politically involved': education and the membership of groups. The authors (1992: 422) argue; 'If there is a single key to political participation in Britain, it must be group memberships', highlighting the ability of groups to mobilise support for particular issues.

The civic voluntarism model, as developed by Verba, Schlozman and Brady (1995) is now commonly regarded as the dominant model in explaining political participation (see, for example, Whiteley and Seyd 2002: 36). The model is built on resource-based explanations for participation (Barnes and Kasse 1979; Parry, Moyser and Day 1992; Verba and Nie 1972; Verba *et al.* 1978; Verba *et al.* 1995). However, the later model refines the analysis of political efficacy and 'requests for recruitment' (Verba, Schlozman and Brady 1995: 272). Verba, Schlozman and Brady (1995: 269) argue that people are unlikely to participate if they lack 'resources' and 'psychological engagement with politics', or if they are 'outside of the recruitment networks that bring people into politics'.

While such approaches highlight many important variables associated with participation they are weak at explaining possible incentives for participation. In

---

[4]These social structural factors are often linked to being brought up in a family with an interest in politics i.e. political socialisation (see Kornberg *et al.* 1979).
[5]Parry *et al.* (1992: 89) reported that 6.8 per cent of their sample of the British electorate were members of a political party in 1984/85.

other words, these approaches are not good at addressing why many of those who enjoy high levels of resources do not become involved in politics, nor exactly why some of them do.  As Whiteley and Seyd (2002: 40) argue: 'What is missing is any understanding of why individuals have a demand for participation, of what incentives they have to get involved in politics.  Many high-status individuals have no such incentives, which explains why they do not participate.  While resources allow one to understand the supply of participation, it is necessary to consider the incentives for participation, or the demand side of the equation, to understand why individuals get involved in politics' (also see Whiteley 1995: 227).  To this end, we turn to rational choice approaches.

## Rational Choice Approaches

Since the 1950s the image of actors making rational choices has been a prominent theme in political science and has inspired a great deal of debate (Aldrich 1993; Barry 1970; Downs 1957; Green and Shapiro 1994; Jackman 1993; Olson 1965, 1971; Whiteley 1995). Downs (1957) applied this to voting behaviour and to party competition, arguing that the voter will vote for the party that provides the highest level of personal utility, and parties will be motivated by the principle of vote maximisation, adapting their policies to gain office.[6]

However, it is the work of Mancur Olson (1965) that has been most widely cited by political scientists in their attempts to explain why people join organisations. Olson viewed individual decisions to participate as being driven by economic cost-benefit analysis and he argued that because individuals were rational and self-interested they were unlikely to participate in activity which aimed to achieve non-excludable collective goods, those goods which are available to everyone in equal measure.  In *The Logic of Collective Action* Olson (1965: 14) argued that public goods are inadequate in explaining individual motivation to collective action because 'they must be available to everyone if they are available to anyone'.  The model predicts that individuals will not be motivated to join if the sole incentives offered are public goods. Through a process of cost-benefit analysis the potential actor will conclude that participation will make no difference to the overall outcome (the imperceptible effect), and that any public goods/benefits accrued by the organisation will be gained without the need for individual participation (the free-rider problem).  Using the union dues payer as an illustration, Olson (1965: 50-51) concludes that participation must be encouraged through the offer of selective utilitarian incentives (private goods) as a supplement to the public goods.  So, the theory predicts that private good incentives will act as the main motivator of individual participation, and that a group's political or collective objectives are a 'by-product' of the organisational efforts to attract members (Olson 1965: 132-5; also see Berry 1984: 69-73).

Olson's theory was regarded as radical at the time because it posed a challenge to traditional pluralist approaches which assumed that individuals would

---

[6]The rational choice approach is alternatively referred to as the economic model of man, the utilitarian model, or value expectancy theory.

be motivated to join with others because they shared common (collective) interests. Truman (1951), for example, argued that people would form groups when they were adversely affected by a 'disturbance'. As Marsh (1976: 258) argues, authors like Bentley and Truman, 'assumed that it is in an individual's self-interest to join an interest group to attain the public policy related goals he shares in common with other group members'. Olson, on the other hand, argued that group or collective interests were not sufficient to motivate the rational individual.

However, Olson's theory was not without problems. Indeed, Olson had some problems identifying what kinds of organisations function in accordance with this model. He writes; 'Logically, the theory can cover all types of lobbies, including noneconomic groups with social, political, religious, or philanthropic objectives' (Olson 1965: 159). However, in the final analysis he restricts his by-product theory to those organisations that are able to clearly demonstrate the existence of private selective incentives. Consequently, he exempts religious, philanthropic and 'lost-cause' groups on the grounds that their participants are 'psychologically disturbed' (Olson 1965: 162).[7] By assuming that the 'by-products' of voluntary organisations or social movements are collective goods, in that they apply to those who participate and those who do not, and that involvement produces little in the way of individual reward, he concludes that participation in these organisations is in fact paradoxical ('the paradox of participation').

However, the work of Olson has been challenged extensively by the political science community (Eckstein 1992; Green and Shapiro 1994; Hindess 1988; Marsh 1976; Whiteley 1995). Other theorists have endeavoured to move beyond the Olsonian analysis of private good economic motivations and attempted to incorporate intangible incentives in their models, including altruism, standards of fairness, emotional ties, and political goals. Prior to Olson, Clarke and Wilson (1961: 130) had developed an 'incentives analysis' of organisations which assumed that 'all viable organisations must provide tangible or intangible incentives to individuals in exchange for contributions of individual activity to the organisations'. Their analysis recognises that a number of different incentives exist beyond economic or utilitarian incentives, referring to material, solidary and purposive incentives (Clarke and Wilson 1961: 134-137). Material incentives involve tangible rewards which could be direct services or the provision of information. Solidary incentives are intangible and derive from social interaction, 'from the act of associating'. Finally, purposive incentives are also intangible but they derive from the stated aims of the organisation itself, what Clarke and Wilson (1961: 135) refer to as 'suprapersonal goals of the organisation'.

In his 1995 publication Wilson (1995: 33-4) outlines four types of incentive: material incentives, specific solidary incentives, collective solidary incentives, and purposive incentives. Wilson's description of material and purposive incentives remains the same as in 1961, however solidary incentives are now separated into two types: specific solidary incentives are intangible rewards which 'arise out of

---

[7]Nevertheless, Olson (1965: 12) recognised that 'in organisations, an emotional or ideological element is also often involved'.

the act of associating that can be given to, or withheld from, specific individuals' (Wilson 1995: 34).  These might include offices, or honorary positions within the organisation.  Collective solidary incentives (Wilson 1995: 34) involve 'the fun and conviviality of coming together' and are not specific to a single individual.

As regards membership of a political party, Wilson (1995: 96) strongly suggests that this is not generally self-interested.  Rather, he argues that 'a major source of incentives for party organizations' is 'purpose, principle, and ideology'.  However, he goes on to illustrate that motivations are exceedingly complex and depend on the type and status of parties. Wilson (1995: 97-106) discusses the importance of material incentives in the days of the party machines in American politics, and he points to dominant ideological motivations in socialist and Marxist parties in American history (the Socialist Workers' Party and the Socialist Labor Party).[8]  In the cases of the Democrat and Republican parties, Wilson (1995: 106) refers to the 'amateur' who is moved to participate by largely purposive goals, or 'the ends of government'; 'a person who finds an enterprise – here, politics – intrinsically rewarding because it expresses a commitment to a larger purpose'.  However, as an explanation of motivations behind party membership in America, Wilson (1995: 110) argues that collective solidary incentives are, ultimately, the most valuable:[9]

> Though we have no survey on this score, it is likely that the majority of persons who are active members of local party organizations seek neither material benefits nor the achievement of large ends, but merely find politics – or at least coming together to work in groups to work at politics – intrinsically enjoyable.  Collective solidary incentives are important to some extent in all political organizations, including the machine and the Communist cell, but they are the dominant incentive in many, if not most, local parties.

Other authors have pointed to the importance of intangible incentives.  Salisbury (1969: 16), for example, in his 'exchange theory of interest groups', points to the importance of 'expressive benefits', 'where the action involved gives expression to the interests or values of a person or group rather than instrumentally pursuing interests or values'.  Unlike Clarke and Wilson's purposive incentives, expressive benefits do not directly derive from the goals of the organisation. They are gained from the very act of expressing a particular set of values (Salisbury 1969: 16).

---

[8]However, Wilson (1995: 103) concedes that this is theoretical speculation: 'We have no careful study of the process by which members of the various Marxist parties were induced to join, and thus it is difficult to speak confidently about the incentives systems employed'. But, he argues, 'For many dues payers, ideology alone must have sufficed, for there were few other awards'.

[9]He cites the work of Salisbury (1965) and Eldersveld (1964) who conducted local level studies of party activists in St. Louis and Detroit.

It is clear that attempts to test and modify rational choice explanations for political behaviour have dominated the work of political scientists in their endeavours to explain membership of organisations. Norris (2002: 219), for example, describes her approach as a 'soft' form of rational choice theory. Interest group studies of environmental participation provide another good illustration of the use of rational choice as a model to test and criticise (Jordan and Maloney 1997: 47-48; Johnson 1998). For example, Jordan and Maloney (1997: 87) challenge the Olsonian approach by highlighting the importance of collective rewards in public interest group membership and make the case for an 'expanded conception of rationality'.

*Mobilisation/Organisational Approaches*

The distinction between people who 'volunteer' to participate in politics and those who are actively 'recruited' by a party or voluntary organisation is commonly recognised in political science (see, for example, Kornberg *et al.* 1979: 97). However, in exploring why people join organisations, researchers tend to focus on one of these aspects: 1. What joiners expect to receive through participation i.e. what benefits they expect from membership or 2. What leaders can do to persuade potential members to join (see Berry 1984: 67). The first approach focuses on individual motivations to join. The second approach tends to involve organisational, top-down analysis.

Wilson (1995: 13) applies the incentives theory first developed by Clarke and Wilson in the 1960s to different kinds of voluntary associations, including civic associations, interest groups and the political party. Wilson's central interest however is organisational maintenance; what organisations have to do in order to attract and hold on to members. As Wilson (1995: 28) explains, this organisational perspective is not a study of individuals:

> Because this is a study of organizations, not of individuals, in the chapters to come attention will be focused on the organization from the perspective of those in charge of maintaining it (they will be called the executives) rather from the point of view of would-be members. In this sense, as in many others, our account will be incomplete. We shall describe (ideally explain) how organizations behave toward persons wanting certain kinds of material and nonmaterial benefactions; we shall not explain, except to offer some passing observations, how it is that certain persons respond to one incentive rather than to another.

In other words, the emphasis shifts from understanding individual-level demand, or satisfaction (the demand side) to organisational supply (the supply side). The focus is on the efforts made by the organisation to attract members, to publicise the group amongst those who might be most attracted to it. Berry (1984: 82) argues that more should be done to understand how organisations attract members, particularly citizen groups functioning within a very competitive environment:

For some interest group leaders, then, it may not be the mix of benefits they offer, but how aggressively they market their organizations, which makes the critical difference in their ultimate success. If they operate in a competitive environment, but offer goods similar to those of other groups, the question is how they reach people and persuade them to join.

Many traditional interest group studies highlight the importance of group entrepreneurs who stimulate potential members into joining. In his exchange theory of interest groups Salisbury (1969) argued that leadership was an important factor in whether people joined groups, as opposed to a Truman type of disturbance. While suggesting that group entrepreneurs were themselves motivated by the offer of a staff job, Salisbury (1969) claimed that the group 'entrepreneur' was competing in an interest group 'marketplace' and that the entrepreneur would be most successful by providing attractive selective incentives to potential members.[10] Expanded versions of this approach also acknowledge that contributing to collective goods can be an important motivation for both the entrepreneur and potential member, thus becoming a significant element in the entrepreneur's attempts to attract members (see Berry 1984: 69-70, Browne 1998: 19-25, and Sabatier 1992: 107-109 for discussion).

More recently, political science scholars have placed even more emphasis on the supply-side i.e. how activity can be stimulated by political elites (Rosenstone and Hansen 1993; Jordan and Maloney 1997; Schlozman *et al.* 1999; Shaiko 1999; Bosso 2003). In their analysis of mobilisation processes, Rosenstone and Hansen (1993) recognise that personal resources can influence perceptions of costs and benefits of activity, but they argue that participation can be *determined* by the mobilisation strategies of political leaders (politicians, political parties and interest group leaders) who target their efforts on people they think may be sympathetic to their cause and in this way pull them into activity.[11] Rosenstone and Hansen (1993: 5-6) argue for 'the centrality of strategic mobilisation' and are critical of traditional approaches which neglect this aspect of participation:

> Political analysts, we contend, have until now told only half of the story of participation in America, the half that stresses the resources, interests, identifications, and beliefs of individual citizens. We complete the story. Political leaders, in their struggles for political advantage, mobilize ordinary citizens into American politics. The strategic choices they make, the strategic decisions they reach, shape the contours – the whos, whens and whys – of political participation in America.

---

[10] Browne (1998: 21) refers to Salisbury's work as a 'fine-tuning of Olson'.

[11] Similarly, Schlozman *et al.* (1999: 446) point out that recruitment strategies are often targeted at those groups who, because of their higher than average socio-economic status, are likely to be more participative anyway. 'In short', they argue, 'when viewed in its entirety, the process of citizen recruitment does not mobilise the marginal and the dispossessed' (Schlozman *et al.* 1999: 446).

Similarly, Jordan and Maloney (1997: 144) emphasise the significance of group behaviour – namely 'professional marketing strategies' – as a mechanism through which members can be encouraged to join. They highlight how a group's marketing approach can manipulate the decision to join, aiming to 'lower the perception of the cost of membership, and to crystalize the predisposed members' concerns' (Jordan and Maloney 1997: 144). Thus, Jordan and Maloney (1997: 3) maintain that 'active marketing by the group can exploit sympathy for causes and encourage the predisposed potential member to join: a decision which might not have been faced without group prompting'. The crux of this argument is that rational choice approaches underestimate the power of groups to influence the individual's decision to join (Jordan and Maloney 1997: Chs 3 and 6).[12] Similarly, Shaiko (1999) offers an analysis of recruitment and retention devices in (US) environmental organisations, including direct marketing, telephone sales and face-to-face canvassing, the first of which is generally most effective. Significantly, these are regarded as tools available to group leaders in their 'nurturing of membership' (Shaiko 1999: 93).

Moe (1980b: 71) also examined the relationship between group leaders and potential members 'with the former offering some combination of selective incentives and collective goods and the latter deciding on the basis of cost-benefit calculations whether to buy the benefits offered'. Moe (1981) points out that when people feel they can make a difference this is often the result of group attempts to manipulate perceptions of efficacy. This is similar to Jordan and Maloney's (1997: 99) description of 'group marketing', where the decision to join is viewed as a low cost decision. For these authors, because individuals do not go through a complex intellectual decision-making process, there should be a shift in focus from the individual to the activities of groups. In other words, the emphasis becomes supply-side, rather than demand-led.

As a general rule, then, the interest group approach concentrates on the behaviour of group leaders as an explanation for membership. Leaders of interest groups are often referred to as 'political entrepreneurs' and emphasis is placed on how leaders can play an active role in shaping how individuals arrive at their decisions. In particular, US interest group scholars have much to say about organizational maintenance issues (see Baumgartner and Leech 1998; Bosso 1991, 1994, 2003; Bosso and Guber 2002; Browne 1998; Cigler and Loomis 2002; Johnson 1995, 1998; Moe 1980a, 1980b; Shaiko 1999; Vig and Kraft 2002).

The supply-side approach can suggest that members are passive actors, manipulated by the marketing strategies of group entrepreneurs. Bosso (2003-10-23) for example, in his look at the 'dynamics of organizational maintenance' of national environmental organisations in the US presents such an image (also see Bosso 1991, 1994; Bosso and Guber 2002). The key characteristics of these groups are passive memberships, staff-driven strategies, and business-like

---

[12]It will be argued later in this chapter, however, that an examination of group recruitment techniques (resource mobilisation) can in fact be accommodated within rational choice models. They are not competing models. The picture of individuals weighing up costs and benefits of membership was developed largely to understand how groups attracted members.

approaches in that the groups are *competing* in 'discrete issue markets', or 'advocacy markets' (Bosso 2003: 402). Furthermore, in many of the groups observed by Bosso (2003: 407) he notes a decline in reliance on individual membership contributions, but an increase in reliance on membership donations. Bosso (2003: 409) suggests that recruiting new members who pay a membership fee and contribute no more can in fact be a financial burden to the organisation unless they can be persuaded to make larger financial donations.

> For most of these organizations, annual dues barely pay the costs of recruitment, but they do get the potential supporter in the door. In this sense, annual dues are a loss leader, the cost of building a base of annual donors who in time may be convinced to go higher on the pyramid of support – where the real money is.

In like fashion, Berry (1984: 86) pointed to the long-term benefits of direct mail strategies. While these tend to have a very poor response (he suggests that a response of 2 per cent is a 'good return'), they can be viewed as a long-term investment, in the sense that recruits may become regular donors: 'If a group can break even when it is searching for new members, it is likely to come out ahead later on when the recent recruits can be asked to donate again'. He continues '..the success so many groups have had with direct mail encourages others to take the risk and invest "seed" money, hoping to uncover a good harvest of donors'. Furthermore, Bosso (2003) suggests that successfully persuading long-term members to contribute more generously explains why many groups have survived despite a flat-lining or even decline in membership numbers. He argues that 'those who stayed on have dug deeper into their pockets to support the cause' (Bosso 2003: 409).

In sum, many interest group scholars argue that groups often look more like 'nonprofit corporations' or 'professional advocacy organizations' than traditional citizen groups (Bosso 2003: 408; also see Baumgartner and Leech 1998). These organisations may simply be seeking financial backing of supporters in order to fund the activities of the professional campaigners. Bosso (2003: 410) also notes the development of 'virtual membership' through the Internet which 'reinforces the perspective that members *as such* are little more than organizational wallpaper, a collective backdrop for professional advocacy'.

*The General Incentives Model*

Recent studies of the Labour and Conservative parties (Seyd and Whiteley 1992, 1995, 2002; Whiteley *et al.* 1994, Whiteley and Seyd 1998a, 1998b, 2002) are based on a general incentives model of participation, used to explain why people join parties and why some become active. At first sight, this approach appears to be an attempt at expanding rational choice explanations. However, Seyd and Whiteley (2002: 89-90; Whiteley and Seyd 2002: 51) describe their approach as a 'synthesis of rational choice and social-psychological accounts of participation'. Like Olson, these authors argue that incentives to action exist – that the perception of costs and benefits plays an important role – although they disagree with the precise nature or characteristics of these incentives. However, Seyd and Whiteley also draw parallels with the field of social-psychology in their assessment of factors like social norms and 'internalized values' (Seyd and Whiteley 2002: 90).

Since the early 1990s, Seyd and Whiteley have identified a number of incentives relevant to the experience of joining the Labour and Conservative parties in Britain. During this time they have refined their model, choosing to rework and apply different labels to motivations behind membership. Most recently Seyd and Whiteley (2002: 90-93) point to five distinct factors which motivate people to join a political party: selective incentives, collective incentives, group incentives, affective or expressive motives, and social norms.[13]

Selective incentives can take a number of forms (Seyd and Whiteley 2002: 91-92). *Selective outcome incentives* apply to the achievement of goals which are private, not collective. These 'private returns' can be experienced only by members. They might include the achievement of elected office, the furtherance of a career in the trade union movement and many other private rewards which come from membership of the party. However, these incentives are most likely to apply to active members and therefore might not be useful in understanding the passive party member. *Selective process incentives* apply to the very act of participating, not the perceived outcome of efforts. The suggestion is that there is inherent value in participation, regardless of the outcome, which might simply amount to meeting 'like-minded and interesting people' (Seyd and Whiteley 1992: 60). However, the authors point out that most members are not active and it therefore also seems unlikely that these 'process benefits' apply to many members. *Ideological selective incentives* are another type of selective incentive. It is argued that party membership might amount to 'giving expression to beliefs', in much the same way as active church-going (Whiteley *et al.* 1994: 85). Thus, Whiteley and his colleagues (1994:85) argue, '...ideological radicalism would motivate individuals to join the party because it allows them to interact with like-minded people and give expression to deeply held beliefs'. However, they again suggest that these motives are only likely to apply to active members.[14]

---

[13]Although in their book on high-intensity participation they point to only four categories of factors: selective and collective incentive, group motivations and expressive motives (Whiteley and Seyd 2002: 52-57).

[14]In the original Labour study, ideological motivations were categorised as altruistic motivations. Seyd and Whiteley (1992: 63) referred to *altruistic concerns*, arguing that 'individuals are motivated by altruism when making decisions'. These are likely to be expressed in terms of idealistic goals, such as 'a desire for social justice', or 'the creation of a more compassionate society'. Seyd and Whiteley (1992: 63) note that these statements have policy implications but that 'the moral imperative is the driving force behind the decision to participate, not the specific goal'. Not separating altruistic motivations from ideological incentives led Seyd and Whiteley (1992: 75) to place responses like 'I wanted to show my commitment to socialism' into the altruism category. In the Conservative Party members book such a response, for example 'an attachment to Conservative principles', was treated as an expressive attachment (Whiteley *et al.* 1994: 96).

Collective incentives relate to policy goals (Seyd and Whiteley 2002: 90). In an early description of *collective positive incentives*, Seyd and Whiteley (1992: 61) challenge the notion that individuals assess only immediate costs and benefits to themselves. They argue that 'individuals can put themselves in the place of the group, and think about the group welfare, rather than just their own individual welfare'. Thus 'one reason why some individuals join is because they believe that the Labour party members collectively make a difference to outcomes' (Seyd and Whiteley 1992:61). Seyd and Whiteley argue that individuals may join the Labour Party simply to help achieve the collective goals or the policy aims of the party. This amounts to a search for a 'collective good'. The underlying assumption is that people choose not to free ride because they know that 'if everyone did that' the policy goal or collective good would not be achieved. However, the collective 'search' might also be negative in the sense that it amounts to getting rid of a collective 'bad', such as a set of Conservative government policies. In other words members can also be motivated by *collective negative incentives*.[15] Seyd and Whiteley (1992: 61; 2002: 90-91) maintain that these incentives can be incorporated in a cost-benefit type of analysis, however an important aspect of this model is the individual's sense of political efficacy and their perception of costs and benefits. Thus Whiteley and Seyd (2002: 54) argue:

> Rational individuals may perceive that their own contribution to the collective good is small, but collective action will still be rational for them if they also see the costs as being very small as well. In other words it is the perceived difference between costs and benefits that matter, not some exogenously defined measure of the benefits alone. In this situation, becoming a member without receiving selective incentives makes sense, providing that the individual believes he or she is making a nonzero contribution to the collective good.

Moving beyond rational choice type incentives analysis, Seyd and Whiteley consider a number of other factors which may influence joining. Seyd and Whiteley (1992: 63-64) claim that 'they are operated within a fundamentally different type of discourse than cost-benefit analysis' and they therefore 'constitute a separate category of motives'. These factors derive from social psychology. *Group incentives* (Seyd and Whiteley 2002: 92) are related to how individuals view the success, or efficacy, of the group. The argument is that individuals are more likely to participate if the group or organisation is viewed as successful, or able to 'make a difference'. Seyd and Whiteley (2002: 92; also see Whiteley and Seyd 2002: 55; Whiteley 1995) argue that such a motivation is not consistent with a 'narrowly defined' rational actor model, as the individual is 'not in a position to

---

[15]Seyd and Whiteley (1992) also note that the political context at the time of joining a political party is very important. Thus, during a time of Labour government, when the party is in a position to deliver policies, positive collective incentives are likely to be more evident. When Labour are in opposition, negative collective incentives are more likely to come to the fore. Indeed the authors (1992:79) argue that 'Mrs Thatcher has been an excellent recruiting sergeant for the Labour Party'.

influence the political effectiveness of a national organization such as a political party'. Thus, they regard such motivations as social-psychological in character. From this perspective, they argue, 'group solidarity engendered by success does provide an incentive to participate, independently of other factors' (Whiteley and Seyd 2002: 55).

*Expressive attachments* first appear as a separate category in the study of Conservative members.[16] They amount to a general emotional attachment to the party; 'Such motives for joining are grounded in a sense of loyalty and affection for the party, which is unrelated to cognitive calculations of the costs and benefits of membership' (Whiteley *et al.* 1994: 88; Whiteley and Seyd 2002: 56). In the study of Conservative members the following responses were included this category: 'an attachment to Conservative party principles', 'belief in the Conservative party leadership', and 'generalised loyalty to the party' (Whiteley *et al.* 1994:96).[17]

Finally, the authors describe *social norms* which 'favour' participation and involve a desire for respect or social approval within a group (Seyd and Whiteley 1992: 64; Seyd and Whiteley 2002: 93). Policy outcomes are almost irrelevant in this context. As in partisan attachment, family norms can be very important.[18] With its consideration of these 'more general social psychological processes', it is clear that the Seyd and Whiteley general incentives approach attempts to move beyond traditional rational choice analysis (Whiteley and Seyd 2002: 56).

## Empirical Studies of Party Membership

General models of participation provide many useful clues as to why people may participate politically. As stated, most recent studies point to 'modes' or types of activities, and suggest that individuals mobilise around different issues and participate in different ways. If we accept this assessment, we might expect membership of a political party to involve a different set of commitments from another form of participation, such as involvement in a community campaign. We would predict, for example, that political beliefs would play a more significant role in party membership (see Verba and Nie 1972; Verba, Schlozman and Brady 1995). However, until recently it has been difficult to explore the question of party membership motivation because studies of party members have been rather thin on the ground.

Moreover, the context and nature of party membership in Britain is very different from that of other countries, such as the US, where the distinction between members and supporters is blurred (see Norris 2002; Scarrow 1996: 210).

---

[16]In other words, they are not applied in the study of Labour members.

[17]This is reminiscent of Parry *et al.*'s (1992) account of expressive participation in which they argue that activity may simply be an expression of political sympathy, symbolic rather than goal-orientated. Examples cited by Parry *et al.* (1992: 15) include attendance at an annual Remembrance Day ceremony.

[18]These social incentives have traditionally been associated with the young Conservatives (Berry 1970: 44).

American parties are very loosely organised and party membership is regarded as rather informal campaign activity at the local level.[19]   This activity is often in support of a particular candidate, and often 'intermittent' and short-term (Wilson 1995: 115).[20]  Within a context of relatively high levels of party identification (see Dalton 1996, 1998), parties have traditionally been rather centralised in Britain and membership 'formal' in character, which we would assume involves a greater degree of psychological investment than simply wearing a badge in support of a party, or attending a local campaign meeting in the US.

Some British studies have examined activism (Barton and Doring 1986; Denver and Bochel 1973; Whiteley 1981), including conference delegates and local council candidates (Brand 1973). However, many of these studies have been local level case studies and simply examined the socio-economic background of active participants, rather than motivations behind membership.  Furthermore, many of the studies that have examined membership have explored this from the point of view of party *recruitment* (Brand 1973; Budge and Farlie 1975; Scarrow 1996).  Brand (1973), for example, studied candidates for Glasgow City council in 1966 by examining recruitment *procedures* as well as the characteristics of those people who became councillors. A more recent study of the main parties in Britain and Germany by Scarrow (1996: 21) also adopted an *organisational*, or 'party-centred' approach, by assessing the value of members to the party organisation, rather than the value of membership to the individual joiner.  Studies of what motivates *individual party members* (passive as well as active) have been few and far between.

The lack of interest in formal party membership in Britain led Seyd and Whiteley (1992: 26) to refer to the 'absence of study of the voluntary partisans'. Indeed, a number of problems have been associated with the study of party membership and activism in Britain.  Berrington (1989: 26) observed that, in the 35 years prior to 1989, studies of political activists and members had been 'sporadic, localised, irregular in scope and variable in their definitions'. Crewe (1984:187) explains the weakness of the research on the unreliability of membership figures (in the case of the Labour and Liberal parties) or the complete unavailability of such figures (in the case of the Conservatives).  Studies conducted in recent years (Bennie *et al.* 1996; Curtice *et al.* 1993; Rüdig *et al.* 1996; Seyd and Whiteley 1992; Whiteley *et al.* 1994) have provided more comprehensive accounts of membership development in the main parties in Britain.  The detailed empirical findings of these studies will be reviewed later, but here we concentrate on motivations for membership highlighted by some important empirical studies of party members in Britain conducted over the last 50 years.  While many of the

---

[19]Wilson (1995: 96) defines a party member as 'a person who involves himself in these coordinated activities, who not only votes for the party candidate, but also attends the meetings of, or undertakes to perform tasks on behalf of, a party organization'.

[20]Wilson (1995: 115) refers to the existence of 'candidate organizations' which are groups of supporters loyal to an individual candidate.  These supporters may be willing to participate during campaigns but their commitment tends to be very short-lived.

authors demonstrate 'resource-based' arguments, most of the analysis has been grounded in a 'soft' form of rational choice'.

In 1954 Gabriel A. Almond attempted to categorise the appeals of Communist party membership in Britain, pointing to economic and social isolation as the key to understanding susceptibility (Almond 1954: 183-184). Almond employed many psychologically bound terms to explain membership. Feelings of isolation, vulnerability and resentment, he argued, may be relieved through affiliating with the communist movement. Almond (1954: 226) argued that susceptibility involved some kind of psychological and social deviance. Almond's work, with its emphasis on social structural stress, deprivation and psychological rewards of membership, was typical of its time. Participation in the British communist party was regarded as out of the ordinary and was explained with reference to psychological states of mind.

Abrams and Little's (1965) study of youth involvement in Britain's political parties (Conservative, Labour and Liberal) highlighted three different factors behind the decision to join: social influence, political principle, and the potential reward of political influence within a party organisation. They found that two thirds of Young Conservative members joined for social reasons, not political ones. The image is of an almost apolitical movement which provides 'organised gregariousness for the children of the middle classes' (Abrams and Little 1965: 319). The Young Socialists at this time were by comparison more militant and more politically active, more 'ideologically engaged, more fervent' (Abrams and Little 1965: 321). As for the Young Liberals, Abrams and Little argued that an influential reason for joining the Liberal Party was the attraction of political power within the party. In other words, the existence of a democratic party organisation acted as a source of encouragement for potential members.

Berry's (1970) study of the Conservative and Labour grassroots in the constituency area of Walton confirmed that the recruiting patterns of the two parties were quite different. In the Conservative Party, Berry argued, there was a much greater emphasis on social activities, as opposed to strictly political activities. The more developed range of social activities offered by the Conservatives served as a powerful recruiting force, whereas the Labour members were more narrowly political in focus: 30 per cent of Labour members cited political reasons (party policies or political principles) for joining the party, only 17 per cent of the Conservatives (Berry 1970: 46). Berry concluded that Conservative members were more socially motivated than their Labour counterparts and, he argued, this helped explain the higher levels of individual membership.

Berry's analysis also revealed that family/friendship networks were an important means of mobilisation for both parties. In response to the question of 'how respondents came to join their party', the most frequently quoted influences were those of family, relatives, husbands, wives, and friends: 63 per cent of Conservatives gave this type of response, 46 per cent of Labour members (Berry 1970: 47). Canvassing and recruitment techniques were almost completely insignificant compared with these family/friendship influences.

In attempting to understand why people become involved in organisations Berry (1970: 60) outlined a model of 'overlapping multiple memberships'. The model indicates that a positive relationship exists between political participation and participation in non-political voluntary associations. Berry noted that the relationship between party activity and activity in other organisations was slightly stronger among the Conservatives than Labour, probably because of the social orientation of Conservative activities, but the relationship held true for both parties. Berry described a group of 'joiners' who, if active in some voluntary associations, were more likely to join a number of others, including political parties.

Denver and Bochel (1973) explored the influence of family and friends in the party recruitment process in their study of the Communist Party activist in Dundee. Considerable weight is attached to socialisation as a factor in party allegiance and recruitment into activity. While Denver and Bochel (1973: 63) established that family strongly influenced support for the Communist Party, they also showed that it was important in socialising respondents into the role of member. Over a quarter of the respondents had at least one parent who was a member before they joined, and over half had a member of their wider family in the party. They were, in effect, 'brought up' in the party. Denver and Bochel (1973: 58) looked at the relationship between party affiliation and religion. They found that a greater proportion of communists than average (25 per cent compared with 3 per cent of Labour activists) said that they were not brought up in any denomination, and from this they concluded that exposure to religious institutions may have weakened the influence of the other agencies tending towards political radicalism. Berry (1970), on the other hand, had found that Conservative and Labour Party members were *more* likely to belong to a local church than the electors as a whole.

There are other events which may help provide an explanation of party membership. Denver and Bochel (1973: 61) classified these simply as 'other experiences'. These may take the form of a single traumatic experience or a gradual accumulation of experiences. Unemployment was one such experience highlighted by Denver and Bochel which they argued socialised a person into support for the Communist Party. Their evidence supported suggestions that the individual grievance of unemployment created a group of people who were susceptible to radical political movements.

In 1980, McCulloch (1990) examined motivations behind membership of British political parties, including the Ecology Party, through a survey of activists who had campaigned in a by-election in Exeter.[21] McCulloch set out to test the economic, rational choice model of Olson and concluded that the model did not explain membership of the political party. This research points to the relevance of what McCulloch (1990: 503) terms 'cultural' and 'ideological' incentives, both of which he regards as normative selective incentives. Cultural incentives refer to feelings of civic duty, 'a cultural norm that the individual should participate in

---

[21]Four parties were included in this local level study – Conservative, Labour, Liberal and Ecology. A questionnaire was sent to local activists, however the sample sizes were very small, and there were only 10 responses from the Ecology Party.

public affairs' (McCulloch 1990: 503). An ideological motivation is a form of political conviction, described by McCulloch (1990: 503-4) as, 'one which derives either from a desire to see a particular set of social arrangements in existence within a particular geographical area, or from a rejection of a desired set of arrangements proposed by some other individual or organisation'. Ideological motivations clearly stand out as the most important motivation in all four parties studied (McCulloch 1990: 513).

More recent studies in Britain of parties have been able to offer more sophisticated attempts to understand the joining process. The empirical studies of Labour and Conservative members stand out in this regard (Seyd and Whiteley 1992, 2002; Whiteley *et al.* 1994; Whiteley and Seyd 2002). Seyd and Whiteley (1992: 74-76) originally argued that, in the case of Labour members, altruistic motives were the most important, representing 42 per cent of responses to an open-ended question on why members joined. Examples included in this category were 'a belief in socialism or left-wing politics' and 'to help the working class'. Selective process incentives proved the next most popular, referred to by 23.9 per cent of cases, followed by collective negative incentives (17.4 per cent). Thus Seyd and Whiteley (1992: 76) argue: '...this data supports the proposition that most people's first priority when they are considering joining the party are altruistic concerns or selective incentives, and not the achievement of specific policy goals'. However, when examining the Conservative Party membership, these authors introduce the new category of expressive attachments, such as 'an attachment to Conservative principles' and argue that these are the most important motives for joining the Conservatives: 22 per cent of the Conservative responses are categorised as expressive attachments. These are followed in terms of importance by collective positive incentives (20.2 per cent), collective negative incentives (15.4 per cent) and selective-process incentives (14.4 per cent) (Whiteley *et al.* 1994: 96-97).

Later analysis by these authors suggests that the motivations of a party's membership can change over time. Panel surveys allow Seyd and Whiteley to compare membership characteristics over a number of years, leading them to the conclusion that the memberships of both parties are becoming 'de-energised', although it is only in the case of the Labour Party that the data spans a ten year period (Seyd and Whiteley 1995; Whiteley and Seyd 1998, 2002).[22] In both the Conservative and Labour parties a decline in activism during the 1990s is noted, and this despite a significant increase in total member numbers in the Labour Party in the run-up to the 1997 general election (Whiteley and Seyd 2002: 95-99).

In a comparison of Labour members who joined the party before and since 1994 (when Blair became Labour leader and the party adopted a more active recruitment strategy) they suggest that the party has been 'recruiting a new type of member' who is likely to have joined the party for different reasons (Seyd and Whiteley 1995; Whiteley and Seyd 1998, 2002). The new member, it is argued, is

---

[22]Two 2-wave panel surveys of Labour members were conducted, the first in 1989/1990 and 1992, and the second in 1997 and 1999. One 2-wave panel of Conservatives took place in 1992 and 1994 (see Whiteley and Seyd 2002: 223).

less likely to have joined due to expressive motives (e.g. 'to make a commitment to socialism') and more likely to have been motivated by instrumental factors (e.g. 'to help get Labour into power') (Whiteley and Seyd 2002: 137). Whiteley and Seyd (2002: 143) speculate that the relative weakness of expressive motives amongst the new members suggests a lack of commitment to the party and goes some way in explaining lower levels of activism amongst this group.

## Explaining Participation in Social Movements

A review of social movement theory as it has developed over the years reveals one overwhelming tendency – a shift from the micro-level of analysis to the broad macro accounts, although some attempts have been made to integrate these explanations, to build micro-macro bridges (for example Diani and McAdam 2003; McAdam *et al.* 1988, 1996; Tarrow 1994).[23] From overview accounts of social movement theory (McAdam *et al.* 1988; Dalton and Kuechler 1990; Scott 1990; Eyerman and Jamison 1991; Della Porta and Diani 1999) a number of models of why people participate can be identified. These can be categorised as classical, resource mobilisation, political process, and European new social movement approaches.[24]

*Classical Perspectives*

Until the 1960s, scholars who studied social movements tended to view them as potentially damaging to democracy and civil society (Arendt 1951; Hoffer 1951; Lipset 1960). This rather sceptical view of social movements is commonly interpreted as a response to right-wing movements in Europe and the US at the time: fascism in Germany and Italy, and McCarthyism in the USA (see for example Zirakzadeh 1997: 7).

The classical social movement theorists conceptualised movements as irrational outbursts of frustration or anger. They associated collective behaviour with the rapid pace of post-war economic and social modernisation. However, the main unit of analysis was the alienated individual, uprooted and socially dislocated by the pace of change. In other words, these classical social movement theories

---

[23]Garner (1996: 45-62) argues that social movement theory can involve three levels of analysis: Micro-level theories which focus on individual mobilisation, and are mainly psychological accounts; middle range theories which look at specific societies, the structural strains which lead to social movement, and the effects of political structures and institutions on the resources, organisation and strategies of movements; and, finally, broad sociohistorical/macrohistorical accounts which focus on the type of society (communist or capitalist, modern or post-modern) in which a social movement exists.

[24]As Della Porta and Diani (1999: 3) argue these should not necessarily be viewed as distinct 'schools of thought' on the grounds that there are quite considerable variations within these traditions. Individual scholars often employ concepts from more than one perspective, and scholars have been known to 'transform' their ideas over time.

were often 'micro' in character, focusing on individual reasons for joining. They tended to offer social-psychological explanations for movement support, arguing that modernisation had created a pool of socially isolated individuals who were susceptible to movement mobilisation. The insecurity of the uprooted and isolated was said to make them easily manipulated by movement leaders.

In sum, it was suggested that an individual's participation could be explained by some psychological or pathological attribute that rendered them susceptible to movement recruitment. Collective action was considered a direct response to frustration-aggression. In other words, those who were personally dissatisfied or deprived were regarded as the most likely to take part. Movements were viewed as 'therapeutic vehicles' through which the disadvantaged could find solace (see McAdam 2003: 282).

*(a) Mass Society*  Mass society theory was born in debates about the rise of authoritarianism and totalitarianism in the early cold war period. The theory had apparently macrosociological starting points but in practice tended to focus on the alienated individual. Actors were seen as disorientated because their traditional environments had been destroyed by modernisation (see Foweraker 1997: 74). Kornhauser (1959), for example, argued that social movements emerged in response to the 'massification of society', the breaking down of local communities, extended families and so on. He suggested that the people most likely to become involved in politically extreme social movements were those alienated from society, seeking comfort in a group setting. Similarly, Arendt (1951: 323-4) referred to 'the completely isolated human being who, without any other social ties...derives his sense of having a place in the world only from his belonging to a movement'.

Kornhauser's (1959) study of anti-democratic movements – fascism and communism – suggested that in mass (and totalitarian) societies there is a paucity of intermediate groups between non-elites and elites, and in such circumstances, non-elites were likely to feel vulnerable and isolated from elite control. Kornhauser (1959: 110-115) argued that the lack of democratic linkage make the individual non-elite highly susceptible to mobilisation by mass orientated elites. Conversely, the diversity of groups and cultures catered for in the pluralist society allowed human beings to find satisfaction and comfort within one of these groups and in this society individuals were less likely to rebel. In constructing his hypothesis Kornhauser relied a great deal on psychological explanations. His text is littered with phrases like 'positive self-conceptions', 'self estrangement' and 'the anxiety accompanying personal alienation'. He sums up the psychological states which are fostered in different societies:

> Non-pluralist society lacks the diversity of social worlds to nurture and sustain independent persons. Furthermore, in non-pluralist society the man who becomes alienated from the prevailing culture is likely to become alienated from himself; whereas in pluralist society there are alternative loyalties (sanctuaries) which do not place the nonconformist outside the social pale (Kornhauser 1959: 110).

Mass society theorists predicted that strong class affiliation would act as a barrier to mobilisation.  According to this perspective, social class ties have the effect of bonding individuals to one group or class, not the common experiences of the mass.  This leads to the expectation that the social types who will be mobilised by totalitarian movements will be the alienated and *unattached* – of *all* classes.  Class rooted counterparts, it follows, will have some if not all of their group needs satisfied by their class identification.  This prediction led Kornhauser (1959: 181) to comment that, 'mass theory looks to the breakdown of class identities as a critical process whereby people are freed to form new ties based on the commonly shared plight of mass men rather than the mutually exclusive plight of class men'.  So, for Kornhauser the secret of mobilisation for totalitarianism was related to mass, not class.

An important category often identified as a potential membership source for these movements was the unattached *intellectuals*. Kornhauser (1959: 184) for example claimed that intellectuals need to be stimulated by symbols and it was they who were least able to suffer a 'vacuum in the symbolic sphere'.  It was predicted that the intellectuals suffered most from solitude and it was they in turn who provided the momentum for mobilisation.

Klapp (1969), like Kornhauser, suggested that some members of society may feel alienated or rejected, and a means of rectifying this may be to seek solace in a social group collective.  In this way 'outsiders' become 'insiders' by finding a personal respect or self-identity.  Central to Klapp's theory is the idea of 'groping' – a form of social action which looks like a search for identity. Different forms of behaviour constitute different stages of this search, and 'the forms of collective behaviour are the fingers of exploration' (Klapp 1969: ix).  Klapp used various other psychologically bound terms in developing his theory ('the seeker' is the person searching for a new self, 'the river' is a metaphor for the collective identity search).

*(b) Collective Behaviour*  Collective behaviour theorists (Blumer 1960; Smelser 1962) placed heavy emphasis on the emergent character of collective behaviour and social movements, and, as Diani and Eyerman (1992: 5) comment, 'The assumption was made that collective behaviour could be analysed within the same set of categories used to explain individual behaviour'.  Personal traits and attitudes were regarded as important in explaining periodic outbursts of political protest, and social movement participation tended to be regarded as reactive, irrational and unconventional by the collective behaviour theorists.  However, this approach contrasted with 'collective psychology' as it represented a 'shift of attention from the motivation of individuals to their observable actions' (Della Porta and Diani 1999: 5). Robert E. Park, Ernest W.Burgess and Herbert Blumer were the leading proponents who pointed to rapid change in social structures – technology, increasingly mobile populations, large scale organisations – which forced individuals to 'search for new patterns of social organization' (see Della

Porta and Diani 1999: 5). Collective behaviour was viewed as crisis behaviour, leading to system adaptation.[25]

The functionalist analysis of Neil Smelser[26] (1962: 384) pointed to 'structural strain' (defined as 'the impairment of the relations among parts of a system and the consequent malfunctioning of the system') as a necessary condition of collective behaviour,[27] and to the resulting anxiety and 'social malintegration' which lay behind receptiveness to movement demands e.g. involvement in the National Socialist movement in Germany. In other words, structural strain – mainly physical or economic hardship – and coexistent frustration was seen as a necessary condition for social movement participation to occur. Smelser (1962: 383) also argued that collective behaviour may involve 'distinctive psychological states' and 'distinctive patterns of mobilization' (the authoritarian leader and followers).

Smelser's general analysis of social movement has been widely criticised for its methodology, a deductivist and positivist approach which assumes the ability to identify 'laws' in the social sciences (Scott 1990: 41), and for its assumption that collective action took the form of 'non-institutionalised irrational outbursts' (Scott 1990: 38). Nevertheless, Smelser's approach contained some sophistication, such as his recognition that collective behaviour could take many different forms. These he referred to as the panic, the craze, the hostile outburst, the norm-oriented movement, and the value-oriented movement. Furthermore, Smelser (1962: 22) recognised collective behaviour was determined by a range of different factors or conditions, not strain alone, including precipitating events (unpredictable events, confrontations or accidents which provided the movement with a focus), and 'mobilisation for action' which involved mobilisation by leaders.[28] The relevance of these other factors, Smelser suggested, explains why strain does not always lead to mobilisation. Indeed, Smelser (1962: 387) states, 'strain must *combine* with the other appropriate necessary conditions to be operative as a determinant'.[29]

---

[25]More contemporary collective behaviouralist have gone on to suggest that movements themselves lead to change by helping to transform norms and existing rules, and, as Della Porta and Diani (1999: 7) describe it, movements are seen as 'meaningful acts driving often necessary and beneficial social change'.

[26]Heavily influenced by Talcott Parsons.

[27]Smelser (1962: 382) defined collective behaviour as 'uninstitutionalized mobilization to reconstitute a component of social action on the basis of a generalized belief'.

[28]Smelser (1962: 22) identifies six determinants of collective behaviour: structural conduciveness, structural strain, growth of a generalized belief, precipitating factors, mobilization for action, and social control. Agencies of social control often acted as 'counter-determinants'; they include the police, religious authorities, and the media. Smelser (1962: 269) suggests that these factors have a logical sequence or order (increasing determinancy) but states that the order is not necessarily fixed or 'temporal'.

[29]This leads Della Porta and Diani (1999: 4) to describe Smelser's approach as 'the most organic formulation of the structural-functionalist approach'.

*(c) Relative Deprivation*   Relative deprivation theorists moved away from the belief that absolute deprivation, in isolation from other groups in society, was sufficient explanation for collective behaviour. The relative deprivation approach attributes activism to a perceived state of deprivation of a group to which an individual belongs. The theory holds that a perceived gap between what a person has and what a person feels they ought to have, be they material possessions or otherwise, leads to a feeling of deprivation and frustration. Deprivation is felt by observing some reference group with the sought after quality, and the frustration brought on by this feeling of deprivation leads to social movement activity with the aim of closing the perceived gap.[30]   While Smelser (1962) and the collective behaviour approach used the idea of general societal 'strains' to explain the rise of social movement activity, the relative deprivation approach focused on much more specific deprivations.   Furthermore, relative deprivation allows for activity as rational action linked to particular grievances, as opposed to some form of 'social pathology'.

Rüdig (1990: 28) documents the history of this perspective, noting that the term was first used by American sociologists to describe the grievances of soldiers in the 1940s. The idea of a reference point was developed and applied by authors like Davies (1959) and Runciman (1966), and the concept was expanded, for example, to include future expectations.[31]   However, since the 1970s, relative deprivation approaches have become less popular. Della Porta and Diani (1999: 256) give very little attention to theories of deprivation in their review of social movement approaches.   In a footnote, these authors argue that 'theories of frustration and deprivation' have steadily decreased in importance to the point where they 'have become entirely marginal in the analysis of social movements in democratic societies'.   Nevertheless, theories can be redeveloped. Rüdig (1990), for example, defends the concept of relative deprivation as an explanation for the emergence of anti-nuclear movements.   He argues that 'nuclear deprivations' are perceived or 'felt', although this is not necessarily in relation to a reference group, and when these perceptions are combined with other key 'intervening' variables collective action can result.[32]

---

[30]A number of assumptions underpin the theory: a) The individual feels part of a group and has a sense of belonging or identification with that group, and b) Individuals have knowledge of another group.  A completely isolated group could not feel relatively deprived because it would have no reference group.

[31]Aberle (1966) used relative deprivation theory to explain participation in his study of the Peyote religion. He argued that the Peyote religion among the Navaho Indians provided solace and meaning through rituals and beliefs.  The American Indians felt deprived by a lack of material possessions, land and livestock.  This deprivation was compared to the more affluent position of White America.  Aberle (1996: 336) writes: 'It [Peyotism] provides a validation of their partial separation and identity, an ethnic adaptive to their social position, a set of compensations for their most pressing deprivations'.

[32]The key variables are a) attribution of blame b) collective experience of deprivations c) high social homogeneity among deprived communities d) perception of political efficacy and e) perceived cost of 'voice' and 'exit'.  Together these variables create a 'Process Model of the Emergence of Social Movements'.  Further, Rüdig (1990: 30) argues that two main

## Resource Mobilisation Theory (RMT)

By the 1970s, a new breed of theorists had emerged. They appeared much more sympathetic to the (democratic) objectives of social movements of the time; the civil rights, anti-war and feminist movements.[33]  They argued (e.g. Rule 1988) that empirical observation of social movement activity contradicted the classical approaches as social movement actors, rather than being marginal, alienated or deprived, were of a high socio-economic status and were more integrated members of society.  For example, women's movement activists (Freeman 1983) and the Three Mile Island protesters (Walsh and Warland 1983) did not demonstrate any direct link between economic strain and collective action (see Knocke and Wisely 1990: 6).[34]  The chief theoretical contender to emerge from the 'second wave' of social movement theorising was the resource mobilisation approach.[35]

Diani and Eyerman (1992: 5) argue that a number of different approaches can be placed in the resource mobilisation category. The common theme, however, is that 'potential for conflict exists in any society and that the actualisation of this potential largely depends upon the proper usage of resources and selective incentives for action' (Diani and Eyerman 1992:5).  The focus is on those with the necessary resources, the most skilled, best-equipped members of society, as movement participants and organisers.  Diani and Eyerman (1992: 6) argue that, 'This had the effect of moving social movement actors from the margins to the centre of society'.

According to the resource mobilisation theorists, grievances and discontent are common characteristics of modern societies but these grievances do not, in themselves, lead people to form or join movements.  While some resource mobilisation theorists do attempt to consider grievances (Walsh 1981; Walsh and Warland 1983), some very radical theorists deny entirely the importance of

---

obstacles must be overcome if relative deprivation is to lead to collective protest.  The first of these involves a move from the private to the political; private dissatisfaction becomes political when there is 'attribution of blame'.  Secondly, there is a move from individual political dissatisfaction to a collective form of action which is most likely to occur when there are 'specific manifestations of deprivation' (nuclear plants) in segmented, homogenous communities with good communication links and high levels of political efficacy.

[33]Zirakzadeh (1997: 15) notes; 'Whereas the earlier generation of movement theorists viewed the prospect of more movements with dread, the newer generation tended to view the prospect as an opportunity to redistribute political and economic power democratically and fairly.  Contemporary movements were seen as signs of increasing political health, not disease'.  While Goodwin and Jasper (2003:5) argue that the civil rights movement was mainly responsible for this change in attitude.

[34]Rüdig (1990: 28) disputes this claim.  He argues that relative deprivation approaches *can* address 'mechanisms for this causal process', by focusing on intermediate variables between deprivation and action.

[35]Resource mobilisation theory was developed in the United States during the 1970s in response to the rapid growth in public interest lobbies at that time.  Britain was slow to respond to the new approach; it was only in the early 1980s that it came to be recognised as a separate approach (see Rüdig, Mitchell, Chapman and Lowe 1991: 131-132).

deprivation. Turner and Killian (1972: 251), for instance, argue that, 'There is always enough discontent in any society to supply grass roots support for a movement if the movement is effectively organised and has at its disposal the power and resources of some established elite group'. McCarthy and Zald (1977: 1215) suggest that grievances or discontent may be created and utilised by issue organisers. The central task, according to these theorists, is to *identify those conditions which transform discontent into actions*. In effect, discontent must be *organised*.

American sociologists McCarthy and Zald (1973, 1977) identified what they believed to be a new type of social movement. These movements were organised by a new elite of movement 'professionals', or entrepreneurs, and received support from public bodies, voluntary organisations and groups of affluent individuals, termed the 'conscience community'. The focus was on the organisations which mobilise people. Organisations with resources (money, people, media skills) were seen to *pull* people into activity. Thus, emphasis was placed on the importance of social movement entrepreneurs at the head of social movement organisations (SMOs). Groups like Greenpeace and FoE were used as examples of elite-led SMOs, which together created a 'social movement industry'.

Jenkins (1983: 533) lists the characteristics of social movement organisations as an indigenous leadership, volunteer staff, extensive membership, resources from conscience constituencies, and actions that 'speak for' rather than involve an aggrieved group. Walsh (1981) points to the importance of social movement professionals in the Three Mile Island protests, and several authors have claimed the environmental movement would not have been mobilised without entrepreneurs.[36]

However, resources vary widely in character. They can be tangible or intangible, internal or external. Freeman (1979: 172-5) uses the distinction between tangible resources (money, facilities, means of communication) and intangible or 'human' assets that form the central basis of social movements and include specialised resources such as organising and legal skills and the unspecialised resource of supporters. Rüdig (1990: 40) documents that Barkan originally distinguished between internal and external resources. Internal resources were seen as the power to persuade, public relations skills such as producing persuasive literature, and financial resources. External resources can be measured in terms of the likelihood of disruption or non co-operation by other actors.

Resource mobilisation theory has a reputation for considering micro-level dynamics at the expense of macro factors or 'broad social transformations' (Scott 1990: 110). However, a number of factors are considered by resource mobilisation theory, from the internal membership of an organisation to the wider political environment, including media organisations and political structures (Gamson 1975; McCarthy and Zald 1977). For these reasons it is now regarded as a form of structural analysis, as opposed to the psychological approaches of the classical

---

[36]For a recent account of the role played by leaders in social movements see Barker *et al.* 2001.

theorists (see McAdam 2003: 282-284).  It examines micro-level developments of organisational recruitment, while noting the existence of parallel macro-level influences such as the linkages among social movement organisations and the wider political infrastructure. Zald and McCarthy (1979: 2) argued that the approach 'depended more upon political, sociological and economic theories than upon the social psychology of collective behaviour'.

McAdam *et al.* (1988: 709) highlight the inter-relationships between macroprocesses and individual actors at any stage of a movement's existence, arguing that 'macro potential' for collective action can only unfold at the micro or 'intermediate institutional' level.  McAdam *et al.* (1988: 709) refer to a 'third level', 'intermediate between the individual and the broad macro contexts in which they are embedded'. They emphasise the importance of the 'meso-level' of action, where macro-structural factors meet individuals, where individuals acquire meaning and develop attitudes towards the macro-level processes, sometimes leading to social movement mobilisation.  For them, the meso-level is 'where the real action in social movements take place' (McAdam *et al.* 1988: 729). Consequently, McAdam *et al.* (1988: 728) suggest that those people most likely to join in collective behaviour are those who already have associations with members of other organisations:

> In our view a wide variety of informal, yet existing, associations of people provide the collective settings within which movements emerge.  The significance of these *micro-mobilization contexts* derive from their potential for translating macro-structural opportunities for action into specific micro-mobilization dynamics.

It is argued that group membership exposes individuals to information about other groups and that social influences encourage them to integrate into these other group formations.  The psychological state at work described here suggests the existence of a socially confident group of people who enjoy participation in many different fields.  For these reasons, we can call them 'joiners', as opposed to the 'alienated' members of society examined by the more traditional social movement theorists.  This approach predicts that those people most likely to engage in social movement activity are those who are already well integrated into society and who are already members of other organisations.

McAdam *et al.* (1988) specify four micro-structural variables which may lead an individual to become active in an organisation.  The first is prior contact with a movement member, which, they argue, has the highest correlation with movement activism (McAdam *et al.* 1988: 707).  Second, is membership in organisations, which is likely to increase feelings of personal efficacy, increase exposure to information on other organisations, and increase the influence of interpersonal relations. Organisational membership is seen to 'drag' people into other organisations through a membership network. The third factor is a history of prior activism.  Partly, this may be due to 'sunk social costs', when individuals invest time, energy and tangible resources in their activities and to exit from activity would be costly in terms of what has already been invested.  Therefore, prior investment encourages future involvement. As for biographical availability, this refers to the personal circumstances associated with periods in a person's life cycle; marriage, family, or job responsibilities. Those people faced with the least number of personal constraints are considered the most 'biographically available'. We might expect students, young people, self-employed, retired and unemployed people to be the most 'available'.[37]

Another important theme of resource mobilisation approaches is participants in social movements are rational, purposeful actors, in pursuit of their own interests. Della Porta and Diani (1999: 9) argue: 'The definition of social movements as conscious actors making *rational choices* is...among the most important innovations of the resource mobilisation approach'. According to resource mobilisation approaches, participants in social movements are rational, purposeful actors, pursuing their own interests, and actions are influenced by available resources. Activity is viewed as 'an extension of the conventional forms of political action' (della Porta and Diani 1999: 7) and is likely to be related to previous activism. As has already been argued, participants are seen to be well-integrated into society rather than socially isolated. Furthermore, this approach predicts that the poorest, most economically powerless, sections of society are the least likely to participate, despite their obvious grievances, because the costs of participation are too great (Piven 1976).

The commonly accepted view among resource mobilisation theorists has been that members are a resource of an organisation and it is therefore important for the organisation to determine how to attract members. As a result, there has been widespread examination of what organisations have to offer potential members in return for their support. Thus rational choice theorists have argued that groups must offer incentives to potential members that out-weigh the costs of membership.

As already noted, the resource mobilisation tradition often points to the importance of 'interaction' and 'solidarity networks' (della Porta and Diani 1999: 8). Since the development of RMT, however, the analysis of networks has moved on and some argue that this now constitutes a separate theory. Zirakzadeh (1997: 13) for example distinguishes between resource mobilisation theorists who emphasise leadership in social movements and an 'indigenous-community' approach which places more emphasis on 'local-level institutions, such as neighbourhood clubs, union locals, and community churches [which] can provide organizational building blocks, communication networks, and leadership skills for later social movements'. However, as Diani (2003a: 12-14) illustrates network approaches vary considerable in their emphasis. Some focus on the impact of networks on individual participation, some on 'interorganizational exchanges', and others on the role of networks in the construction of meaning and ideas. The Diani (2003b: 318) approach is a broad analysis of the dynamics of networks, 'processes connecting events, activities, and ideas, and not only ... those linking individuals

---

[37]Echoing these arguments, a recent study of the 2000 fuel protest in Britain pointed to 'informal networks, prior experience of action and the resources provided by workplace ties' as factors behind these protests (Doherty *et al.* 2003: 11).

or organizations'. Indeed, a network underpinned by a shared collective identity is central to Diani's definition of a social movement (1992: 13). While the network theme is compatible with the resource mobilisation theorists, the RMT approach was much more narrowly focused on the links between individuals and organisations, as opposed to cultural processes and the construction of identities. In fact, the recent network approaches appear to have more in common with 'new social movement' analysis, with its emphasis on movement identity (see below).

*Political Process Models*

By the mid-1980s the political process model had evolved, sometimes referred to as the political opportunity approach. This approach also involved a rational view of collective action, but it concentrated to an even greater extent on macro-level factors, linking protest activity with institutional political actors. An early version of this approach was provided by Jenkins and Perrow (1977) who argued that grievances were 'relatively constant and stable' and that the mobilisation and outcomes of farmers movements had more to do with the behaviour of political and economic elites. In essence, political process theorists argued that broad political circumstances, including constitutional arrangements, national level politics and styles of decision-making, had an effect on an actor's decision to participate in a movement, and also influenced the strategy and success of the movement. The concept of 'political opportunity structure' was used to describe a set of factors which facilitate or constrain the development of social movements (Gamson and Meyer 1996; Kitschelt 1986, 1989; Kreisi 1995; McAdam *et al.* 1996; Tarrow 1989, 1994, 1996). These factors include the degree of openness or otherwise of a political system, the receptiveness of political elites to the demands of social movements, and the existence of organisational support groups (Diani and Eyerman 1994: 6).

Political opportunity approaches all explore the interaction of movement and institutionalised politics, but two different styles of analysis are apparent. The first involves exploring how changes to some aspects of a political system can affect a social movement. These tend to be detailed historical case studies of single movements and are typical of early American approaches. Tarrow's (1989) study of protest politics in Italy is an example of this approach in a European context. The second approach involves cross-national study of comparable movements, and this is characteristic of most European approaches. One of the most commonly cited studies to employ this approach is Kitschelt's (1986) analysis of the anti-nuclear movements in Sweden, France, West Germany and the USA. Kitschelt argued that states which are open and weak provide opportunities or access points for movements to work within established institutions, but states which are closed and strong exclude movement actors and lead to confrontational strategies outside traditional decision-making spheres. Kitschelt focuses on institutional structures and party systems which are relatively inert aspects of opportunity.

Political process theorists focus on a wide range of political, social, economic and cultural factors to explain the development and impact of social movements. However, the relevant factors are widely disputed. Some theorists examine aspects that are deeply embedded in political institutions and culture, factors which tend to change very slowly if at all. Others look at aspects which are relatively volatile, shifting with 'events, policies and political actors' (Gamson and Meyer 1996: 77).

Kreisi (1995) emphasises formal political institutions, informal political practices and procedures, and what happens in arenas of conventional party and interest group politics. His focus is on 'aspects of the political context that have to be taken as given by the challenging actors'. Kriesi identifies a number of factors which influence movement development: the degree of territorial centralisation; the degree of separation of power between executive, legislature and judiciary; the coherence of the public administration; and the configuration of power in the party system, which depends mostly on the electoral system. In these ways, Kriesi distinguishes between open and closed states. Switzerland and Germany are said to be relatively open, while France is the most closed. Tarrow (1994: 85) defines a political opportunity structure as 'Consistent – but not necessarily formal, permanent, or national – signals to social or political actors which either encourage or discourage them to use their internal resources to form social movements'. In other words he considers not only formal state structures but also 'conflict and alliance structures'. Tarrow develops the idea that partially opened access to political systems encourages protest i.e. neither fully closed nor fully open types of system. For example, the movement for democratisation in the former Soviet Union and Eastern Europe in the late 1980s was given new opportunities for political action by perestroika and glasnost.

Others focus on more dynamic aspects of political opportunity, those that can change very quickly. Gamson and Meyer (1996) consider more general, cultural aspects of political context as an explanation for social movement development. Gamson and Meyer (1996: 279) refer to the different approaches as 'institutional versus cultural' and they refer to the importance of 'the cultural side of opportunity'. They argue that 'opportunity has a strong cultural component and we miss something important when we limit our attention to variance in political institutions and the relationships among political actors'. Gamson and Meyer (1996: 287) include an analysis of the media, arguing that the media's openness to social movements is in itself an important political opportunity. The authors argue that the media can play a central role in the construction of meaning and culture, and journalists' beliefs of how important different actors are in a policy arena can be very important.

There is in fact little agreement on which variables should be considered part of a political opportunity structure. McAdam (1996: 25) notes the lack of consensus: 'To the extent that the concept is defined or used in very different ways, it threatens to be of very little use to anyone...Conceptual plasticity...threatens to rob the concept of much of its analytic power'. Often the variables identified by POS writers are not all 'political'. McAdam (1996) argues that political opportunities (structural changes lend power shifts) should not be conflated with other facilitating conditions e.g. the important role of the media in structuring processes. Similarly Rootes (1997: 81) argues that the term POS should be confined to those factors which are genuinely structural and that many factors considered to be part of the POS are often in fact contingent – they change relatively quickly and are themselves shaped by other institutional arrangements. Rootes (1997:83) is also critical of Kitschelt's approach because 'it conflates genuinely structural features of political systems with...*contingent* features of those systems'.

The reason for this confusion according to Rootes (1997: 83) is that there has been 'slippage between the way the term structure has generally been used in political science and the way it has been used by sociologists'. Traditionally, political scientists deal with formal political structures, in particular governmental institutions as structures, while sociologists have examined less formal, social institutions, regarding these also as structural. Political scientists have been forced to consider the importance of informal processes in their attempts to explain collective behaviour which takes place outside the governmental-institutional sphere and have 'borrowed' the language and expression of sociologists. The result is confusion over factors which should be considered 'structural'. Rootes (1997: 84) provides many examples of this confusion. For instance, to what extent are electoral systems structural? They are often regarded as structural but Rootes (1987: 86) challenges this: 'Most that follows from the electoral system is better described as the *contingent product* of this aspect of the political system than as anything structural in its own right' he argues. Rootes (1997: 93) notes that British governments have differentiated between movements and been quite accommodating to the environmental movement, not so the anti-poll tax movement, and he argues that these different approaches are underestimated by a strictly structural analysis. As an alternative to a strictly structural analysis, Rootes (1997: 94-100) outlines three different 'dimensions of context' which influence collective action, and he attempts to assess their 'relative fixedness or variability', starting from the most fixed (least variable), moving towards 'the most contingently or conjuncturally variable'. *Political institutional structures* are the relatively fixed, formal institutions which Rootes would regard as genuine political opportunity structures. Perhaps inconsistently, Rootes (1997: 95) includes electoral systems here because they 'are usually remarkably stable over time', but he notes that party systems and political alliances are more problematic, because they are relatively stable but ultimately contingent upon genuine political structures. *Social and cultural contexts*, according to Rootes (1997: 96), are 'in a state of eternal flux'. They tend to change gradually, and appear stable *and* changing because of the long term nature of change. Finally, Rootes (1997: 97) points to the *ideas, knowledge, values and repertoires* of actors. This applies to the relatively small proportion of the overall population who are crucial to social movements, but the mass population may also be important in terms of their response to the action of the movement, and the values and perceptions of official decision-makers are also relevant. Rootes notes that ideology can determine forms of action, whatever the political opportunity setting. So, the values and beliefs of actors, as well as their adversaries, are just as important as formal political structures. These may create opportunities or may prevent other opportunities from being taken.

*European 'New Social Movement' Approaches*

US researchers were the first to utilise social movement theory and were heavily influenced by the resource mobilisation approach. In contrast, European social scientists since the late 1960s have been more concerned with macro-societal, structural changes in advanced industrial societies, arguing that social movements have resulted from and contributed to these changes. Attention has been focused on 'new social movements', the movements of the 1960s and 1970s such as feminist, environmental and peace groups. The 'new politics' movements are said to be the manifestations of a new set of conflicts in contemporary, or 'post-industrial' society, thus challenging traditional Marxist interpretations (Melucci 1989; Offe 1985). As Scott (1990: 153) illustrates, many European sociologists have attempted to explain the 'newness' of these movements by analysing broad transformations in social systems, or societal structures:

> New social movements are assumed to 'reflect' broader societal developments such as the shift of focus within the economic base from production to reproduction (Castells); industrial to post-industrial society (Touraine); or from liberal to late capitalism (Habermas). It is argued that these structural developments have thrown up qualitatively new forms of opposition within society.

A common argument is that the development of advanced capitalist societies – based on an active Keynesian state, welfare provision, and the expansion of the service sector – has produced a new set of conflicts. The 'old politics' prioritised economic affluence, political order and strong military defence. The 'new' brand of movement politics appears identity based and is said to involve a very different set of demands: equal rights for minorities; greater democratisation; concern for the environment; military disarmament and so on (Melluci 1989; Offe 1985).

Central to these developments is the 'new middle class'. The 'old' middle class relates to those who still control the means of production. The 'new' middle class, it is argued, derives its power from knowledge. Partly this is a result of an active welfare state, which creates a new class of non-commercial, professional educationalists, social and health workers and so on. However, another important new middle class group are the people with scientific and technical expertise who are increasingly important in modern economies. These new middle class groups are regarded as the natural constituents of social movements, however the motivations behind new middle class support for these movements is widely debated. Some interpret this as an instrumental attempt to protect new middle class interests, others as an act of altruism (Byrne 1997: 52-54). A closely related argument is that advanced by the political scientist Ronald Inglehart (1977, 1990).

Diani and Eyerman (1992: 7) argue that the new political conflicts involve 'symbolic goods', meanings, lifestyles, personal and collective identities, rather than traditionally political or economic goods. In this respect, the European new social movement analysis might be described as 'identity orientated', as opposed to the 'strategy orientation' of resource mobilisation and political process models.[38] Indeed, European scholars are often critical of the resource mobilisation approach for concentrating on resources controlled by a small number of movement 'entrepreneurs' (a top-down approach) and thereby underestimating structurally determined conflicts (bottom-up factors) and, at the same time, overestimating the rationality of collective action. For example, action by dispossessed groups which is based on 'emotion' may not be properly accounted for by resource mobilisation approaches (see della Porta and Diani 1999: 9). Dalton and Keuchler (1990: 9-10) criticise resource mobilisation theory on the grounds that it is 'apolitical' and is indifferent to the ideological content of the new social movement message.

A number of characteristics are commonly associated with the new social movements. These include the promotion of an alternative set of *values* to the ones which dominate, including active participation, collective responsibility and post-materialism, a *strategy* aimed at changing public opinion, an *organisational structure* which reflects the ideals of democratic participation, and a distinctive *social basis* of support, including young people and the 'new middle class' (see for example Hallsworth 1994; Martell 1994: 112-113). Dalton and Keuchler (1990: 11) argue that these features of new social movements are *determined* by the ideological demands and values of the movements. In other words, advocacy of quality of life issues, democracy, participation and opportunity strongly influences the type of supporter, organisational structure and political style or choice of political tactics. Such an argument leads to the conclusion that one can only fully understand recruitment to new social movements if one considers their ideological appeal. To sum up, the European approaches have in common the claim that new social movements are not only 'chronologically new', 'they also represent a qualitatively new aspect of contemporary democratic politics' (Dalton and Keuchler 1990: 11).

Criticisms of this approach include the view that new social movement theorists have difficulty accounting for the link between conflict and action; and their tendency of 'positing certain coincidental traits – in particular the illustration of novel elements among actors in new collective movements – as absolutes' (see della Porta and Diani 1999: 13). As Scott (1990: 30) suggests, the aims and demands of new social movements are 'highly diverse' and it is often very difficult to distinguish between old and new social movements. Furthermore, Scott (1990: 68) argues that macro-level, social-structural approaches shift emphasis away for the questions of mobilisation discussed by resource mobilisation theory and therefore say very little about motivations behind membership, what he calls the 'means/ends calculation involved in decision-making'.

In recent years scholars of social movements have continued to develop their ideas in areas such as the emotions of protest (Godwin *et al.* 2001; Melluci 1996), the role of social networks in movements (Diani and McAdam 2003), the global character of many movement activities (Bryner 2001; Giugni *et al.* 1998; Keck and Sikkink 1998), and the institutionalisation of social movements (Giugni

---

[38]Zirakzadeh (1997: 15) refers to 'identity-formation' theorists.

*et al.* 1998; Meyer and Tarrow 1998; Rucht and Neidhardt 2002). Scholars have also recognised the need to integrate approaches, to construct 'comprehensive and synthetic approaches to the study of social movements' (Meyer 2002: 3; also see Eyerman and Jamieson 1991; Johnston and Klandermans 1995; Klandermans *et al.* 1988; Meyer 1999; Tarrow 1994). Most notably, there have been attempts to link identity approaches and political process ideas (Meyer *et al.* 2002). As Meyer (2002: 5) argues, 'states create the conditions in which particular identities develop'. Whittier (2002: 289) refers to a 'multi-layered' view of social movements, which acknowledges the interdependence of meaning and structure. Whittier (2002: 306) recognises that 'Meaning, consciousness, interaction, organization, cultural contexts, and political opportunities are all important to understanding how people work to change the world'. Nevertheless, these attempts at synthesis in the literature remain underdeveloped.

*Can Political Scientists Learn from Sociological Approaches?*

The review of social movement theory reveals a rich mix of theoretical approaches in the study of social movement participation, each with something to offer in understanding why people join social movements. As Zirakzadeh (1997: 19) argues, the classical approach 'reminds us that humans are reactive animals who respond to changes in their environment'; resource mobilisation perspectives reveal that 'humans are far-seeing animals who contemplate consequences, benefits, and disadvantages associated with different available courses of action'; and the identity-orientated approach highlights that 'humans are interpretive animals who constantly reimagine their situations and identities'.

In contrast, the political science community's attempts to explain political participation are more clearly dominated by the rational choice approach. Membership of the group or party is seen as the end result of some kind of cost-benefit analysis on the part of the joiner. The approach itself is widely criticised and modified (Barry 1978) and, more often than not, the original models provide a benchmark against which actual political behaviour can be measured (Ward 1995: 91). However, political scientists have perhaps relied too heavily on rational choice in their assessment of political behaviour. Ward (1995: 92), in an attempt to assess the status of rational choice within political science, strongly suggests it is a mistake to look to rational choice alone as an explanation for political behaviour:

> Human beings are psychologically complex, frequently act irrationally and operate within meaning systems that are difficult to comprehend fully when seen from a rational choice perspective. This suggests that the domain of application of rational choice theory will by no means cover the whole domain of political life, and also that other approaches to human action are as indispensable as rational choice itself.

Political scientists often employ similar terms and ideas to the sociologists but the models employed are more narrowly focused. For example, political science studies of green interest groups contrast with sociological studies in terms of the theories employed and the scope of the analysis. While the political science studies of groups focus on a range of questions, including internal organisational dynamics and levels of group influence, they are often very descriptive and/or adopt a critical rational choice approach. This contrasts with studies of the peace movement (primarily CND) which regard the group as part of a peace *movement* and relate support for the CND to much broader developments in society, including changing values and social structures (Byrne 1988; Parkin 1968; Taylor and Pritchard 1980).[39]   Parkin's analysis examines different forms of alienation in modern industrial society and Byrne's study reviews and employs many of the social movement theories outlined above to explain the development of CND. As Rüdig *et al.* (1991: 130) note, Byrne's study stands out as unusual because he was a political scientist and in fact 'social movement approaches have played a marginal role in British movement research'. In Britain the pressure group approach has dominated the study of the environmental movement (Rüdig *et al.* 1991: 128).

Nevertheless, it is interesting that the methods employed (survey research) and the conclusions reached by social researchers, whether political scientists or sociologists, are not dissimilar. Rüdig *et al.* (1991: 135-136) refer to two dominant themes in social movement research in Britain: the social characteristics of members and activists, and the influence of the movements in the political system. Furthermore, collective, purposive motivations behind membership are dominant in these studies, often described as *moral* reasons for joining (Parkin 1968). Clearly, there is scope for a greater degree of communication and collaboration between sociologists and political scientists. Jordan and Maloney (1997: 67) illustrate this point in their comparison of social movement and pressure group/interest group approaches:

> The wide attention given to social movements (as indicated in the range of papers, books, and articles that have appeared in recent years in contrast to the paucity on interest groups) has been imperfectly related to the interest group literature. It has assumed that interest groups are more formally organised with regularized membership arrangements than are in fact routinely covered in the range of the interest group world. Undoubtedly, the social movement literature is dealing with a material that is also covered by interest group writers – particularly those concentrating on cause groups or those who accept the concept of the unorganised group.

Similarly, Burstein (1995: 1) notes that social movements, political parties and interest groups, while sharing a number of common characteristics, are studied separately: 'There is, essentially, a separate subdiscipline for each type of organization, with its own history and theories'. Often, according to Burstein (1995: 13-14), political scientists and sociologists 'are studying the same thing without realizing it'.[40] Burstein (1995: 12) argues that political scientists would

---

[39]Rüdig *et al.* (1991: 133) note that the peace movement has been subject to more quantitative survey research than any other movement in Britain.
[40]See Scott (1990: 26) for a similar argument.

gain from greater recognition of the importance of social movement organisations and their influence in democratic politics, although, he claims, 'sociologists could benefit even more by paying more attention to formal democratic institutions'.

This is not to say that political scientists have been uninterested in social movements (see Rüdig 1990; Wilkinson 1971). The political scientist Paul Wilkinson (1971) for example was the first political scientist in Britain to conduct an extensive review of social movement literature, producing a detailed typology of social movements (Rüdig *et al.* 1991: 122). However, most studies of social movements in Britain have taken the form of largely atheoretical case studies of individual movements. Furthermore, while some political scientists *have* shown an interest in the integration of political science and sociological approaches (Rüdig 1990; Scott 1990), these recommendations have not been followed up to any significant extent.

The consequences for academic study are missed opportunities to learn from different disciplines (see Meyer 2002: 5). Different assumptions and different vocabulary obfuscate our attempts to understand the many forms of social and political behaviour. There is clearly a need to learn from other approaches to the same social phenomenon. In this study of Scottish Green Party membership, it is assumed that political science can learn from the social movement approaches outlined above. In other words, both political science and sociological approaches will be used to inform the analysis of party membership.

## Choosing Testable Theories: A Framework for Analysing Scottish Green Party Membership

The theoretical review unveiled a rich mix of approaches to participation and the question of why individuals join political parties or social movement organisations. Table 3.1 summarises the themes on who joins as members, how members join and why members join. From this outline it should be possible to identify a series of testable propositions.

Joining can involve being subject to the influence of multiple factors. When applied to specific movements or organisations each of the theoretical approaches can appear very convincing. There will inevitably be cases when movements rise up from socially isolated individuals, or economically deprived groups, and in these cases frustration aggression approaches are a relevant explanation.[41]

---

[41]Wallis (1984) for example considers recruitment to 'new religious groups' (e.g. Scientology, Krishna Consciousness and the Unification Church). He describes the recruitment base of these 'world-rejecting' movements as social groups marginal to, or suddenly marginalised by, the prevailing social order; a rejection of a world that has rejected them (Wallis 1984: 119). Studies of commune members reveal a similar tendency (Abrams and McCulloch 1976; Rigby 1974). Abrams and McCulloch (1976: 93) argue that in most cases motivation for communal living stems from a 'sense of personal estrangement from feelings of threatened or frustrated individuality'. Abrams and McCulloch argue that commune joining is often about taking stock before re-entering society; it is a transitional

Evidence of mobilisation of members by highly active movement entrepreneurs is evident in many studies. Furthermore, political setting and cultural identities also have indisputable effects on all aspects of movement development. However, each theoretical approach has a tendency to concentrate on a limited number of influences and thereby tell only one part of the story. For example, a focus on the recruitment techniques of groups neglects the other aspects of a society that help shape attitudes and behaviour, including the media. Many interest group scholars seriously underestimate these wider societal factors. Furthermore, many of these theories have been based on empirical studies of groups and social movement organisations. Therefore the conclusions may be 'movement-specific' and not generalisable. The individual who joins the Jehovah's Witnesses (Beckford 1975) will probably do so for very different reasons from the person who decides to join a trade union. So motivations behind membership depend on the *type* of organisation being studied.

Moreover, different theories may be applicable at different stages of a movement's development. Rüdig (1990) for instance, while constructing a process model for the emergence of a new social movement, defends the relative deprivation theory, claiming it has much to contribute. However, only at the initial stage of the movement's life does he make a strong defence of the approach. He suggests that once a movement has been born, relative deprivation explains very little.

Under these circumstances, is it possible to develop an integrated understanding of joining? A useful attempt to integrate approaches is provided by McAdam *et al.* (1988). This model of movement emergence and development includes an exhaustive list of micro-level and macro-level factors, which can be summarised as the interactive dynamics between (a) the individual, (b) the organisation, and (c) the political/structural environment. The study involves an analysis of individual level accounts of movement emergence (psychological, attitudinal, rational choice and relative deprivation accounts) and micro-structural accounts that highlight the need for a structural vehicle (the need for prior contact, membership in organisations, history of activism and biographic availability). It also considers some of the micro-processes at work during movement development; the production and maintenance of meaning and ideology, resource maintenance, sustaining membership commitment.

The utility of this approach is its recognition that membership can result from the *interaction* of many different variables. For example, a section of the population may be susceptible to a movement, either because of a desire for social integration or because they are ideologically committed to the movement's objectives, but they are unlikely to join unless they interact in some way with other members of the community and/or movement. In other words, it is impossible to consider individual level variables in complete isolation from the behaviour of organisations which people join and the macro-political context in which individuals take the decision to join. The decision to become, or remain, involved

---

course to help in the process of integration into society. Similarly Rigby (1974) describes the process of 'dropping-out' of society involved when people join communes.

in an organisation will inevitably be influenced by the resource mobilisation activities of organisations in their attempts to attract members, and by the opportunities for involvement inherent in different societies. For these reasons we cannot avoid 'middle way' attempts to explain participation which focus on the 'meso' level, the intermediate level which involves the relationship between micro and structural levels. This assessment of *micro-mobilisation contexts* involves an integration of 'demand side' and 'supply side' perspectives.

**Table 3.1  A Summary of Approaches**

| Who (individual characteristics) | How ('push' or 'pull' relationship with organisation) | Why (reason join) |
| --- | --- | --- |
| **Classical approaches** | | |
| Irrational/alienated /discontented. | Individual may 'seek out' membership or 'respond' to movement recruitment techniques. | Psychological reasons, e.g. desire for integration. |
| Deprived individual or member of relatively deprived group. | Individual may 'seek out' membership or 'respond' to movement recruitment techniques. | Search for solution to deprivation. (stimulus-response). |
| **Resource Mobilisation/Rational Choice Accounts** | | |
| The rational self-interested individual makes cost-benefit analysis. Likely to be integrated members of society and economically secure. | Exchange relationship ('push' and 'pull') but emphasis on organisers/ membership networks who 'pull' sympathisers into membership. | Attracted by tangible/intangible rewards. May be selective or collective incentives. |
| **European New Social Movement Approaches** | | |
| New middle class. | Individual may 'seek out' membership or 'respond' to movement recruitment techniques. | Attracted by ideological content of movement message. |

The McAdam *et al.* (1988) approach clearly illustrates the potential multi-dimensionality of the joining decision.  However, some of the aspects of joining outlined by McAdam *et al.* (1988) are very difficult to test empirically. Cultural influences, for example, are very difficult to assess.  The researcher must choose to focus on ideas that can be explored with data available to them.  Social-psychological variables are not, strictly speaking, testable properties. The political scientist or sociologist cannot infer from questionnaire responses that a member of a party is 'socially inadequate', 'alienated' or 'estranged from family and friends'. However, using individual level questionnaire data we are able to identify the social 'types' of participants, their political experiences, and the participants' self-declared reasons for involvement. The 'micro-mobilisation contexts' described by McAdam *et al.* (1988) provide us with another set of testable ideas.  How important is social integration and organisational experience in the individual's decision to become involved?  Are members 'pulled' into membership by movement organisations?  Is the act of 'joining' one organisation likely to lead to involvement in another?  These questions can be explored with the use of questionnaire data on movement participants, in this case the Scottish Green Party. It should be possible to create a profile of membership characteristics and motivations.

Such an approach amounts to more than a simple account of social characteristics of members; it considers the relationship between the individual's decision and the behaviour of movement organisations.  Through an examination of *who* participates, *how* they become involved, *why* they participate, and *when* they decide to become involved, we will concentrate on the micro-level and meso-level aspects of movement emergence and development. The study is based on individual accounts of the membership experience but these are inevitably interweaved with the micro-structural dynamics of organisational behaviour, and they are also in some way related to the cultural and political setting in which the decision to join was taken.  Although the book does not examine in detail those macro-structural dynamics which influence society's values and attitudes, these factors become relevant when they are perceived to be important by the participants, and when they influence the timing of joining.  Indeed, the *timing* of joining – the social and political environment at the time of joining – is under-explored by much of the literature on participation. It will be argued that the decision to join the Scottish Greens is related to the political events of the day.

*Joining: Testable Propositions*

*(i) Who joined the Scottish Greens*  It is a relatively straight-forward exercise to identify the socio-demographic characteristics of Scottish Green members.  The surveys explored a wide range of social background variables: gender, age, education, occupation, mobility, housing tenure, religion, marital status, and perceptions of class.  In addition, the surveys explored the members' experiences of other groups and parties.  In this way it is possible to assess whether members are economically insecure and marginalised, or whether they are economically prosperous and belong to the 'new middle class'.  And we can test for

'biographical availability' (are these party members people with time on their hands?). Furthermore, we can explore the extent to which members appear 'integrated' in the sense that they belong to social or political networks.

*(ii) How the members joined* Another objective is to look at the mechanics of joining the Scottish Green Party and assess the levels of self-initiative involved. However, as the literature reviewed reveals, it is very difficult to determine exactly how members become involved in an organisation. For example, a potential member may sympathise with the general objectives of a group but he or she may not be aware that the group exists. A press advertisement may alert the potential member to the group's existence, and the individual may then make contact with the organisation. Under these circumstances, should we assume that the member joined through their own initiative, or were they responding to group advertising techniques? The participation literature would suggest a combination of 'push' and 'pull' tends to be involved, however, the resource mobilisation type theorists place much greater emphasis on the organisation's ability to *attract* members. As has already been argued, this approach can appear rather 'apolitical' in that potential members are viewed as resources of the organisation that can be pulled into membership as and when the organisation requires financial assistance. Academics who adopt this approach run the risk of under-estimating the individual's independence of thought when deciding to join an organisation. While recognising the difficulties associated with these questions, the 1990 survey of Scottish Greens attempted to explore the level of self-initiative on the part of members, by asking them exactly *how* they became members. This was separated from influences on the decision to join, and the precise question of *why* the respondents joined. In this way, it should be possible to identify the main 'pathways to membership' of the Scottish Green Party. For example, what proportion of members responded to a membership appeal? How many got a membership form from a friend or colleague?

*(iii) Why the members joined* The alternative approaches to understanding participation will be addressed. For example, is there any evidence of a desire for social integration? Or do members join in order to counter what they see as a form of deprivation? Although economic deprivation is unlikely in the case of Scottish Greens, the experience of environmental problems may be regarded as a form of deprivation. The book develops the idea of 'environmental deprivation', the suggestion being that environmental problems can be 'felt' and may have some influence on the decision to join. If membership of a green organisation is the result of negative environmental experiences, we may be able to resurrect theories of relative deprivation.

The discussion to follow will attempt to examine a number of membership incentives, as illustrated by expanded rational choice approaches. Much of the literature reviewed can be divided into two broad categories: organisational approaches, which examine the benefits to the organisation of attracting members (Johnson 1995, 1998; Jordan and Maloney 1997; Rosenstone and Hansen 1993; Scarrow 1994, 1996; Schlozman *et al.* 1999; Shaiko 1999) and member-centred approaches which focus on the benefits gained by members (McCulloch 1990; Seyd and Whiteley 1992, 1995, 2002; Whiteley and Seyd 1994, 1998a, 1998b, 2002; Rüdig *et al.* 1996; Curtice *et al.* 1993). This study falls squarely into the second of these two categories. One hypothesis to be tested is the extent to which membership of the Scottish Greens can be explained by selective or collective incentives. As a small green party is not in a position to offer many selective incentives to its members, it is likely that collective incentives are at the core of membership. However, the precise nature of these incentives requires detailed investigation. Based on survey responses to detailed batteries of questions on joining, the book explores general influences behind the decision to join, as well as reasons given for joining. The importance of different types of collective incentives will be assessed. Resource mobilisation types of approaches will be challenged because they assume that social movement leaders organise discontent, and they neglect the importance of collective, political beliefs. Nevertheless, it will be suggested that perceptions of organisational effectiveness, the ability of the organisation to promote the collective good, *is* a key ingredient in membership of the Scottish Greens.

Furthermore, the book considers the importance of socialisation in the environmental movement. Indeed, it is possible that members of a green party may have more in common with members of other green organisations, that is green pressure groups, than traditional political parties. We might expect a green party member's motivations to be different from those of a member of a large, traditional party. For instance, Seyd and Whiteley's (1992) collective positive incentives appear plausible in the case of a major party with every likelihood of forming a government, but we might question whether this applies to members of small parties who are unlikely to be given the opportunity to implement their policies. Nevertheless, 'making a difference' could simply amount to pressuring the other parties. We should not rule out this type of motivation in the case of the Scottish Greens.

*(iv) When the members joined*  The book argues that the act of joining and motivations behind joining are likely to be related to the time of joining. It will be suggested that a wide cultural and political environment will have a bearing on why members choose to join at a particular point in time, indeed whether they join at all. For example, increasing tangible evidence of environmental degradation – in the form of scientific reports and environmental accidents – which is widely reported in the media, creates a unique set of political circumstances which are likely to influence the decision to join a green party. The hypothesis to be tested here is that individuals who joined the Scottish Greens at the end of the 1980s will offer different reasons for joining from those who joined the party before the height of interest in the environment. Furthermore, the 2002 survey allows us to consider SGP membership in the context of significant constitutional change. Is there any evidence to suggest that the members in 2002 were influenced by the very different political context of the day? Have different social types joined the party, and do they have different motivations and expectations now that the

Scottish Parliament is up and running and the Greens now have more of a prospect of contributing to Scottish politics?

Following on from this, it will be suggested that political process/political opportunity structure approaches offer some useful insights into the joining decision, in that to fully understand membership one must also consider the wider political context in which the decision is taken.[42] For instance, mobilisation may occur at a time of economic prosperity, or when electoral systems change, or when new governments are formed. Many of the traditional approaches reviewed can be criticised for neglecting this important aspect of the joining decision. Micro-level variables must be viewed in the context of macro-level developments. In the case of the Scottish Greens, this involves consideration of a wide set of variables – critical environmental events, elite responses, the media reporting of these events, and constitutional changes to name but a few. In other words, to explain long-term membership patterns of such a party, including any sudden upturns in membership, contextual developments are important. It will be suggested that the decision to join should be treated as a rational act because it involves the pursuit of some interest, be this individual or collective. However, to fully understand the joining decision we must place it into political context.

---

[42]As has already been argued, as a conceptual tool of analysis, the 'political opportunity structure' approach is problematic. The concept is often stretched to breaking point in an attempt to embrace the multitude of contextual factors. The result can be confusion and a loss of meaning – there is a risk that the concept is stretched to the point where it becomes meaningless. Nevertheless, the broad ideas of political opportunities and context may yet be relevant in understanding social movement.

# Chapter 4

# Who Were the Scottish Greens in 1990?

Theories of political participation and social movement approaches provide some testable questions concerning *who* participates in politics (chapter 3). Some classical theorists predicted that those people most likely to participate were alienated, marginalised or deprived individuals. Klapp (1969: 41), for example, referred to those who were on an 'identity search', attempting to counteract the 'disharmony' of their lives. Other theorists focus on the mobilisation of resources and suggest that socially integrated individuals are the most likely to become involved. Parkin (1968: 16), for example, argued that participation in politics was 'fully compatible with social integration'. New social movement observers similarly predict that the socially confident and integrated – the 'new middle class' – will be movement actors.

Similar debates exist in the green literature. Dobson (1994: 158) refers to one school of thought which predicts that the 'agents for social change' are likely to be those members of society who are marginalised and alienated from the process of production and consumption: '...it is the distance from the process of consumption and the degree of permanence of this isolation that currently determine the capacity of any given group in society for radical green social change'. A number of writers point to a 'disenfranchised' and 'excluded' group or groups within modern society who are most susceptible to the radical green perspective. Gorz (1985: 35-36) refers to a 'socially marginalised' group, a 'post-industrial proletariat of the unemployed, occasionally employed, short-term or part-term workers, who neither can nor want to identify themselves with their job or their place in the production process'. Similarly, Alber (1989: 205) argues that 'the typical supporter of the Greens... is young, highly trained, and unemployed or not economically active'.

This position contrasts with the view that socially integrated, middle class members of society will perform the role of agents for change (Porritt 1994: 116). The middle class are said to have benefited from post-war structural changes in society – the expansion of higher education, the rise in living standards – and have experienced a shift in political values from materialist to post-materialist 'quality of life' concerns (Inglehart 1977; 1990; 1997). This changing value system combined with an expanding set of 'new' non-commercial middle class occupations (health workers and educationalists) is said to have produced a new middle class, likely to be at the forefront of demands for environmental protection (Byrne 1997; Cotgrove 1982: 95).

Previous empirical research on participation clearly indicates that those most likely to become involved in any form of social organisation are the socially skilled middle class and integrated members of society (for example Kornberg *et al.* 1979; Norris 2002; Parry *et al.* 1992; Verba *et al.* 1995). Participation in social movement organisations is no exception to this general rule but we find that a particular section of the middle classes appears to be attracted to environmental and peace movements. A number of studies of CND members have pointed to a distinct character of member; middle class, well educated and likely to be employed in a non-market-based occupation (Byrne 1988; Parkin 1968; Taylor and Pritchard 1980). And more recent studies appear to confirm the predominantly middle class character of green or peace movement participants. In their study of environmental public interest group members, Jordan and Maloney (1997) highlight the middle class qualities of participants – high levels of education, professional occupations and high levels of income – while arguing that members are also more likely to be young and female. They describe the average member of Friends of the Earth or Amnesty International as 'a well educated middle-class female under 45 in a professional/managerial occupation from a relatively affluent household, who is a member of other campaigning organizations...and votes for a centre-left party...' (Jordan and Maloney 1997: 121).

Previous research on green party members in the UK (Rüdig *et al.* 1991) suggests that the typical UK Green is similarly economically secure and well educated, s/he enjoys many middle class comforts and does not appear marginalised from the rest of society. However, a feature of the typical UK Green is that s/he 'has made some choices which set him or her apart, not just from the rest of the population but also from other "middle class" professionals' (Rüdig *et al.* 1991: 30). These choices involve studying for a degree in the arts and humanities and working in a 'caring' profession (teaching, health, social work). These characteristics might be interpreted as 'indications of a certain detachment from a world in which economic growth and profits play a dominant role' (Rüdig *et al.* 1991: 30).

This chapter establishes the sociological characteristics and political experiences of Scottish Green Party members in 1990. Were they marginalised and alienated or were they socially confident, integrated members of society?

## Social Background of Scottish Greens

The 1990 survey enables us to create a sociological profile of party members at this time, and allows us to compare the demographic characteristics of Scotland's general population. When appropriate, the results of the study of UK Greens and other empirical studies of environmental and peace movement actors (Byrne 1988; Cotgrove 1982; Jordan and Maloney 1997; Parkin 1968; Taylor and Pritchard 1980) are also considered, along with characteristics of other party members in Britain in the early 1990s (Bennie *et al.* 1996; Curtice *et al.* 1993; Seyd and Whiteley 1992; Whiteley *et al.* 1994). Table 4.1 introduces some of the prominent characteristics of Scottish Greens relating to gender, age, education and occupation.

*Gender*

Evidence of a gender gap in political participation and political attitudes is far from clear cut (see Schlozman *et al.* 1995). While there is evidence to suggest that women are under-represented in political organisations generally (Seyd and Whiteley 1992) some studies indicate that women have different issue priorities and that they are more likely than men to support environmental causes (Jordan and Maloney 1997: 109; Young 1991: 77-108). In the UK study of Greens, females were under-represented but only slightly (Rüdig *et al.* 1990: 17). Did women make more of an impact on the membership of the Scottish Greens?

Table 4.1 reveals that, of the Scottish sample, 54.7 per cent were male and 45.3 per cent were female. In 1990, 52 per cent of the 1990 Scottish population were female (Central Statistical Office 1992: 33), meaning that women appeared to be under-represented in the party, and a little more so than in the UK Greens where 47 per cent of members were female (Rüdig *et al.* 1991: 17).[1] In addition, women in the Scottish Green Party were considerably less likely to be active than men, and a little less active than women in the UK party. Almost every indicator of party activity pointed to male dominance. Women were less likely to attend local party meetings, take part in local campaigns, hold a local party office, or stand as candidates in elections. For example, 24.3 per cent of men had been local election candidates but only 15.5 per cent of the female members. The only activity that attracted more women than men was the organising of coffee mornings! At the area and national levels, the trend of male dominance was even more evident.

Are peace groups and other environmental organisations more successful at mobilising female members? Byrne (1988: 57) found a more equal split between the sexes in his study of CND members in 1985; in all age categories, females numbered almost exactly 50 per cent of the sample. The Jordan and Maloney (1997: 108) analysis of environmental group membership in the UK reveals a clear *over-representation* of women. The authors found that women made up 59.3 per cent and 56.4 per cent of Friends of the Earth and Amnesty members respectively. Jordan and Maloney (1997: 109) suggest that public interest groups may attract more women than men because these groups are unlikely to provide material selective incentives and women may be less interested in these types of incentives. Certainly, it is possible that women are attracted to the non-party political approach of pressure groups; they may be put off by party status. It is a fairly well established fact that women tend to be under-represented in traditional political

---

[1]These figures take into account some problems in administering the survey which meant that joint members received only one survey between them. In the UK survey, analysis of the returns revealed that in the majority of these cases the respondent who completed the questionnaire was male. It was therefore necessary to recalculate the overall proportion of female members, assuming that the majority of joint memberships consisted of one male and female. However, this was not a serious problem in the Scottish sample. There was only a marginal difference in the number of male and female responses. Of 120 joint responses, 63 were male and 57 female. Following recalculation, the percentage of females overall moved from 44.7% to 45.3%.

parties. Compared to the UK Labour Party, the Greens in 1990 were quite successful at attracting females: only 39 per cent of Labour members were female (Seyd and Whiteley 1992: 32). The Conservatives however had a greater proportion of females than the Greens in their ranks: 49 per cent of Conservative members were women (Whiteley *et al.* 1994: 43). Overall, the Greens looked quite successful at attracting females. However, there were signs that environmental and peace pressure groups were even better at this. However, the evidence is not conclusive. In Taylor and Pritchard's (1980: 22) study of the 1958-1965 membership of CND 20 years on, only 35 per cent of members were women.

**Table 4.1  Social Profile of Scottish Green Party Members 1990 (%)**

|  | Scottish Greens | Scottish Population |
|---|---|---|
| **Sex** | | |
| Female | 45 | 52 |
| Male | 55 | 48 |
| | | |
| **Age** | | |
| 16-44 | 75 | 43 |
| 45-64 | 19 | 22 |
| 65 and over | 6 | 15 |
| | | |
| **Education** | | |
| Completed education by age of 16 | 16 | 22 |
| Studied/studying for degree | 81 | 8 |
| Highest degree postgraduate | 25 | - |
| Highest degree Honours | 50 | - |
| | | |
| **Occupation** | | |
| Professional/technical | 53 | 15 |
| Self-employed | 17 | 10 |
| Unemployed | 7 | 8 |

*Age*

The age distribution of the Scottish Green Party in 1990 was weighted quite heavily towards the young. As Table 4.1 indicates, three quarters of members (75 per cent) were below the age of 45, compared to 43 per cent of the Scottish general population in 1990 (The Scottish Office 1991: 3). And the party in Scotland had a slightly more youthful profile than the party in the rest of the UK: 66.9 per cent of UK Greens belonged in this category (Rüdig *et al.* 1991: 17).

At first sight it appears that the party in Scotland was successful at mobilising young people into membership. However, a closer look at the overall age distribution of the party members reveals that the very young (those below 25) were actually underrepresented in comparison with the 'middle aged' groups (between 25 and 44): 12 per cent of the Scottish Greens belonged in the 16-24 age bracket, compared to 63 per cent of members between the ages of 25 and 44 (Figure 4:1). Furthermore, the under-25s in the party were also under-represented by comparison with the general population: 14 per cent of the Scottish population were between 16 and 24 in 1990 (Scottish Office 1991: 3). Clearly, the middle-aged contingent provided the core of Scottish Green Party membership in 1990. Most members were between the ages 25 and 44 and the mean, or average, age of party members was 39.[2]

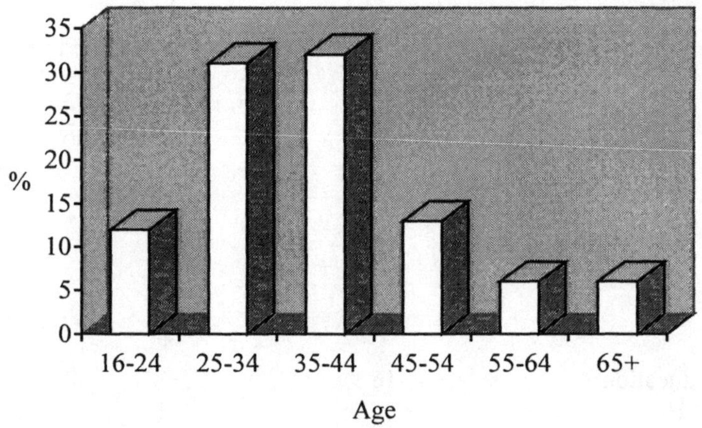


**Figure 4.1 Age of Scottish Greens 1990**

Nevertheless, compared to the large UK parties, the Greens in Scotland and the rest of the UK had a very youthful profile. Less than half – 48 per cent – of Labour members were aged 45 or below (Seyd and Whiteley 1992: 39); and less than one in five – only 16 per cent – of Conservatives (Whiteley *et al.* 1994: 43). The Liberal Democrats were nearly as old as the Conservatives: just over a quarter were aged 45 or younger (Bennie *et al.* 1996: 136).

The age structure of the Greens appears more similar to those found in studies of environmental organisations and peace groups. Byrne's 1985 sample of CND members found that 24 per cent of members were below the age of 25 and nearly half – 47 per cent – were between 25 and 40 (1988: 57). Jordan and Maloney (1997: 116) found that 59 per cent of Friends of the Earth members were between 25 and 44.

---

[2]The mean age of UK Greens was 41 (Rüdig *et al.* 1991: 17).

The relatively youthful profile of the Greens suggests that these members may have been 'biographically available' when they became members (McAdam *et al.* 1988). Younger people are less likely to have family and work commitments making them potentially more 'available' as party recruits. Snow *et al.* (1980: 794) also point to the importance of demographic availability arguing that people who become involved in social movements often lack extraneous commitments and have time to participate. Furthermore, Snow *et al.* (1980: 794) suggest that because social movement recruits are often at a particular stage in demographic development, this is why they sometimes appear to be socially isolated individuals.

With these points in mind, the Scottish Green Party questionnaire of 1990 asked members to indicate their 'marital status': 33.4 per cent described themselves as 'single', 54.5 per cent said they were married or living with a partner, 10.1 per cent were divorced/separated; and 2 per cent were widowed. Just under half of the membership (49 per cent) indicated that they had children. How do these statistics compare with those of the general population? In 1991, 26.6 per cent of Scottish households contained one person (The Scottish Office 1991: 51). In 1991, the proportion of households in Scotland with 'dependent children' was 30 per cent (Central Statistical Office 1993: 48). While these figures are not strictly comparable, they suggest that the party members in this study were not significantly more 'demographically available' for recruitment than members of the general population. For many, party membership was combined with family responsibilities. Whether or not the members appear 'available' in terms of their occupational background will be discussed below.

*Education*

The level of education of 1990 Scottish Green Party members was spectacularly high. Only 16 per cent had completed their education by the age of 16; in Scotland, 22 per cent of 16 year olds at the time did not stay on at school or go on to further education, but this figure is much higher for older generations (Central Statistical Office: 59).[3] Even more impressive is the extent of educational achievements of Scottish Greens. For example, respondents were asked to state the highest degree they had been awarded (Table 4.2).

This table illustrates the high educational attainment of the Scottish sample. Of all Scottish respondents, more than one in four had a postgraduate qualification. In Scotland at this time (1991) only 8 per cent of the Scottish working population had a degree (Central Statistical Office 1992: 88). In response to a separate question, an exceptional 81 per cent of the Scottish Greens indicated that they had either studied, or were at the time studying, for a degree at an institution of higher education. Of those who had studied, or were studying, for a degree, 6.2 per cent went to Oxford/Cambridge, 67.7 per cent went to another university, 9.2 percent a Polytechnic, and 16.9 per cent another college.

---

[3] 28% of the Scottish Greens attended a fee-paying independent school: 7% of the British population attended such a school (Foster 1990: 150).

**Table 4.2  Highest Academic Degree (%)**

|                      | Scottish Greens | UK Greens |
| -------------------- | --------------- | --------- |
| Phd/DPhil            | 5.7             | 3.4       |
| MA/MSc/MPhil         | 14.7            | 9.8       |
| Postgraduate diploma | 6.3             | 5.0       |
| BA/BSc Honours       | 14.3            | 18.5      |
| BA/BSc               | 9.2             | 6.4       |
| HND                  | 4.1             | 3.1       |
| Other                | 8.6             | 7.3       |
| No degree/No answer  | 36.9            | 46.5      |
|                      |                 |           |
| N                    | 509             | 4,357     |

Furthermore, Scottish Greens appeared better educated than their UK party counterparts: 'only' 67 per cent of the UK Greens had studied or were studying for a degree at the time of the survey (Rüdig *et al.* 1991: 21).  This probably reflects the generally higher levels of educational attainment in Scotland.  For example, in 1990/1991 more 16 year olds continued their education in Scotland than in any other region of Britain (Central Statistical Office 1992: 24).  Nevertheless, the educational achievements of the Scottish Greens were impressive.

None of the studies of party members in Britain revealed such high levels of education. Of all the major parties, the Liberal Democrat members were the most likely to have a  degree, but this amounted to just under 50 per cent of members (Bennie *et al.* 1996: 137). Again, the Greens in this sample appear rather more like pressure group members. Parkin (1968: 177) found that 54 per cent of his respondents had had some form of higher education. In 1978, only 19 per cent of Taylor and Pritchard's (1978: 23) respondents had ended their education at the minimum school leaving age and 73 per cent had a degree or a professional qualification.  In 1985, only 15 per cent of CND members had completed their education by the age of 16, and 57 per cent had a degree or diploma (Byrne 1988: 58).  Jordan and Maloney (1997: 111) found that 54 per cent of Friends of the Earth members had a degree or postgraduate qualification.

The choice of subjects of Scottish Greens who had studied for a degree is also noteworthy: 27.9 per cent studied arts and humanities (e.g. languages, philosophy, history), and another 27.4 per cent social sciences (e.g. sociology, psychology, politics, economics).  Overall the Scottish Green Party members with a degree were much more likely to have a background in arts and social sciences than the graduate population in Britain (Foster 1990: 269). A similar preference for arts and social science subjects was highlighted in Parkin's (1968: 172) study: 70 per cent of his CND respondents specialised in humanities or social sciences while only 17 per cent specialised in pure or applied sciences.

These findings raise a number of questions about the effects of education.  It has been suggested that education, in particular higher education, can have a radicalising effect.  Parkin (1968: 169) for instance argued that 'exposure to the liberating and critical influences of the universities can have the effect of creating liberal or radical dispositions in those of previously more orthodox or conservative outlook'. Parkin was suggesting, in other words, that higher education makes a person less likely to endorse conventional attitudes and values. Parkin (1968: 171) states:

> The tendency for advanced education to make inroads upon young people's acceptance of middle class political values is more marked in some fields of study than others. In general, the process would seem to be especially marked in the social sciences and humanities, and least so in fields like engineering, technology and other applied sciences.

This study provides some support for this argument. However, the preference for arts and social science subjects amongst Greens can be interpreted in a number of ways. It is possible that the experience of higher education encourages the development of a socially critical, non-conformist perspective but it is also possible that participants are already sympathetic to this outlook before they experience higher education and they choose degree subjects in line with these values. The second of these explanations might lead us to expect that, for some, the choice of degree subject reflects already established values and represents the first step in the choice of career path.

*Occupation*

Is there any evidence that Scottish Green Party members in 1990 were alienated from the mainstream process of production and consumption? Can we identify the existence of a '*post-industrial proletariat*' (Gorz 1985), or '*frustrated academic plebeians*' (Alber 1989: 205)? It has already been established that the party members were exceptionally well educated, but did they go on to become excluded from mainstream economic activity? A distinctive feature of the Scottish Greens' work status was the sizeable number in full-time education, constituting one in ten members (10.6 per cent).[4] Nevertheless, the number employed in full time work (51 per cent), unemployed (6.6 per cent), and part time workers (11 per cent) was pretty close to the Scottish national average. For example, in 1990 the unemployment rate in Scotland was 8 per cent (Central Statistical Office 1992: 83). Overall, the Scottish Greens were a little *more* likely to be economically active than the general population, partly explained by the age structure of the membership; the 25-44 age group which was over-represented in the party is the most likely to be economically active (Central Statistical Office 1992: 81). Furthermore, the retired over 65s were severely under-represented in the party.[5] There is little indication here of 'frustrated drop-outs' who have suffered from

---

[4]The UK average at the end of the 1980s was less than 2% (Foster 1988: 269). Fewer UK Greens (8.4%) were in full-time education at the time of the survey (Rüdig *et al.* 1991: 25).
[5]Conversely, only 29% of UK Conservative members were in full time work, again explained by the age profile of the membership (Whiteley *et al.* 1994:46).

'blocked mobility chances' (Alber 1989: 205).  This observation is confirmed by assessing the occupations of Scottish Greens (Table 4.3).

**Table 4.3  Occupation of Scottish Greens 1990 (%)**

| | |
|---|---|
| Farmer or farm manager | 2.0 |
| Farm worker | 0.4 |
| Skilled manual worker (e.g. plumber, electrician fitter, driver, cook, hairdresser) | 4.9 |
| Semi-skilled/unskilled manual (e.g. postman, machine operator, assembler, waiter, cleaner, labourer) | 4.7 |
| Clerical worker (e.g. clerk, secretary, telephone operator) | 7.3 |
| Sales worker (e.g. shop assistant, commercial traveller) | 1.8 |
| Professional/Technical (e.g. doctor, teacher, social worker, accountant, computer programmer) | 53.3 |
| Manager or senior administrator (e.g. company director, executive officer, local authority officer) | 4.9 |
| Other | 19.6 |
| | |
| N | 450 |

The professional background of Scottish Green Party members at this time is clear.  Nearly six in every ten of the economically active members had a professional, technical or managerial occupation, in comparison to around one in eight of the 1991 general population who were employed as managers or administrators, or in associated professional and technical positions (Central Statistical Office 1992: 88).  The dominance of professionals was evident amongst all UK Greens but was even more prevalent in Scotland: 49.5 per cent of the UK respondents were employed in a professional or technical occupation (Rüdig *et al.* 1991: 26).

The high incidence of 'middle class' professionals in green and peace groups has been noted previously. Taylor and Pritchard (1980: 147) classified 83 per cent of their respondents as non-manual and 12 per cent as manual (5 per cent unknown).  Byrne (1988: 58) described 74 per cent of his CND respondents with an occupation as having 'middle class occupations'; 22 per cent had skilled or manual occupations and 5 per cent were unemployed or retired.  In Jordan and Maloney's study (1997: 112) just under half (48.0 per cent) of FoE members had a professional or technical occupation, and 52.2 per cent of Amnesty members. Another 11.0 per cent and 15.2 per cent, respectively, were managers or senior administrators.

It has been suggested that environmentalists might be likely to seek employment in particular fields i.e. the public sector in 'caring' occupations such as social work, health and education (Byrne 1988; Cotgrove 1982; Parkin 1968; Taylor and Pritchard 1980).  This study provides further evidence of such a trend

(Table 4.4). Only one in five of the Scottish respondents worked for a private firm, well below the national average (Central Statistical Office 1992: 86-87). In total 49.1 per cent of the economically active Scottish Green respondents were employed in the public sector, a slightly higher figure than for UK Greens, 44.2 per cent of whom worked in the public sector (Rüdig *et al.* 1991: 26).

**Table 4.4  Type of Employer (%)**

|                                | Scottish Greens | UK Greens |
| ------------------------------ | --------------- | --------- |
| Private firm                   | 20.1            | 26.8      |
| National industry              | 5.4             | 6.4       |
| Local authority                | 18.6            | 15.5      |
| Health/hospital                | 8.6             | 7.3       |
| Primary or secondary education | 4.4             | 5.6       |
| University/College education   | 12.1            | 9.4       |
| Never had job                  | 2.5             | 0.8       |
| Self-employed                  | 19.9            | 18.9      |
| Other                          | 8.4             | 9.2       |
| N                              | 478             | 3,971     |

Given Scotland's greater reliance on the public sector as an employer these differences are perhaps unsurprising (see Kellas 1990: 62). Nevertheless, the 'caring' professions were definitely over-represented in the Scottish Green Party. Again, this can be interpreted in two ways; individuals who work in these professions may be more susceptible to becoming Green party members, or members may consciously choose a profession which is 'outside the mainstream of economic activity' (Rüdig *et al.* 1991: 27). The latter of these explanations would be consistent with party members choosing degree subjects which are compatible with the values fostered in 'caring' occupational fields.

Parkin (1968: 180-181) had identified the concentration of CND members in 'welfare and creative' occupations, teaching being the most common, and he identified a link between professional values and political values, suggesting that different occupations fostered different types of values. Business and commerce were said to rest on the values of profitability, efficiency and material reward, while welfare and creative occupations involved values like service to the community, human betterment, welfare, self-expression and creativity. Welfare occupations, which presented middle class people with first hand knowledge of social problems, were portrayed as a challenge to dominant middle class values.

Parkin (1968: 182) assesses the idea of *status inconsistency* as an explanation for the occupational profile of CND members in the 1960s. According to Parkin, welfare professionals experience a discrepancy between educational and economic status.

In other words, these occupations demand high educational qualifications, but the returns economically are low compared to many other commercial and business occupations. Parkin argues (1968: 183):

> Indeed, it is commonly argued that the salaries of those in welfare professions should be comparatively low, in order that the 'right sort' of people be attracted to them, and not those mainly concerned with material reward.

He reviews the argument that the strains caused by this status inconsistency may in some way be related to a radical political outlook. However, Parkin (1968: 185) ultimately finds this argument unconvincing, concluding that CND members in his study are not reacting against strain; nor did they adopt the value system of the profession while working in the field. Rather, the CND members in his study were already radical before entering the profession. In other words, they chose occupations that were compatible with their value orientations:

> The clustering of radicals in the welfare and creative professions is not best explained as a product of status inconsistency, but as the result of *occupational self-selection* on the part of radicals, stemming from their desire to avoid direct employment in capitalist economic institutions (Parkin 1968: 188-189).

Byrne (1988: 59-60) confirmed the tendency of CND members to work in the public sector, and the 'non-commercial' nature of their occupations: 37 per cent of his respondents were employed in the public sector, 26 per cent in the private sector (37 per cent no response). Respondents 'lower down the occupational scale' were more likely to be working in the private sector: 64 per cent of skilled manual/manual worked in private sector, only 35 per cent of the middle class occupational group. About half of Byrne's respondents worked in non-commercial occupations; 25 per cent of his respondents worked in the education field alone.

Cotgrove (1982: 19-20) identified a similar clustering of non-market occupations in his survey of 'radical environmental associations' (FoE and Conservation Society). Cotgrove argues that there are two distinguishing features of environmental group members; their relation to the market place and their political beliefs and values. He attempts to explain the apparent congruence between occupations and values, confidently concluding that 'environmentalists will try to choose occupations congruent with their public post-material values and social ideals' (Cotgrove 1982: 45). In other words, strongly held beliefs have been responsible for pointing them in a particular career direction. However, Cotgrove (1982: 72) also suggests that once in a particular field of employment, the environmentalist critique of industrialism is reinforced:

> The predominantly 'middle class' supporters of environmentalism are especially vulnerable and exposed to the stress points in market civilisations. Their occupational roles locate them outside the market place. As teachers, social workers, doctors, research scientists and academics, their roles

sensitize them to the limits of economic self-interest, and indeed, to the
needs of the casualties of the market place.

The result, according to Cotgrove (1982: 97), is that a particular section of the
middle class (the 'humanistic intellectuals') have interests and values different
from other, more technocratic, sections.

These accounts are consistent with the findings of this study. There is little
evidence to suggest that, at least in terms of occupation, Scottish Greens are in any
way socially or economically excluded. They are very likely to be 'middle class'
professionals employed in responsible positions. Very few of the Scottish Green
respondents can be termed 'socially unattached intellectuals', those people 'whose
general economic position tends to be somewhat marginal and precarious' (Parkin
1968: 97). Of those people who were employed, there is a strong tendency towards
public sector, non-market based employment. The overrepresentation of the
caring, humanistic professions must in part be explained by self-selection of
occupation, and in turn, it is likely that choice of occupational field is influenced
by values, a proposition which will be explored further in chapter 5.

Another interesting feature of the survey results is the large number of
Scottish Greens who were self-employed in 1990. One in every five of the Greens
(Scottish and UK) described themselves as self-employed, which was twice the
national average in 1990 (Central Statistical Office 1992: 83.) It is impossible to
tell however if these members were employed in what are commonly regarded as
green areas such as organic farming, or if they were the more professional self-
employed. If they were predominantly green occupations we might interpret this
as evidence of avoidance of capitalist organisations. However, such questions
were not explored by the 1990 survey.

The Greens in 1990 (Scottish and UK) were not as likely to work in the
public sector as UK Labour members, almost two in every three of whom worked
in the public sector (Seyd and Whiteley 1994: 34). By contrast, only 31 per cent of
Conservatives worked in the public sector. The greatest similarities were between
Green and Liberal Democrat members: 49 per cent of Liberal Democrat members
worked in the public sector, and two thirds of them could be described as members
of the salariat. In the same way that many Greens have middle class public sector
occupations, 'Liberal Democrat members appear to come from a particular section
of the middle class, the better educated in society who choose employment in one
of the caring professions in the public sector' (Bennie *et al.* al. 1996:138).

*Housing and Area of Residence*

The housing pattern of Scotland is a little different from the other regions of the
UK. In 1990, there was a smaller proportion of owner occupiers and a larger
percentage renting from local authorities (Central Statistical Office 1992: 24).
However, Scottish Green Party members were very likely to own their own homes,
and much less likely to be living in council accommodation than the Scottish
general public: 61.5 per cent of Scottish Greens owned their home and 8 per cent
rented from a local council, compared with 51 per cent of the population who

owned their home and 40 per cent who rented council accommodation (Central Statistical Office 1992: 48).  Because the party membership consisted of a smaller proportion of very young people than the general population, one would expect them to be more likely to own their own homes but the differences are significant nevertheless, a reflection of the class background of party members.  Scottish Greens were only a little less likely to own their homes than the UK Greens, 69 per cent of whom owned their houses outright or had a mortgage (Rüdig *et al.* 1991: 24).[6]

The Greens in this study did not reveal very high levels of mobility.  The respondents were asked 'How often have you moved during the last five years over a distance of more than ten miles?': 52.5 per cent of the sample had not moved at all.  Of the 47.5 per cent who indicated that they had moved in the past five years, half had moved only once and 36 per cent two or three times.  These do not look like people who are continuously 'seeking' a comfortable social location.

Most of the population of the UK live in urban areas (suburban and inner city). This is true also of Scotland, although the population density of Scotland is lower than in the rest of the UK (Central Statistical Office 1992: 172). Green party members in Scotland, however, were most likely to live in rural areas and small communities: 40.4 per cent of Scottish Greens described the area in which they lived as rural, 32.8 per cent as suburban, and only 27 per cent as inner-city. Indeed, the Scottish Greens were considerably more 'rural' than UK Greens.  More than one in five of the Scottish respondents lived in a community with a population density of less than 500 people, compared to less than 10 per cent of the UK Greens.

A fairly large section of the Scottish Greens – 25 per cent – described themselves as English when asked 'Would you describe yourself as English, Scottish or Welsh?': 61 per cent said they were Scottish, 2 per cent Welsh, and 12 per cent 'other'.  Cross-tabulation of national identity by population size of area of residence reveals that 28 per cent of the English respondents lived in a village/town containing less than 500 people, and only 15 per cent of the Scots. This finding evokes stereotypical images of English 'immigrants' living in small, remote communities in Scotland.

*Class Identity*

So far, the data on the Greens in Scotland reveals that they were exceptionally well educated, and many of them worked in 'caring' public sector professional occupations.  Objectively, these people were solidly middle class in profile.  However, in terms of their own perceptions, many of the respondents were reluctant to classify themselves in these terms (Table 4.5). When asked if they ever thought of themselves as belonging to a particular social class, 41 per cent said that

---

[6]Interestingly, the Scottish Greens (and UK Greens) were less likely to own their own house than Labour or Conservative members: 75% of Labour members and 91% of Conservative members owned their houses outright or had a mortgage.  This again is probably explained by the older age profile of these parties' members.

they 'never thought of themselves in class terms'.  This is probably a rejection of traditional class based politics, or it may be a form of 'status-distance' when an individual, 'is able to derive gratification and self-respect from his public disavowal of bourgeois values, without at the same time taking the drastic step of abandoning his middle class status for one lower in the social order' (Parkin 1968: 53).  In other words, middle class individuals may attempt to distance themselves from the values commonly associated with that status.[7]

However, the respondents were, in effect, forced to choose between two classes and the majority then identified themselves as middle class (Table 4.5).[8] This finding stands in stark contrast to the vast majority of Scottish voters – over 70 per cent – who regarded themselves as working class at this time (Bennie *et al.* 1997: 102; Brown 1999: 62).

**Table 4.5  Perceptions of Social Class (%)**

|  | Scottish Greens 1990 | Scottish Population 1992 |
|---|---|---|
| Working class | 11.9 | - |
| Lower middle | 12.5 | - |
| Middle class | 30.6 | - |
| Upper middle | 4.0 | - |
| Never think in class terms | 40.9 | - |
| N | 496 | - |

When asked to choose between two classes:

|  | Scottish Greens 1990 | Scottish Population 1992 |
|---|---|---|
| Working | 27 | 74 |
| Middle | 73 | 26 |
| N | 483 | - |

*Religion*

How religious were the Scottish Greens in 1990?  Less than one third – 28 per cent – described themselves as 'belonging to an organised religious group'.  This was very low in comparison with the proportion of the Scottish population who

---

[7]Greens appear only a little more averse to these class labels than members of the other (UK) parties.  For example, only 62% of Conservatives said they thought of themselves as belonging to a particular class (Whiteley and Seyd 1994: 47).  73% of Labour members regarded themselves as belonging to a class (Seyd and Whiteley 1992: 34).

[8]Respondents were asked, 'If you had no choice but to place yourself in one of two classes, which one would it be: working class or middle class?'.

regarded themselves as belonging to a religion. Only a quarter of the 1992 Scottish Election Study respondents considered themselves to be *non*-religious (Bennie *et al.* 1997: 117).[9] Amongst those people with a religious affiliation (see Table 4.6) we find that the main denominations are under-represented, while Quakers and Buddhists are over-represented. An almost identical pattern was evident in the UK responses (Rüdig *et al.* 1991: 29). Parkin (1968: 27) found that 58 per cent of his CND respondents described themselves as 'non-believers', 40 per cent as 'believers'. Of the 'believers', 14 per cent were Church of England, 10 per cent Quaker, 5 per cent Methodist, 4 per cent Presbyterian, 2 per cent Baptist, 2 per cent Catholic and 1 per cent Jewish. Taylor and Pritchard (1980: 23) found that, of CND members between 1958 and 1965, 41 per cent had a Christian religious belief: 35 per cent of these were Anglican, followed by a high proportion of Quakers (28 per cent). By 1978, religious affiliation had declined – only 32 per cent then said they had a religious belief. Byrne's 1988 analysis of CND members revealed that only 23 per cent were 'practising members' of any church or religion. Of these, 37 per cent were Church of England, 25 per cent were Roman Catholic, 10 per cent were Quakers and 6 per cent were Methodist.

**Table 4.6  Religious Affiliation (%)**

|                       | Scottish Greens |
|-----------------------|:---------------:|
| No religion           | 72.3            |
| Roman Catholic        | 3.1             |
| Church of England     | 3.7             |
| Church of Scotland    | 8.8             |
| Methodist             | 1.0             |
| Quaker                | 4.7             |
| Other Christian       | 2.0             |
| Jewish                | 0.2             |
| Buddhist              | 2.4             |
| Other Non-Christian   | 0.4             |
| Religious Movement    | 1.4             |
| N                     | 504             |

While different question wordings make comparisons of different studies, and indeed comparison of the Greens and general public, difficult, a number of themes emerge from the studies of environmentalists and peace movement activists. A generally low level of religious belief is evident; the underrepresentation of traditional denominations; and the overrepresentation of non-traditional religions, in particular Quakers. The findings support the proposition that the highly

---

[9] 41% of UK Labour members were 'non-believers' (Seyd and Whiteley 1992); and only 11% of Conservatives (Whiteley *et al.* 1994).

educated middle class often shed their religious beliefs, a result of learning to question established truths and the general liberalising effect of education (Parkin 1968: 178).

## Political Background of Scottish Greens

Having explored the social profile of Scottish Greens, this section explores the political experiences of the members, another way of assessing the extent of integration. It will be shown that Scottish Greens in 1990 had a great deal of political experience outside of their involvement with the party.

### Party Political Experience

More than one in four – 28 per cent – of the Scottish respondents had been members of other political parties: 12 per cent Labour; 6 per cent SNP; 2 per cent Conservative; 6 per cent Liberal; 1 per cent SDP; and 1 per cent Liberal Democrat. Of those who had been members of another party, more than half claimed to have been active in their previous party (25 per cent not at all active, 19.3 per cent not very active; 30 per cent fairly active; 17.1 per cent very active and 8.6 per cent extremely active). Around 30 per cent had held a party office or had stood as a party candidate, nearly all at the local level. The findings so far suggest the existence of a significantly large group who were inclined towards political activism before they joined the Greens. In other words, for more than a quarter of members, it was not the party *per se* that attracted them to political participation. Nevertheless, the majority of Scottish Greens did not have any experience of formal party political membership before they joined.

A comparison of the party membership records of Scottish and UK Greens highlights the very different party systems (Table 4.7). Nevertheless, the largest proportion of Greens with a previous party affiliation came from Labour in both cases (Rüdig *et al.* 1991: 31). In Scotland, however, former SNP members account for a fifth of members with previous party membership experience. One in six Scottish Greens who had previously been a member of a party belonged to another small party, such as the Communists.

Unsurprisingly, the studies of CND members showed higher numbers of political party membership, a result of the CND's affiliated relationship with the Labour Party at the time. Parkin (1968: 16) found that 51 per cent of his sample were members of a 'political organisation or political party'. Taylor and Pritchard (1980) found that 51 per cent of CND members between 1958-1965 were members of the Labour Party, and less than a third (31 per cent) did not belong to a political party or other political group (this had risen to 34 per cent by 1978). However, Byrne (1988:63) found that two thirds of his CND respondents did not belong to any political party (25 per cent were Labour members, 3 per cent Greens, and 2 per cent Alliance members).[10]


**Table 4.7  Membership of Other Political Parties (%)[11]**

|                         | Scottish Greens | UK Greens |
| ----------------------- | --------------- | --------- |
| Conservative            | 7.8             | 12.3      |
| Labour                  | 42.6            | 51.3      |
| Liberal Party           | 24.1            | 24.5      |
| SDP                     | 2.1             | 7.3       |
| SLD (Liberal Democrats) | 2.8             | 3.0       |
| SNP                     | 20.6            | 0.6       |
| Others                  | 15.6            | 12.5      |
| N                       | 141             | 1,225     |

Those SGP respondents who had previously been members of other parties were asked to choose the most decisive/important reasons for leaving their previous party (most recent party).  The most frequent reasons given involved party principles or party policy:  45 per cent indicated that 'disagreement with the party's fundamental aims' was decisive or very important in their decision, 43 per cent had a 'disagreement with an important change in policy', and 19 per cent thought that there were 'better ways of achieving the party's aims'.  It is perhaps significant that there were few cases which involved negative experience of the party e.g. only 6 per cent said that 'activities were too boring'; and 4 per cent claimed 'I was not able to attain a position of influence within the party', although a larger group (15 per cent) said that 'ordinary members had few opportunities to participate'. Friendship ties appear completely insignificant in this context.  None of the respondents indicated that 'most of my friends had left the party'. Therefore, for those Greens who had been members of another political party it was not so much their experience of internal party decision-making that turned them against the party.  They don't appear all that concerned about opportunities for democratic involvement.  Rather, policy programme and/or political principles appear to be the key to why they left their previous party.  Friendship ties were the least important reason of all.

The questionnaire also explored the voting record of party members: 9 per cent of members said they had not voted in any General Election since 1970. Most of the members (over 50 per cent) had voted Labour in a General Election since 1970, and more than half had also voted for the centre parties (Liberals or Alliance), although this was considerably lower than in other parts of the UK

---

[10] 10% of Byrne's CND respondents said that they supported the Green party in elections.

[11] % of those who were members of other parties. Figures add up to more than 100 because some respondents were member of more than one party before they joined the Greens.

(Rüdig *et al.* 1991: 38). Nearly a third (28.7 per cent) of the Scottish Greens had voted nationalist.

Not all of the Scottish Greens had actually voted Green. When asked if they had ever voted for the party (or one of its predecessors, People or the Ecology party) in a national election (including European Elections), just over three quarters of the members – 76.9 per cent – said they had, marginally more than in the rest of the UK where the figure was 75.1 per cent (Rüdig *et al.* 1991: 38).

Having assessed the party experiences of the Scottish Greens, the main finding is that, although a significant minority had belonged to another party, a large majority of the Scottish Greens in 1990 did not look very much like party political animals. Most had no previous experience of party membership. They did not appear to be people who experimented with parties, moving from one to the other. What about other forms of social movement activity? We find that, although a minority of Scottish Greens came to the party with experience of party involvement, most members were by no means new to membership of the wider environmental movement. In fact, most of the respondents appeared to have had a fairly long-term commitment to the environmental cause in the form of pressure group membership.

*Experience in Environmental Groups: Multiple and Overlapping Membership*

Respondents were asked if they were or had ever been members of an environmental group, and, if so, for how long they had been members (see Table 4.8).[12] The environmental groups most popular with Scottish Greens in 1990 were Greenpeace and Friends of the Earth. Just over 50 per cent of all the respondents had been members of Greenpeace, and over 40 per cent had had membership experience of Friends of the Earth. And the length of commitment to these organisations was rather impressive. In fact, nearly 30 per cent of all respondents claimed to have been members of Greenpeace for between three and ten years. Nearly 40 per cent of 1990 Scottish Greens claimed to have been members of CND. The next most popular groups were the RSPB, the National Trust, Amnesty International, and WWF, although a third said they had been members of some other environmental group. The extent of membership overlap between the party's membership and environmental pressure groups might be considered surprising, as the historical relationship between the green parties and environmental groups in Britain is said to have been one of competition rather than co-operation (Byrne 1989: 110).

Interestingly, membership of local level environmental and peace groups amongst the Scottish Greens in 1990 was less apparent than that of the big, nationally organised groups. A fifth of the Scottish Greens had been part of a local amenity group or conservation society; one in eight of the members indicated that they had taken part in a local protest against nuclear energy; and a very small number (6.8 per cent) had been part of an 'anti-nuclear campaign'. These findings

---

[12]In other words the question referred to current membership *and* past membership.

suggest that many of the 1990 Scottish Green members were not inclined towards grass-roots campaigns and protests. Rather, the large environmental organisations, with their largely passive memberships, had greater appeal. However, the number in Scotland who had taken part in a local protest against nuclear energy (15.3 per cent) was higher than in the rest of the UK. Rüdig *et al.* (1991: 33) found that 8.7 per cent had participated in such an activity.

**Table 4.8  Overlapping Membership Between Scottish Greens and Environmental Groups (%)**

| | Less than 1 year | 1-2 years | 3-10 years | Over 10 years | Total % ever been members |
|---|---|---|---|---|---|
| Friends of the Earth | 3.3 | 14.1 | 20.2 | 3.7 | **41.3** |
| Greenpeace | 4.1 | 17.9 | 26.7 | 2.0 | **50.7** |
| National Trust | 2.9 | 6.7 | 12.8 | 4.7 | **24.5** |
| RSPB | 3.3 | 6.9 | 9.8 | 5.5 | **25.5** |
| Ramblers Association | 0.6 | 2.2 | 1.4 | 0.8 | **5.0** |
| WWF | 4.1 | 7.1 | 9.6 | 2.0 | **22.8** |
| RSPCA | 1.2 | 2.6 | 3.7 | 1.0 | **8.5** |
| Local amenity group/ conservation society | 2.9 | 6.7 | 8.4 | 2.9 | **20.9** |
| Other environmental group | 5.1 | 11.4 | 12.2 | 3.5 | **32.2** |
| Anti-nuclear campaign | 0.6 | 2.2 | 2.8 | 1.2 | **6.8** |
| Local protest against nuclear energy | 2.9 | 6.1 | 4.7 | 1.6 | **15.3** |
| CND | 1.6 | 9.8 | 20.8 | 6.9 | **39.1** |
| Other peace groups | 1.2 | 3.1 | 8.1 | 1.6 | **14.0** |
| Amnesty International | 5.3 | 7.7 | 8.8 | 2.4 | **24.2** |
| Anti-Apartheid | 2.6 | 5.7 | 3.3 | 1.0 | **12.6** |

These results reveal a large degree of *overlapping membership* between environmental organisations, which is consistent with Berry's (1970) model of 'overlapping multiple memberships'. The model indicates that a positive relationship exists between political participation and participation in non-political voluntary associations. Berry described a group of 'joiners' who, if active in some voluntary associations, were more likely to join a number of others, including political parties. This is similar to Parry *et al.*'s (1992) argument that membership of one group increases the chances of joining another. Scottish Green Party members in 1990 certainly appeared to be part of an overlapping network of environmental membership. In all, a remarkably small minority of party members

– 10.2 per cent – had never belonged to any environmental or peace group, and many had belonged to more than one group. Overall, the Scottish Greens had belonged to an average of 3.4 environmental and peace organisations. The UK figure was 2.8 (Rüdig *et al.* 1991: 34).

Similar trends of multiple and overlapping membership are evident in other studies. For example, UK Labour Party members were also likely to have joined a number of organisations  (Seyd and Whiteley 1992: 92).[13]  Furthermore, many Labour members belonged to more than one group at the same time e.g. over 50 per cent of Amnesty members were also members of CND.  Seyd and Whiteley (1992: 93) describe a 'network of highly active people within the party who are clearly involved in many kinds of political campaigns as well as in the party organisation'.[14]  Parkin (1968: 16) found CND members in 1968 to have high levels of membership in non-political/voluntary organisations, including Trade Unions and professional associations, and welfare and humanitarian groups.  He found that only 16 per cent of the members did not belong to any other organisation; more than one third of the respondents belonged to three or more.[15] Parkin found that they were also likely to have held positions of responsibility within these organisations – 46 per cent of all respondents had held an elected post or position of responsibility within these other organisations.  Byrne (1988) categorises 30 per cent of his 1988 respondents as belonging to a voluntary organisation. However, he describes many more as 'supporters' of campaigns: 60 per cent of respondents had supported campaigns of groups other than CND, the most popular ones being those associated with the environment (22 per cent) (e.g. Greenpeace and FoE) and what Byrne calls 'moral campaigns' (29 per cent) (Anti-Apartheid and third world groups); 16 per cent supported left-wing political campaigns and 11 per cent trade union campaigns.  Jordan and Maloney (1997: 119-120) also point to the trend of overlapping membership in their study e.g. 32 per cent of FoE members and 34 per cent of Amnesty members were members of Greenpeace, and 74 per cent of Amnesty respondents said they were members of another environmental or campaigning organisation.  Their explanation for this

---

[13]Labour Party members were most likely to be members of the following interest groups: Campaign for Nuclear Disarmament (18.9%); a local community action group (18.8%); a local tenants' or housing group (16.5%); Greenpeace (16.0%); the Anti-Apartheid Movement (11.8%); and Friends of the Earth (8.2%).

[14]These findings contrast with those for the Conservative Party membership.  Whiteley *et al.* (1994: 186-188) reveal that Conservative members were rather unlikely to have involvement in other organisations. The most popular groups amongst Conservative members were: National Trust (27%); World Wildlife Trust (12%); British Legion (8%); Consumer's Association (7%); RSPCA (6%); NSPCC/RSPCC (6%); Women's Institute (6%); Christian Aid (5%); Age Concern (5%) (Whiteley *et al.* 1994: 186). Conservative were not only less likely to be involved in other organisations, they were less likely to belong to political organisations. Whiteley *et al.* (1994: 187) conclude that Conservatives are not particularly integrated or networked.

[15]The breakdown of responses was as follows: Membership in 1 or 2 – 49%; Membership in 3 or 4 – 24%; Membership in 5 or more – 11%; Membership in none – 16% (N=358).

rests on the marketing strategies of groups who often exchange membership lists and target similar demographic groups, indeed sometimes the *same* individuals.

The existence of distinct overlapping environmental memberships in the ranks of the Scottish Green Party suggests that involvement in the environmental movement may be a key to understanding membership. However, it will be argued that the dynamics involved extend beyond the behaviour and tactics of movement or group leaders. A concentration on leadership strategies neglects the importance of individual motivations, the influence of friends and many other factors.

*Experience in Other Political Movements*

Respondents in the Scottish Green Party survey were asked a number of questions about social movement activity outside the environmental movement, revealing high levels of commitment across the board.[16] Respondents were asked to look back over the entire period of their involvement in political campaigning and to describe their 'own level of activity' within various movements outside party politics. They were then asked to describe their level of activity in the party. Unfortunately, 'activity' is a rather ambiguous term and can be interpreted in many different ways. Nevertheless, the results, displayed in Table 4.9 again suggest the existence of an active minority of members who had been committed to a wide range of social movements: 41 per cent described themselves as extremely, very or fairly active in the environmental movement, and 30 per cent claimed to have been as active in the peace movement. 38 per cent of the respondents said they were at least fairly active in the Greens, although this did leave more than six in every ten of the members who indicated they were not very or not at all active. In addition, 12 per cent said they had been active in the 1960s and 1970s in the 'student movement', and 10 per cent indicated that they had been involved in the protest movement against the Vietnam War. The members on the whole appeared positively inclined towards radical forms of political protest. When asked if they thought that non-violent direct action and civil disobedience had 'weakened or strengthened campaigns of groups such as the Campaign for Nuclear Disarmament?' 70 per cent felt that it had strengthened the campaigns (8 per cent said weakened, and 22 per cent said they didn't know).

These questions covered activity over a long period of time, but what about more recent activity in these movements? Respondents were asked to think about how much time they had devoted to activism in a number of different movements

---

[16]Just under half of the members belonged to a trade union or staff association (36 per cent were members of a trade union and another 11 per cent belonged to a staff association), which is a little higher than in the population at large. In the Scottish population in 1990, 48.5 per cent of males and 39.5 per cent of females belonged to a trade union or staff association (Central Statistical Office 1993: 98). Byrne (1988: 63) found that 37% of his CND respondents belonged to a trade union, and a further 24% to a professional association. This compares with 67% of Labour members and 36% of Conservative members who belonged to a trade union, staff association or professional association (Whiteley *et al* 1994: 257).

*in the previous year* and to state how many hours they had devoted on average per week. Of all the party members, 36 per cent claimed to have been active in the environmental movement (outside the party); 26 per cent said they had been active in the conservation movement; 18 per cent said they had been involved in the peace movement; 13 per cent in the anti-nuclear movement; and 12 per cent in the animal rights movement. On average, the members who had been at all active in these movements in the preceding year had devoted 1 or 2 hours per week. The impression given so far is that up to 40 per cent of the members were active in some way in one or more social movements, including the party itself. However, it is important to note that most of the members were in fact rather *passive*.

**Table 4.9  Activity in Social Movements (%)**

|  | Extremely/very active | Fairly active | Not very active | Not at all active |
|---|---|---|---|---|
| Conservation movement | 9.2 | 18.9 | 26.9 | 45.0 |
| Environmental movement | 14.7 | 26.7 | 25.3 | 33.2 |
| Animal rights movement | 4.9 | 12.0 | 18.9 | 64.3 |
| Anti-nuclear movement | 9.3 | 19.4 | 24.8 | 46.5 |
| Peace movement | 11.1 | 19.1 | 24.0 | 43.9 |
| Feminist movement | 5.5 | 8.4 | 14.9 | 71.2 |
| Urban movement | 4.3 | 5.1 | 7.1 | 83.5 |
| Trade union movement | 5.3 | 6.5 | 14.9 | 73.3 |
| Green Party | 14.7 | 23.4 | 38.9 | 23.0 |

Activity is only one measure of support for a political cause. Another is financial donations. Respondents were asked to indicate how much money, if any, including membership subscriptions, they had donated to the party and other organisations in the preceding year. Scottish Greens were particularly generous in their donations to the party, and to charities and environmental pressure groups, while contributing in large numbers to animal rights groups and anti-nuclear or peace groups. For example, 42 per cent of respondents claimed to have donated between £11 and £50 to the party, and another 32 per cent gave a similar amount to environmental groups. Even if not directly active, many Scottish Green members in 1990 were 'doing their bit' for a number of environmental causes through financial support, an activity made less difficult by the members' relatively high levels of disposable income.

The picture to emerge from this analysis is that many of the Scottish Greens in 1990 had a great deal of political experience in a wide range of political movements. This commitment was both historical and current. It is fair to say that the majority of Scottish Greens at this time had some kind of social movement experience or political involvement. In other words, they did not look like new recruits. Rather, membership of the party appeared to evolve from a network of multiple and overlapping memberships. A common theme emerging, however, is that as members of the Scottish Green, most of these environmentalists were in fact *passive*. The following section explores the distinction between activists and passive party members who do very little other than contribute their membership subscription.

*Level of Activity in the Scottish Green Party*

Assessing the level of activity of Scottish Greens in 1990 we find that the majority were rather inactive. This conclusion is based on a variety of different indicators.[17] As reported above, when the members were asked to assess their own level of activity in the party over the entire period of their political involvement, 62 per cent indicated that they had been 'not very active' (38.9 per cent) or 'not at all active' (23 per cent). Another question asked the members: 'During the last year, how many hours did you devote to party activities in the average week?'. 60.5 per cent of the members replied that they had not devoted no time whatsoever to the party, 25.4 per cent of members claimed to have spent one or two hours on party activities, and 14.1 per cent said they devoted three or more hours to the party.

The questionnaire explored the activity of members at the local, regional and national levels of the party. The respondents were asked; 'How would you best describe your involvement with the local party branch? (Table 4.10). The results confirm the suggestion that the majority of members (50-60 per cent) were not active in the party: 58 per cent had no contact with the party beyond receiving a local newsletter. In Scotland, the number of members with no local branch in their area was considerably higher than in the UK study where only 4.6 per cent of members did not have a local party (Rüdig *et al.* 1991: 41).

In contrast to the passive members, around 20 per cent of the respondents demonstrated a regular commitment to party activities, and not just at the local level. For example, 21 per cent had attended an area party meeting in the last year, and 11.3 per cent had on at least one occasion attended a national UK Green party conference. 12 per cent of the members at one time held an office within the party at regional or national level, and 15 per cent indicated that they belonged to one of the party's working groups or other internal party groups.

A similar proportion of the members had been prepared to stand in an election for the party: 20.6 per cent had been a Green candidate in local elections. While only 3.6 per cent of the members had been selected as a PPC for the 1992 General Election, 10 per cent indicated that a PPC had not yet been chosen in their area and that they were thinking about putting themselves forward. Only 3.5 per cent had ever been a Green candidate in a European Election or a General Election.

Overall, between 50 and 60 per cent of the members were passive, around 30 per cent were occasionally active, and 20 per cent were more regular activists (17.6 per cent felt that their Green party activity in the last year had cost them in

---

[17]Furthermore, one must also assume that active members are the most likely to return a questionnaire of this kind and therefore passive members are probably under-represented.

the form of lost earnings, unpaid expenses etc.). The super-activists – those that were willing to stand in elections, speak in public for the party and so on – were drawn from this final group and constituted between five and ten per cent of the members.

**Table 4.10 Involvement with Local Party (%)**

| | |
|---|---|
| There is no local branch in my area | 12.2 |
| I have no contact whatsoever with the local party | 11.6 |
| I receive the local party newsletter but have no other contact with the local party | 34.2 |
| I occasionally go to local party meetings | 26.9 |
| I regularly attend local meetings | 23.6 |
| I help to organise coffee mornings, jumble sales etc. | 17.9 |
| I help with information stalls | 13.8 |
| I help organise local campaigns | 17.9 |
| I speak in public (outside party meetings) on behalf of the local party | 9.8 |
| I convene and/or chair local branch meetings | 6.7 |
| I hold an office within the local party | 8.1 |

*Conclusion: Who Were the Scottish Greens in 1990?*

The predominantly middle-class profile of Greens has been documented extensively elsewhere (Rüdig *et al.* 1991; 1993). The composition of the Scottish Green Party membership in 1990 was little different in this respect. The members were educated to an exceptionally high level and the majority worked in managerial or professional positions. Overall, the socio-demographic profile of the Scottish Greens in 1990 was distinctly middle class. It is important to note however that these party members tended to belong to a *particular section* of the middle class, what is commonly referred to as the 'new' middle class. Scottish Greens to a very large extent resembled the 'humanistic intellectuals' referred to by Cotgrove (1982: 97). As well as being very well educated they were likely to have specialised in humanistic degree areas and they tended to be employed in public sector, 'caring', non-commercial based occupations.

Based on evidence of social background (upbringing, education and occupation) these party members did not appear in any way socially or economically excluded. As Alber (1989: 203-4) may have predicted when he linked green support to the 'education revolution', the Greens in this study revealed impressive educational achievements, but when we consider their role in the economic sphere, they cannot be considered to be 'outside the labour force' suffering from 'structurally blocked mobility'. Very few of the Scottish Green respondents can be viewed as 'socially unattached intellectuals' (Kornhauser 1959), those people, such as artists, actors, writers and freelance journalists 'whose general economic position tends to be somewhat marginal and precarious' (Parkin

1968: 97). There is little sign here of economic deprivation, disorientation, frustration or aggression.

Furthermore, the Scottish Green Party members in 1990 appeared to be very well connected to other individuals and groups. They had a history of involvement in a number of causes, including political party membership, and support for social movements, either through direct activity or financial support. The party members were by no means inexperienced politically. They looked to be integrated into an environmental network. This form of collective action does not look like 'irrational outburst' (Smelser 1962). McAdam *et al.* (1988: 728) argue that group membership exposes individuals to information about other groups and that social influences encourage them to integrate into these other group formations. The psychological state at work here suggests the existence of a socially confident group of people who enjoy participation in many different fields. For these reasons, we can call them 'joiners', as opposed to the 'alienated' members of society. The dominant political science and social movement approaches predict that those people most likely to engage in politics are those who are already well integrated into society and who are already members of other organisations. The findings of this study so far are consistent with this line of argument.

So far, theories of political alienation appear rather irrelevant in understanding this party's membership. However, it may be too early to completely reject the idea of alienation as an explanation for membership. There may be different types of alienation. Parkin, for instance, outlines three different forms of alienation – social exclusion, powerlessness, and value based isolation. Parkin (1969: 19) argues that the first of these – social isolation – did not apply to CND members in his study. However, Parkin (1968: 178) argues that alienation (or 'deviance syndrome') may be applicable if one focuses on *values* held by members; '...the minority of the non-manual stratum which has undergone formal intellectual training beyond the sixth form constitutes a permanent source of potential opposition to certain commonly accepted socio-political values, and therefore provides also a source of potential recruits to movements like CND'. Parkin thus identifies a link between educational experience, occupation and political values, and these political values he regards as 'deviant' because they do not reflect dominant middle class values. Both Byrne (1988) and Cotgrove (1982) describe a similar relationship. Cotgrove (1982: 19-20) for example argued that the two distinguishing features of his environmental group respondents were their relation to the market place and their political beliefs and values and he argued that the former partly determined the latter. Of those respondents who were economically active in the Scottish Green sample, there was certainly a strong tendency towards public sector, non-market based employment. It is likely that choice of occupational field both influences, and is influenced by, interests and values. However, by concentrating on descriptive social background factors, we have so far been unable to explore the importance of this kind of motivation.

Identifying the socio-demographic characteristics of individuals who were involved as Scottish Greens in 1990 does not in itself allow us to effectively assess the value of the different approaches – rational choice approaches, political process models, new social movement approaches and so on. Analysis of *who* the members are is useful in identifying the kind of people likely to participate in some way – it points to a pool of potential participants.  However, this approach does not explain why people choose to join a specific organisation like the Scottish Green Party.  It doesn't fully illuminate the decision-making process involved in the act of joining.  Why do people with similar resources and personal backgrounds, faced with the same issue stimuli, take different decisions about joining organisations? After all, the vast majority of middle class professionals who supported environmental causes in 1990 *did not* join the Scottish Green Party.  To understand fully why people join a particular organisation we can examine the mechanisms through which they become members, and the declared reasons given by members for their decision to join. We turn now to *how* and *why* the respondents came to be members of the Scottish Greens.

# Chapter 5

# How and Why Did the 1990 Members Join?

While it is useful to identify the types of people who participate in green politics, this does not explain why people choose to join a specific organisation like the Scottish Green Party. It does not explain the decision-making process involved in the act of joining. Why do people with similar resources and backgrounds, faced with the same issue stimuli, take different decisions about joining organisations? After all the vast majority of middle class professionals who supported environmental causes in 1990 were not members of the Scottish Green Party.

While incentives behind membership have been the subject of much academic research, this analysis has been overwhelmingly conceptual and theoretical rather than empirical. To fully understand why people join a particular organisation we can examine declared reasons given by members for their decision to join. However, as Snow *et al.* (1980: 795) suggest, understanding why people join social movements involves more than an analysis of subjective reasons for joining. They argue that an examination of *how* members come to be recruited often reveals the importance of organisational 'pull' or 'persuasion', which builds on or helps to create a set of motivations for membership in the mind of a potential movement participant. Alternatively, social or friendship ties may be more important. The pertinent point is that there can be a relationship between *how* a person joins an organisation and *why* they join that organisation. Therefore we can examine the mechanisms through which members become involved, as well as the declared reasons given by members for their decision to join. We turn now to *how* and *why* the respondents to the survey came to align themselves with the Scottish Green Party.

**How the Members Joined**

One of the debates in the literature is over *how* a person comes to be a member of an organisation. Do they in some sense seek membership and 'push' themselves into membership or are they 'pulled' into membership by the organisation? Are they 'volunteers' or 'recruits' (Kornberg 1979: 97)? While some classical approaches point to the self-starter who makes contact as part of a search for identity or cure for deprivation, more recent approaches focus on the organisation's ability to pull sympathisers into membership. The potential member, it is argued, has to be informed about and introduced to a particular organisation. This involves an exchange relationship between potential member and organisation; while an individual may be sympathetic to a cause, he or she actually joins when presented with the opportunity to do so (see Bosso 2003; Rosenstone and Hansen 1993; Schlozman *et al.* 1999).

In this context, it is important to identify exactly how the Scottish Greens and party organisation came together in the first place. A number of factors can be considered. Did the party make face-to-face contact with the potential member, or was contact made through mediated forms of communication, such as television or telephone? Did joining occur in a public forum, such as a public meeting or rally, or did joining take place through more private mechanisms, like personal relationships, or direct communication through mail or telephone? In other words, we can attempt to assess the 'sociospatial settings in which movements and potential participants can come into contact', and the different forms of communication between movements and potential members (Snow *et al.* 1980: 789-90). According to this approach, the settings may be private or public; information dissemination may be face-to-face or mediated.

While it is indisputable that an individual will not join an organisation if he or she is completely unaware of its existence, the relationship between 'seeking' and 'pulling' is unclear. If an individual independently seeks out information on groups promoting a cause and then decides to join one of them can we assume that membership resulted from 'prior contact with a recruitment agent'?. While some members of organisations will have been in some way persuaded to join by the organisation, others will have *approached* the organisation using a greater degree of self-initiative. Whiteley *et al.* (1994: 77) recognise this distinction when they distinguish between party members who are 'self-starters' – those who 'took the initiative to join on their own' – and 'recruits' who 'joined as a result of initiatives from other members or the party organisation'. So the potential member may take the initiative to seek out information about the organisation and how to join, rather than the organisation itself making first contact. Identifying the degree of member initiative is therefore important. Did members independently approach the party, or were they persuaded to join as the result of a membership campaign? With these points in mind, respondents in the Scottish Green Party survey were asked *how* they became involved in the party as a member (Table 5:1).

*Interpersonal Ties*

Social ties (private channels) did not appear to be very important in answers to the question on how the 1990 members joined. Only 15.7 per cent said they got a membership form from a friend or a relative. The relative unimportance of social links is confirmed by a question asking members if, at the time of joining, they already had friends in the party whom they would meet regularly: only 16 per cent answered affirmatively. And once they had become members, 63 per cent of respondents indicated that they never or rarely met party members socially outside party meetings. This is consistent with Jordan and Maloney (1997: 131) who found that a very small number of their respondents had been influenced by social ties; less than 10 per cent of FoE and Amnesty subscribers 'got a membership application form from a friend, relative or work colleague' (another 1.7 per cent of FoE respondents received their membership as a gift).


**Table 5.1  How Members Joined the Scottish Green Party (%)**

| | |
|---|---|
| At local party meeting/stall/rally | 17.5 |
| Got membership form from friend or relative | 15.7 |
| Phoned/wrote to local party representative | 15.0 |
| Filled in membership form from party advert in national press | 14.2 |
| Responded to membership appeal received through post | 3.7 |
| Contacted national party office independently | 27.4 |
| Responded to party canvasser on doorstep | 0.4 |
| Other | 6.1 |
| | |
| N | 492 |

However, the study of Conservatives (Whiteley *et al.* 1994: 78) had very different results.  A large proportion of Conservative members joined through personal contact with other members: 23 per cent joined as a result of 'social contacts'; 22 per cent 'family contacts'; 10 per cent through a Conservative club or work contacts; and another 12 per cent responded to a doorstep canvasser.

Although friendship ties so far appear relatively unimportant in joining the Scottish Greens, the key here might be that, prior to membership, the Greens had friendship links to members of a wider environmental movement that can be regarded as a compatible network.[1]  In other words, it is possible they had friends who were members of other environmental groups. As chapter 4 documented, many of the respondents belonged to environmental groups and it is possible that information received through this network encouraged membership of the party.

*Self Versus Organisational Initiative*

While it is very difficult to precisely identify the initial point of contact – exactly where and when the members became aware of the party in the first place – it would appear that a large number of the survey respondents are 'self-starters', rather than 'recruits' as they took the initiative in contacting the party.  In fact, *the* most common pathway to membership of the Scottish Green Party was contacting the national party office independently.  More than one in four of the members claimed to have contacted the national party, and another 15 per cent phoned or wrote to their local party.  As Table 5.1 shows, 42.4 per cent of the responses indicated clear self-initiative in the joining process (they 'phoned/wrote to a local party representative', or 'contacted the national office independently'), a significantly higher percentage of members than joined through other routes such

---

[1]As opposed to 'alternative networks' which are countervailing influences – involving ties that can compete – and can make people less likely to join (Snow *et al.* 1980).

as contact with friends. Indeed many of the party members in this study appeared to be willing to 'seek out membership'. For these members their relationship with the organisation appeared to be predominantly one of membership 'push' rather than organisational 'pull'. We can certainly conclude that there is relatively little evidence of the party directly approaching the individual and that mobilisation was more indirect than direct (Rosenstone and Hansen 1993: 26-28).

The Scottish Greens were less likely to be self-starters than Labour members, but more likely than Conservatives. An overwhelming 71 per cent of Labour members said they approached their local party, compared to 21 per cent who 'were approached', leading Seyd and Whiteley (1992: 84-85) to conclude, 'most appear to recruit themselves'. 51 per cent of Conservative members said they were approached by the local party, as opposed to only 33 per cent who said they approached the local party (Whiteley *et al.* 1994: 78).

The picture of fairly highly motivated individuals seeking out membership is rather different from those in many studies of group members (for example, Godwin 1988; Johnson 1998; Jordan and Maloney 1997). Godwin (1988: 51) surveyed a number of groups in the US (environmental groups, political action members and political party members) who attracted members through different mechanisms and outlined two main routes into membership – social networks and direct marketing. Godwin classifies social network recruits as those who joined 'because of friends or who were given a membership', and direct marketing recruits as those who came to be members by responding to direct marketing techniques, such as direct mail. Jordan and Maloney found that responding to a group advertisement, media campaign or postal membership appeal was much more significant than social ties, indeed more important than any other route to membership: 23.6 per cent of FoE members contacted the office after seeing a press/media campaign; 28.2 per cent of Amnesty members responded to a press advertisement; and 22.6 per cent of FoE members and 18.5 per cent of Amnesty members responded to a postal membership appeal. Jordan and Maloney interpret these results as confirmation that membership is a response to the activities of groups. Overall, Jordan and Maloney (1997: 132) argue that 'these sorts of organisations are largely constituted by Direct Marketing Recruits (DMRs)', as opposed to Social Network Recruits (SMRs) e.g. 65 per cent of the Amnesty sample were classified as DMRs, only 12 per cent as SNRs.

These results are interesting from the point of view of the Scottish Green Party organisation. Could the party recruitment agents have done more to make contact with potential party members? The party's attempts to recruit members varied considerably in their effectiveness. Doorstep canvassing did not prove significant, although this is undoubtedly related to the small numbers of party activists. Similarly, a very small number of respondents claimed to have responded to a membership appeal they received through the post. National press advertisements were much more effective, as were local party events such as stalls and rallies. If the results are applied to Snow *et al.*'s (1980) analysis of recruitment, we find that public channels of communication are the most important, and face-to-face forms of recruitment appear a little more effective than the mediated forms. However, it is difficult to come to very definite conclusions about the effectiveness of different recruitment techniques. At this time, party membership appeals were very infrequent and did not reach a very large constituency. If the party had devoted more resources to such a strategy this might indeed have been an effective way of attracting members.

### Local-National Divide

Another consideration when assessing the empirical evidence is the importance of different levels of party organisation. Are members more likely to join through local level mechanisms (local party stalls, rallies and so on) or do they join through national party structures such as national party membership appeals? On balance, more members joined through local level mechanisms than national, although this is only if we categorise 'receiving a membership form from a friend or relative' as a local level mechanism.[2] In this respect, the party members in this study are different from pressure group members. The decentralised structures of most political parties, and the Greens in particular, mean that members can join through and have an affinity with a local organisation. Very few of Jordan and Maloney's (1997) respondents joined at a locally organised meeting: 4.8 per cent of FoE members and 3.6 per cent of Amnesty members. Fewer still joined at a national meeting or event (0.8 per cent and 1.7 per cent respectively), although 8.3 per cent of Amnesty respondents joined at a rock concert (U2, Peter Gabriel). The Greens in this study appear to have had more contact with their organisation at meetings and events, most of which were organised by local parties.

### Four Pathways to Membership

While it is very difficult to identify the level of independent decision-making and/or action on the part of the joiner, there appear to be four main routes to Scottish Green Party membership that correspond with four types of joiner (see Figure 5.1).

*Responders* These members responded to a party membership appeal and constituted around one in five of the total membership in 1990. They may have responded to a party canvasser, a party advertisement at the local or national level, a membership appeal received through the post, membership appeals following a party election broadcast, membership forms contained in election material, membership forms in public places, or advertisements in environmental magazines/ecological press. They appear to be responding to party recruitment techniques. However, the respondents sometimes suggested the process was a little more complicated. For example, they may have bought a copy of the party's newsletter, in which they found a membership form. Even members who appear rather passive and appear to have responded to party behaviour or campaigns may

---

[2]Even when members joined through national level mechanisms, they became a member of a local party.

in fact have previously shown an interest in green politics, if only by buying a green magazine.

*Networkers* These members joined through a green or radical politics network and represent around a fifth of members.    Included in this category are those who joined while in attendance at a local event – party meeting, stall or rally – and those who indicated that they had joined as a direct consequence of their involvement in movement activity.

*Socialisers* These members joined through family or friendship connections. Family members or friends were responsible for bringing the member and party together. Approximately 15 per cent of the members belong in this category.

*Independents* These members displayed clear self-initiative and a high level of motivation in the way that they joined the party, suggesting that they made first contact with the party rather than the other way around.  These members form the largest group – around 45 per cent of the membership – and include those who contacted their local party or the national party office independently.

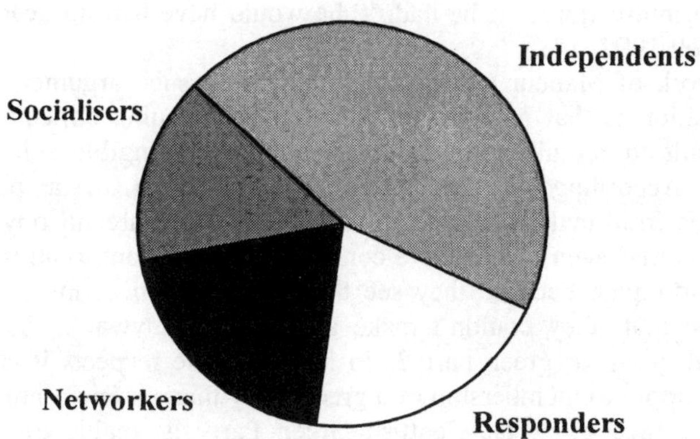


**Figure 5.1  Pathways to Membership**

Overall, a minority of members in 1990 looked like pure 'responders' to party recruitment tactics.  More significant were those who were involved in some way with what might be considered a green network. The largest group of members (nearly half) were those who displayed a large level of independent initiative when joining the Scottish Green Party.

## Why the Members Joined

*Membership Incentives*

Tocqueville (1988: 190) believed that people formed and joined groups to promote common interests. However, much of economic theory has challenged this basic idea. Public choice theorists argue that individuals are motivated by self interest and utility maximising. Self interest, according to this perspective, would not include altruism or public good in an explanation of behaviour. As Vernon Van Dyke (1995: 135) explains, 'If utility-maximising persons do good for others, it must be in order to gain advantage for themselves. They are completely selfish'. An anecdotal story about the US President Abraham Lincoln illustrates the point. He is said to have argued that all altruistic behaviour was prompted by selfishness. While travelling on a coach he was explaining this theory to a travelling companion when they came to a bridge over a muddy ditch. They heard a sow crying and distressed because her piglets were drowning. Lincoln got out of the coach and rescued the sow's piglets. His fellow traveller pointed out that he had refuted his argument himself. Lincoln replied that he had rescued the piglets for purely selfish motivations. If he hadn't, he would have had no peace of mind all day (O'Connell 1997: 14).

The work of Mancur Olson (1965) builds on such arguments. The broad Olsonian position is that a group or organisation pursuing collective goods will find it difficult to recruit unless it is able to offer tangible selective material incentives. According to this analysis, membership of a public interest organisation is irrational and paradoxical because there are no obvious benefits. Olson suggests that even if collective concerns are important to an individual they still won't participate because they see their contribution as insignificant. They would believe that 'they couldn't make a difference anyway'. So why join an environmental group or green party? In fact, in some respects it is less obvious what benefits apply to membership of a green party than an environmental pressure group. On the face of it, the Scottish Green Party is unable to offer political influence or other selective incentives like the free gifts offered to new contributors of groups like the RSPB, although the party is more likely to provide opportunities for democratic participation within its organisation.

However, the assumption that all human behaviour is motivated by selfish interest has been widely criticised. James Q. Wilson (1995: 31) stated that public choice theorists 'tend to underestimate the power of motives, such as duty or fairness, which seems at odds with any conception of immediate self-interest'. The large number of members belonging to interest groups and political parties supports Wilson's argument, as the return for membership is not obvious in economic terms.

In order to explain the so-called paradox of participation, there has been an attempt to expand the boundaries of rationality by focusing on non-material or 'soft' incentives for membership (see chapter 3). This has resulted in a list of incentives that organisations use to attract members. Clarke and Wilson (1961) referred to material, solidary and purposive incentives, only the first of which they described as 'free-rideable'. Solidary incentives (Wilson 1995: 33-34) refer to intrinsic enjoyment gained from being part of a group, but according to Wilson (1995: 34) purposive incentives are the key to understanding involvement in political parties: 'These are intangible rewards that derive from the sense of satisfaction of having contributed to the attainment of a worthwhile cause'. Furthermore, Wilson (1995: 23) argues that behaviour which stems from 'feelings of personal moral worth' can be regarded as completely rational. Salisbury pointed out that purposive incentives may involve an element of material incentive (e.g. a belief in tax cuts) and identified expressive incentives which are about the value of expression only and are non-free-rideable. Opp (1986: 88) uses the term '*soft*' incentives to refer to non-material economic inducements. These include moral motivations, social influences, entertainment value, prestige, and self esteem. Parry, Moyser and Day (1992) describe communitarian incentives (a feeling of civic duty, a belief in the public good and a desire to contribute to the community). We must assume that some mix of incentives is responsible for membership of any organisation, but are there any types of incentives which appear more important than others in the case of the Scottish Greens?

## *Difficulties Measuring Membership Incentives*

Explaining the meaning of social action is fraught with difficulties (Skinner 1972), and there are a number of problems associated with attempts to explain why individual agents become involved in social action. Measuring incentives behind membership of a group or political party is an exceptionally difficult task. What factors determine the act of joining? One possible approach is to ask the participant and cite their motives for performing the social action, on the grounds that only the members can make this calculation. However, to cite an agent's motives points to 'lawlike connections' between stimulus and behaviour (Skinner 1972: 139) when in fact action is likely to derive from a combination of many different motivations.

Furthermore, reasons for joining may be perceived differently after a period of membership. A form of social reconstruction may occur, which often takes place after participants join organisations or movements. Motives for joining are often very difficult to identify because these motives are 'generally emergent and interactional rather than prestructured' (Snow *et al.* 1980: 795). In other words, it can be during the period of involvement, through interaction with the movement organisation and other members, that participants are provided with justifications for joining and for remaining members. Vocabularies of motive can be developed after the event. Therefore, the rationale for participation might partly be provided by the organisation. For these reasons the researcher must always be cautious about empirical findings and aware that social action is likely to stem from a complicated mix of motivations, influences and interactions.

*Why Join the Scottish Green Party?*

A number of questions were asked in 1990 in an attempt to identify reasons for joining the Scottish Greens. Table 5.2 displays the responses to the question, 'When you made up your mind about joining the Green Party was your decision influenced by any of the following factors?'. This was an attempt to identify influences in the period running up to the decision to join. Table 5.3 contains responses to the question, 'A number of reasons why people might join the Green Party are listed below. Please indicate how important a role each reason played in your decision to join'. This question is more specific and attempts to examine the decision at the time of joining.

The responses to these two questions give a good indication of the factors that were and were not important to Scottish Green Party members in their joining decision, as well as the effectiveness of party recruitment activities.[3] The overwhelming sense from the responses is that selective incentives were not very significant motivators and collective incentives were of paramount importance. However, a number of different incentives appear to be in operation and it is often very difficult to separate them.

*Selective Incentives*

At first sight it may not appear that the Scottish Green Party in 1990 could offer much in the way of selective incentives to party members. Membership was very unlikely to involve private reward in the form of an occupation or political power, and the party was unable to reward members with material incentives in the way that wealthy environmental pressure groups can and do. Nevertheless there are some obvious rewards for party membership which would be unavailable to non-members. These include opportunities to participate in the party, information incentives, and solidary incentives.

*The opportunity to participate* Green parties are well known for their democratic and decentralised decision-making structures. The organisational structure of the Scottish Greens in 1990 (and now) provided excellent opportunities for any member to become involved in internal party decision-making. Compared to other parties, the Greens had very democratic decision-making procedures, allowing every member the opportunity to attend party conferences, and contribute to policy development, candidate selection and so on.

---

[3]A number of the respondents (48% of all respondents) indicated that some 'other factors' were a relevant influence on their decision to join the party, many of whom wrote a comment in the space provided for other factors. In fact, most of these comments simply clarified their responses, rather than pointing to a different set of reasons for joining, thus making 'other' influences appear artificially high.

## Table 5.2  Influences on the Decision to Join (%)

| | Decisive | Very Important | Important | Not Very Important | No role |
|---|---|---|---|---|---|
| Watching a Green Party political broadcast. | 5.1 | 6.4 | 8.4 | 12.9 | 67.1 |
| Reading the Green Party manifesto/literature. | 20.5 | 18.1 | 24.8 | 10.3 | 26.3 |
| Talking to a member (canvasser on doorstep, relative, friend or work colleague). | 14.5 | 12.8 | 13.7 | 9.0 | 50.0 |
| Reading newspaper/magazine article/book. | 15.1 | 23.0 | 23.2 | 11.2 | 27.4 |
| Watching TV programme/documentary/film. | 8.9 | 16.7 | 21.5 | 12.1 | 40.9 |
| Being confronted with a specific environmental problem locally. | 11.0 | 14.2 | 13.8 | 16.1 | 45.0 |
| Learning about a particular event highlighting national or global environmental problems. | 22.1 | 23.5 | 23.9 | 8.5 | 21.9 |

*(Average N = 449)*

The opportunity to become involved in democratic decision-making was acknowledged as a relevant reason for joining by more than half the members; 65 per cent stated that this was at least important (Table 5.3). However, only 13.2 per cent of the respondents claimed that this was a decisive reason, and compared to the other options available, this was actually one of the least relevant reasons for joining. On this evidence, the opportunity to satisfy personal political ambitions was not a very relevant selective incentive.

A number of other questions attempted to assess the members' views of internal party democracy. It is possible that the members felt there ought to be *more* opportunities available to participate in the party. The members were asked to assess the power of different organs within the party, from individual party members and local parties, to the party speakers and executive council. The responses suggest that the members were perceived as having considerable influence: 70 per cent said that individual members had an important to decisive influence on the party's 'political direction and internal functioning'; and only 25 per cent felt that the party should 'adopt a *more* decentralised structure'. However, the national party positions (Scottish Executive, National party speakers etc.) were definitely viewed as most powerful and the respondents expressed a clear desire for members to be given more influence. Over 50 per cent said that individual members and local parties had either too little or far too little influence. Overall, the members' views on internal party democracy were rather contradictory which makes any conclusions on membership involvement as a selective incentive rather tentative. However, compared to other motivations behind the decision to join they seem relatively unimportant.

*Information incentives*   Many environmental groups produce a magazine or newsletter. Likewise, the Scottish Green Party keeps in touch with its members through a newsletter. How important are these in terms of attracting members? Mitchell (1979) concluded that these were not incentives in the Olsonian sense as they are secondary rather than primary in motivating membership. In other words, the aims of the organisation can be the primary motivation and not simply a by-product of group activity.   Similarly, Jordan and Maloney (1997: 78-79) distinguish between environmental groups who offer a front-end premium such as a piece of stationery ('a minor inducement offered given to all recipients of the mail shot') and those who offer a back-end premium, for example a free wildlife video ('the inducement only for those who contribute'). They argue that only the back-end premium resembles the type of material incentive described by Olson and for the vast majority of environmental groups selective material incentives are not very important, although there are always exceptions, as in the case of the National Trust which has a large membership many of whom will have joined for the selective incentive of entry into National Trust properties.[4] The Scottish Green Party can offer no such incentives.

However, a large section of the members did indicate that they had read the party manifesto or newsletter or election material before joining and that this had influenced their decision: 63.4 per cent said the party manifesto or green literature had been important (38.6 per cent said decisive or very important).   Also, the members were very positive about the quality of party publications. When asked for their general opinion of party publications, 76.6 per cent said they were interesting rather than boring (9.8 per cent boring); 54.1 per cent well designed (21.2 per cent badly designed); 69 per cent easy to understand (11.5 per cent incomprehensible); 62.6 per cent well written (13.2 per cent badly written); 27.9 per cent appealing to ordinary citizens (47.5 per cent preaching to the converted); and 51.5 per cent persuasive (23.3 per cent dull and repetitive).

---

[4] Furthermore, precisely because most people join the Trust for the selective rewards it is doubtful whether the organisation should be classified as an environmental public interest group at all.

**Table 5.3  Reasons for Joining (%)**

| | Decisive | Very Important | Important | Not Very Important | No role |
|---|---|---|---|---|---|
| As a member I can join like minded & interesting people fighting for the environment. | 22.2 | 21.6 | 33.8 | 13.4 | 9.0 |
| There are many good people in the party that I support. | 5.4 | 11.4 | 32.0 | 26.8 | 24.5 |
| The Green Party is the only party not to compromise its principles. | 26.6 | 24.7 | 23.3 | 13.2 | 12.2 |
| I don't agree with everything in the Party programme but I want to make sure that its point of view is heard. | 25.5 | 31.8 | 22.4 | 11.3 | 9.0 |
| The party provides the best Opportunity to achieve the political claims I support. | 46.3 | 17.1 | 18.8 | 10.8 | 6.9 |
| Ultimately, the Green Party can probably do little to save the destruction of the planet, but one has to try to do everything possible to avert such a catastrophe. | 37.5 | 18.4 | 18.4 | 12.3 | 13.3 |
| Unlike other parties the Party allows members to play a meaningful, active role within a democratic framework. | 13.2 | 20.5 | 31.2 | 16.7 | 18.4 |
| The Green Party helps to fulfil my spiritual needs. | 7.2 | 8.3 | 14.9 | 19.6 | 50.0 |

*(Average N=485)*

Although party literature does not resemble the free gifts offered by many groups, it might be interpreted as specialised *information* which acts as a selective incentive.   Johnson (1995: 23) reports that many environmental groups view mailed information as a 'valuable educational activity', and that for many people, direct mail is the main source of information about the environment. Certainly, being a member of the Greens opens up access to information on green politics that non-members would not receive.  However, the member would have to agree with the aims and policy of the party in order to gain satisfaction from party material, and these are collective, non-material incentives.  There is an obvious difficulty in attempting to disentangle selective incentives from collective incentives.

Rothenberg (1988) argues that membership of groups can involve a very general search for information on the group and the issues.  In a study of the public interest group Common Cause in the US Rothenberg (1988: 1132) builds on the idea that individuals joining groups do not have perfect information, in line with the work of Moe (1980a).  However, where Moe effectively argues that people make mistakes and join groups with an escalated view of their own influence, Rothenburg (1988: 1132) suggests that '..the decision to join makes sense as a strategy by individuals who recognise their lack of knowledge.  Members join groups to learn about them, and as they acquire knowledge, some can be expected to leave'.  He refers to this as 'the politics of experiential search'. So, membership can be about the search for information, a way of educating oneself about groups and issues. *Membership may be an information gathering technique.*

*Solidary incentives* Parkin (1968: 49) argued that the 'middle class radicals' in his survey attempted to lessen a hostile political environment by selecting friends who shared their beliefs:  65 per cent of his respondents had friends who approved of the campaign, 23 per cent of friends were indifferent and only 3 per cent were hostile. Furthermore, Parkin (1968: 145) identified the importance of 'family socialization into radicalism'. In a sample of CND supporters between 15 and 21, more than six in every ten of this group had at least one parent who actively supported CND or approved of its aims and methods (mothers more likely to be supportive than fathers).   The Scottish Greens gave very similar answers to Parkin's respondents when asked about attitudes towards the party amongst friends, family, work colleagues and employers (see Table 5.4).

The data reveals a very high level of approval from friends and family, less so from work colleagues and employees, suggesting that friendship ties may be an important factor in membership after all. Furthermore, nearly 60 per cent said that they discussed politics frequently/very frequently with their friends, and 40.7 per cent said they discussed politics at least frequently with their work colleagues. Most Greens also had families that approved of the party, and the survey data reveals that the Scottish members came from fairly political family backgrounds, with a high degree of interest in political matters and current affairs.

**Table 5.4  Attitudes Toward Greens (%)**

|  | Mostly approved of the party | Mostly indifferent to the party | Mostly hostile to the party |
|---|---|---|---|
| Friends | 71.8 | 26.2 | 2.0 |
| Family | 56.5 | 37.4 | 6.1 |
| Work colleagues | 28.0 | 33.4 | 8.7 |
| Employees | 13.8 | 66.7 | 19.6 |

(*Average N=443* )

With these facts in mind, we might expect social contacts/solidary incentives to have played an important part in membership of the Scottish Greens, either in the form of social benefits or the avoidance of social punishment. In actual fact, there is little evidence from the survey that solidary incentives were very significant when it came to joining the party. Most members (just under 60 per cent) indicated that 'talking to a member' (either a relative, friend, work colleague or canvasser) was uninfluencial in their decision to join the party, and only a few members suggested they joined because of 'good people' they supported in the party. And when asked if they had friends in the party at the time of joining, an overwhelming 84 per cent said they did not.

Furthermore, when the members were asked about their experiences of membership in the party, there was little sign of strong friendship networks. When asked how often, at the time of the survey, they met party members socially outside party meetings, 63 per cent indicated never or rarely, 21.8 per cent sometimes and only 15.2 per cent quite often or very regularly. There does not appear to have been a great deal of social contact between members. Overall, Scottish Greens were well 'integrated' into other organisations, and their friends and family tended to be supportive of the Greens. However, family and social contacts did not appear very important in the actual decision to join the party.

*Networks*

We have already established that social links (interpersonal ties) did not appear very significant in the decision to join the Scottish Greens. There is very little evidence that intensive interaction with party members was responsible for the initial period of party involvement. However, these influences may still be important in the context of *movement networks*. As discussed in chapter 3, a number of studies have pointed to movement networks and the general membership overlap of many groups and organisations. Parkin (1968: 162) for example illustrates the operation of an active network amongst young members of CND, a large number of whom were involved in politics outside CND. Parkin (1968: 163-4) claims that for many young people CND acted as a 'transmission belt into radical politics of a wider kind', and of those young members who were members of a political group, 62 per cent joined *after* they joined CND (also see Berry 1970; Byrne 1988; Finger 1994; Parry *et al.* 1992; Seyd and Whiteley 1992; Taylor and Pritchard 1980).

These studies tend to provide support for the idea that political participation is cumulative – that 'conventional' and 'unconventional' political participation is not mutually exclusive. Indeed much evidence points to the existence of a set of rather committed political animals. This is true also of the Scottish Greens. Certainly, party membership does not appear to have been their first involvement with the environmental movement. While the majority of members were new to party political membership and had joined the Greens in the previous two years, most had had some involvement with environmental pressure groups. Chapter 4 outlined a wide-ranging network of multiple and overlapping memberships, with over 50 per cent of Scottish Greens having membership experience of Greenpeace alone. And there was a high level of support for environmental organisations through the making of donations. There definitely appears to be a link between experiences of activism (membership of groups) and current levels of activism (membership of Greens). Furthermore, the party members in the study give every indication that they are exceptionally well informed about political events (also see chapter 4).

The impression given here is that membership of the party was part of a *gradual process of learning, conviction and participation*, that in some way, a general interest in environmental matters and membership of other groups lead to membership of the party. A number of respondents offered written explanations/clarifications as to why they joined, and these confirm this link between a long-held concern for environmental issues, commitment to environmental organisations and membership of the Scottish Greens; in other words the existence of a green network. One respondent described their party membership as a 'natural progression from anti-nuclear politics'. A number of the respondents argued that pressure group activity had been important to them, but that it was now time for *political action*.

The survey evidence suggests that the Scottish Greens in this study were not new to political involvement. It appears that many of these members had a 'proclivity to join' (Johnson 1995: 31). However, it is not entirely clear whether the respondents were *accumulating* (collecting) memberships of different organisations (multiple membership) or if they were experimenting with different groups and then moving on, which would look more like a search for a comfortable membership home. Some of the members did suggest that they had moved from support for pressure groups to supporting the party. However, the evidence reported in chapter 4 on the members' extensive involvement in other organisations suggests the first explanation is probably most valid. And the evidence from other studies (chapter 3) definitely points to membership accumulation (multiple memberships).

*Personal Experience of Environmental Problems*

Concern about environmental problems is likely to involve collective incentives, as environmental problems often affect members of a population in equal measure, and if these problems are solved the collective group benefits. However, it is possible that membership of a green party may involve more selective motivations, if the individual demonstrates a personal desire to avoid a particular environmental problem. To what extent was membership of the Scottish Greens in 1990 a response to being personally confronted with environmental degradation? According to classical social movement approaches, the individual is likely to act in response to feelings of frustration or deprivation (see chapter 3). It is possible that personal experience of environmental problems could produce such feelings and that the decision to join the party is a response to this 'environmental deprivation'. In other words, support may be related to objective environmental conditions and to personal experience of environmental deterioration. Experiencing environmental threats may stimulate the individual to join collectively with others (see Shaiko 1999).

The work of social psychologists (for example Finger 1994) connects experiences 'in and with' the environment and environmental behaviour. Finger (1994: 153) argues that 'environmental behaviour can almost exclusively be explained as a result of environmental experiences', in most cases experiences with nature, and exposure to environmental catastrophe. Hallman and Wandersman (1992: 182) illustrate the high levels of stress associated with environmental problems and the threat of damage to one's health, because they are mainly invisible and difficult to control, and how this can lead to collective coping strategies. Opp (1988: 854) assesses reactions to the Chernobyl accident in West Germany, identifies a 'shock effect' amongst people who were not sensitive to these issues before the incident, and relates this to social movement participation. However, the work of Walsh and Warland (1983) suggested that active protest following the Three Mile Island accident was not strongly related to discontent following the incident, but pre-accident solidarity and ideology instead.

The survey of Scottish Greens was able to assess whether the members had been confronted with any local level environmental problems and whether this had been influential in their decision to join the party. A significant number of respondents (39 per cent) indicated that the experience of a specific local environmental problem had influenced their decision to join; just over 25 per cent said that such an experience had been decisive or very important (Table 5.2). Respondents were asked to specify what these environmental problems were. A total of 125 respondents provided written answers, a number of who identified multiple problems. Four or five broad themes emerge from the answers.

Many pointed to *problems they experienced in their local urban environment*. They indicated a sense of exasperation at the general mess of their local urban environment, including a lack of recycling services. Examples include 'dirt and rubbish everywhere', 'rubbish in streets, dog waste, noise pollution', and 'general disgust with the urban environment'. One respondent referred to 'the general destruction of the local environment and green belt'. Another common urban problem identified was traffic and the associated problems of congestion and pollution, including difficult conditions for cyclists.

A number of the respondents referred to problems they associated with the *food industry* and links with poor health. They spoke of ineffective agricultural practices and the detrimental effects of the use of pesticides and food additives. For example, there was reference to 'food additives, and the radiation of food' and to 'perpetual outbreaks of sickness in the locality, related to farming/the use of chemicals'.

One of the most common responses was reference to problems of *industrial pollution* in Scotland, and in particular of the rivers and seas.   A significant number referred specifically to sewage disposal in the Moray Firth and its detrimental effect on dolphins that enter the Firth.   One respondent passionately described how a particular local industrial plant had been absolutely decisive in their decision to join: 'The building of that filthy Petro Chemical Plant at Moss Morran, an environmental obscenity perpetrated upon the people of Fife jointly by Esso and the Fife Regional Council thugs and permitted by public apathy'.

Another source of concern was *Scotland's nuclear industry* (power stations and weapon bases).   Respondents pointed to pollution resulting from the nuclear industry and other safety threats, including the transportation of nuclear waste through Scotland. Dounreay was most commonly mentioned.   And the existence of (decommissioning of) nuclear submarine bases on the West coast worried a number of the respondents.

Overall, one quarter of all respondents highlight local environmental problems that appear to have had some influence on their decision to join the party. Other issues highlighted included land use in Scotland – the reforestation programme in Scotland, landfill sites, logging, quarrying and so on – but the responses to this question were dominated by the four issues of urban environment, food quality problems, pollution, and nuclear issues.

Given the difficulty of distinguishing between directly experienced environmental problems and perceived problems it was necessary to explore this question further.   Another question attempted to assess direct negative experiences of environmental problems.   Respondents were asked if they personally (or anyone very close to them, like family or friends) had suffered 'any significant negative effects from any environmental problem': 26 per cent claimed that they had definitely, another 19 per cent said that they had probably, 25 per cent did not know and 30 per cent said no.   If the respondent answered yes to this question they were then asked to give written details of the environmental problem and the effect it had had in their particular case.   Looking at those who said they had definitely or probably suffered negative effects, most commonly the respondents identified general environmental problems associated with traffic (12 per cent); air pollution (11 per cent); industrial pollution (9 per cent); general environmental degradation (9 per cent); and industrial pollution (8.7 per cent).   Smaller numbers pointed to personal experience of more specific problems: 5 per cent referred to the problems associated with being a cyclist; 4 per cent cited problems with food quality; and 4 per cent referred to sea pollution.   More significant than these were the numbers indicating that global environmental problems had affected them personally – Chernobyl (9 per cent), and global problems (7 per cent).

How should we interpret these findings? To what extent is membership a response to being personally confronted with environmental degradation? Overall, a significant minority of around 45 per cent pointed to having had 'environmental experiences', but for the majority of members (over 60 per cent) being confronted with a specific environmental problem at the local level appeared unimportant as an influence on the decision to join the party (Table 5.2). Overall, environmental experience was a relevant but not very significant factor in the decision to join the party. There is very little evidence to suggest that self-interest or 'NIMBYism' was a prominent motivation behind membership.

Overall, while only a minority claim to have had first hand experience of environmental problems it seems likely that the party members in this study will have had heightened *perceptions/awareness* of these problems. Cotgrove (1982: 15) noted that the environmentalists in his survey were very different from industrialists and members of the general public in this respect; they were very aware of environmental damage, environmental shortages and the destruction of natural habitats. The most important influence which emerges from Table 5.2 is *'learning about a national or global environmental event'*, which provides support for the idea that it is not so much direct experience of ecological problems that motivates potential members, but awareness of problems that exist, and in this case it is perceptions of national or global problems that seem to have had the biggest impact.

Finger (1994: 147) discusses the relevance of *fear* as a motivation for environmental behaviour. He identifies a group of people who seek information on the environment to help cope with fear and anxiety. And Byrne (1988: 67-68) identifies 'fear' as a reason for joining CND: 7 per cent of his respondents explained their joining in these terms. It is possible that fear of the magnitude of global environmental catastrophe provided some motivation for membership of the Scottish Greens but it is difficult to test such an hypothesis with the available data. There were certainly a considerable number of examples of the 'survivalist' or 'eco-doomster' position in written answers. One respondent stated 'fear', one highlighted 'anxiety about the whole future of the world', another referred to 'anxiety over environmental, political, social and economic distress internationally', and another to 'the growing need for urgent action necessary to avoid destruction of the plant'. Such comments suggest fear of environmental disaster can be a motivation for membership.

It has been suggested that fear of the environment is related to having children (Hallman and Wandersman 1992: 112). Of Byrne's (1988 67-68) respondents, 6 per cent referred specifically to 'fear for the future safety of their children' as the reason for joining CND. In outlining 'other' relevant factors on their joining decision a number of the Scottish Green respondents stated that they feared 'for the future' and that their concern was over the health of their children (or grandchildren) and the quality of the community in which they had to raise their children. As one respondent commented, 'the SGP seemed to be the only party that was not only concerned about this generation but of all generations to come'.  Fear of the magnitude of global environmental catastrophe was certainly a motivation for some of these party members.  There was genuine concern about the ecological risks of modern society identified by Beck and other writers (Beck 1992; 1996; 1997; Giddens 1998).

*Political Aims/Goals*

Olson suggests that large groups need to finance their political activities through the sale of selective incentives.  This is a very non-political view.  Byrne (1988), Cotgrove (1982) and others (Moe 1980a; Parkin 1968; Taylor and Pritchard 1980) place much greater emphasis than Olson on the goals of the organisation, arguing that purposive incentives can be an important motivation.  In other words, groups may exist for political reasons and members may join for political reasons.

Researchers in this field often give the impression that motivations are primarily *moral*.  Taylor and Pritchard (1980) did not ask their respondents a specific question on why they joined, but they asked about their primary objection to nuclear weapons: 39 per cent referred to moral-religious reasons; 13 per cent to political reasons; and 48 per cent to equally moral and political reasons.  Thus, Taylor and Pritchard distinguish between political protesters and *moral protesters*, although this is not a very useful distinction as the two sets of motivations are not exclusive of each other.

We would predict that political beliefs would be somewhat more important in the membership of a political party.  The 'non-political' analysis may have some relevance in the interest group world, but it is less likely to be relevant in understanding motivations behind a political party's membership.  In a party, we would *expect* purposive goals to be important.

Seyd and Whiteley's research illustrates how difficult it is to separate collective incentives, ideological incentives and altruistic incentives (Seyd and Whiteley 1992, 1995, 1999, 2002; Whiteley *et al.* 1994; Whiteley and Seyd 1998a, 1998b, 2002).  However it is clear that, in the words of Seyd and Whiteley (1992: 61) there is much evidence of 'collective rationality' in these party studies, when 'the individual thinks collectively [about the welfare of the group] rather than individually'.  The research indicates that party members believe their party can make a difference in policy terms.  In the case of the Greens this may just amount to putting pressure on the other parties, but it is clear that policy, and the implementation of green ideas is important.

Scottish Greens indicated that *the* most decisive reason for joining was 'the party provides the best opportunity to achieve the political aims I support'.  Nearly half of the respondents described this as 'decisive' when joining, and over 80 per cent indicated that this was at least important.  Such strong support for this statement indicates the existence of political aims or principles on the part of the members. It is possible that some of the respondents might have interpreted this statement to mean the fulfilment of political ambitions – achieving a certain position within the party for example – which would obviously be a selective incentive, but the responses to other questions suggest that the political aims referred to are collective, purposive incentives, based on a central concern for the environment. In line with this interpretation, another very important reason for joining was that the party was the only party not to compromise its principles; just over 50 per cent indicated that this was decisive or very important and another 23.3 per cent said this was at least important. And, as has already been reported, a relatively large number of the respondents revealed that reading a party manifesto or literature had been important in influencing their decision to join: 63.4 per cent said this was at least important, suggesting that agreement with party policies (purposive incentives) was extremely influential.

The greens in the study appeared quite familiar with the policies and manifestos of the party: 40 per cent of the membership had bought and read the Manifesto for a Sustainable Society, and another 15 per cent had read someone else's copy; 29.3 per cent had bought and read the 1989 Manifesto for the European Elections, and another 15.7 per cent had at least read it; and 35.2 per cent had read the 1987 General Election Manifesto (with another 16.3 per cent having read someone else's copy). Furthermore, a significantly large number of the members (one in ten) added that party policies had been an 'other' important influence on their decision to join. Some referred to specific issue areas while others pointed to the overall policy programme and radical agenda.

There seems little doubt that Scottish Green Party members in 1990 were concerned about policy. Members were asked what measures they felt the party should take to build upon its 1989 success, and the responses clearly indicate that development of policy was a priority, rather than internal party reform, or matters of strategy such as exploration of pacts with other parties or concentrating on non-violent direct action: 87.2 per cent agreed with the view that the party should 'concentrate on grass-roots campaigning on key environmental issues' (just under 50 per cent strongly agreed); 84.5 per cent felt that the party should 'improve its media image as a responsible party with sensible policies' (again just under 50 per cent strongly agreed with this statement); 75.5 per cent thought the party should 'devise a set of more detailed policies to cope with the environmental challenges of tomorrow'; and 69.8 per cent wanted the party to 'put greater emphasis on social issues and representing the underprivileged in society'. Moreover, when asked if 'the party should always stand by its principles even if this loses votes', 86.3 per cent agreed or strongly agreed, suggesting a relatively strong attachment to green principles.

Conversely, only 16.6 per cent wanted to see the party 'explore the possibility of pre-election anti-Thatcher pacts with other parties'; and only a quarter (25.8 per cent) agreed that the party should 'adopt a more decentralised internal structure', although 41.6 per cent wanted the party to 'elect one party leader'. 43.7 per cent agreed with the suggestion that the party ought to 'employ non-violent direct action and civil disobedience to campaign on green issues'.

An apparently contradictory result was the strong agreement with the statement, 'I do not agree with everything in the Green Party programme but I want to make sure that its point of view is heard'. One in every two members said this was decisive or very important; only 20 per cent of members indicated this was *not* important. On the one hand, this suggests that members are not fully supportive of party policies. On the other, it suggests that the members are *aware* of the party programme, that membership has involved some intellectual assessment of what the party stands for, and that policy/purposive incentives are at work in some way. This is backed up by the fact that six out of every ten of the respondents claimed that reading (a book, magazine article or newspaper article) had been an important influence on their decision to join (Table 5.2).   These respondents were asked to specify which books, magazines or newspapers had been so influential.  Of the three, books appeared to be the most influential. The most commonly noted text was 'Seeing Green' by Jonathon Porritt, but the books and authors referred to were very wide-ranging: David Icke's 'It Doesn't Have to be Like This', E.F. Schumacher's 'Small is Beautiful, Rachel Carson's 'Silent Spring', Fritjof Capra's 'Turning Point', Ben Elton's 'Stark', and the 'Green Consumer Guide' all elicited a number of responses.   Other authors referred to included R. Bahro, Aldous Huxley, J.E. Lovelock, Andre Gorz and Petra Kelly.  60 members (39 per cent of those who pointed to a publication, 12 per cent of entire sample) highlighted the importance of newspapers, the Guardian being the most influential and 50 respondents referred to the influence of a wide range of journals and magazines including the Ecologist, the Economist, National Geographic, New Internationalist, New Scientist and Green magazine.  Overall, the members appeared to be well read and to have been influenced by a wide range of intellectual sources, although Porritt's 'Seeing Green' stands out as the most influential source of all.  It is clear that for a substantial number of these respondents, membership of the party represented an intellectual engagement with green ideas.

The evidence suggests that most party members in this study were motivated by a mix of collective and purposive incentives. While members appeared to agree with the positive collective objectives of the party, a concern for the environment must by definition involve a desire to avoid environmental problems (negative collective incentives). As Wilson (1995: 46-7, 101) points out, there are probably many different types of purposive incentives.  He refers to goal oriented and ideological purposive incentives, the first being based on a concern for specific public policy goals or single issues, the second involving a distinct political vision of the world, a 'systematic world view'.  We can't assume from the data available that all the Scottish Green members were strongly committed to a radical green perspective.  Some mix of goal oriented and ideological members is more likely. However, it is sensible to assume that the incentives at work here amount to a mix of 'purpose, principle and ideology' (Wilson 1995: 96). These members became members for non-material reasons. They may not be have been deeply ideological, in that protection of the environment may have been their goal rather than deep ideological conviction, but they showed every sign of being *committed to the cause*.

*Values*

The preceding chapter argued that the classical approach to alienation had little explanatory value.  Scottish Greens are not socially marginalised.  However, the concept of alienation might still be useful if we expand its definition. Frank Parkin (1968: 11-32) refers to three possible types of alienation: alienation as social isolation, alienation as powerlessness, and alienation from dominant values. The third form of alienation developed by Parkin (1968: 21) refers to 'non-acceptance or rejection of certain values which may be regarded as central to the social order, and...commitment to alternative values which, simply as a matter of definition, can be classified as deviant'. Values that Parkin (1968: 22) describes as 'comparatively marginal to the social order' include rejection of monarchy, capitalism, religion and militarism. To this we might add rejection of industrialism and materialism. Parkin is pointing to a measure of normative integration, rather than social or psychological integration. Parkin (1968: 29) concluded:

> ...CND supporters' overall position in relation to central societal values points to what might be called a 'deviance syndrome' – that is, the propensity to endorse minority or deviant standpoints on a broad range of public issues. Such an attribute would obviously be an important factor in helping to account for involvement in CND.

Parkin argues (1968: 3; 29-30) that, because of their beliefs, these people would have been 'prepared' for membership before the question of nuclear weapons became a topical political issue.

Cotgrove (1982: 138) also argues that a belief system or collection of values is the key to understanding involvement in the environmental movement: 'It is commitment to a set of values which explains why people join a particular group and why these different types of environmental organization should recruit different types of member'. Cotgrove (1982: 27-34) argues that the belief structures of the environmentalists in his study represent an 'alternative environmental paradigm' based on the core values of non-materialism (self-actualisation), a belief in the intrinsic value of the natural environment, and a desire to live in harmony with nature, as compared with the values of the traditional or dominant paradigm – materialism (economic growth), viewing the natural environment as resource, and a belief in domination over nature. These values distinguish environmentalists from nature conservationists who support a more traditional paradigm and do not envisage any radical change in society. For example, conservationists do not share an anti-industrial position and nor are they postmaterialists.

In an attempt to assess the importance of postmaterial values in the Scottish Green Party, respondents were presented with Inglehart's list of goals and asked to choose which were most important to them.[5] There were few surprises here with the Greens prioritising the postmaterial responses rather than the more traditional concerns. 'Giving people more say in important government decisions' and

---

[5]Question: "There is a lot of talk these days about what this country's goals should be for the next ten or fifteen years. Here is a list of some of the goals that different people say should be given top priority. We ask you to choose from them the two goals that are most important to you. Place the number '1' beside the goal that appears to you most important, and a '2' beside the second most important goal: Maintaining order in the nation; Giving people more say in important government decision; Fighting rising prices; Protecting freedom of speech."

'protecting freedom of speech' were given priority over 'maintaining order in the nation' and 'fighting rising prices' by 80 per cent of the membership. Unfortunately, this question is a rather rudimentary attempt to assess the complicated dynamics of members' value systems, but the strength of direction of the responses illustrates that membership of the party was strongly correlated with postmaterial attitudes.

In the green political literature, some authors have attempted to prove that the left-right political spectrum is a manifestation of traditional politics and is less meaningful to participants in the 'new' environmental movement. Cotgrove (1982: 90) cites as proof of the radicalism of his sample the fact that 37 per cent of his environmentalists classified themselves as either centre or no position. However, this approach tends to conceal the fact that the left-right political spectrum is still a useful tool for movement participants in understanding the political world and in assessing their own position. In fact, only 16.8 per cent of Cotgrove's 'environmentalists' said they had 'no position' on this scale: 45.8 per cent of these respondents described themselves as left or mildly left, and another 19.9 per cent as centre.[6]

The Scottish Green Party membership was even less likely to reject the left-right spectrum. The members were asked to consider the party system in Scotland and place the parties on a seven-point scale from left to right (Table 5:5). Only 12 per cent of members were unwilling to place themselves on the scale, and only 11 per cent did not place the party on the scale.

The Scottish Greens obviously considered themselves and the party to be left of centre: 70.1 per cent described themselves as left of centre, and 77.2 per cent consider the party to be left of centre. However, few of the members had an extreme left position. Nor did they want the party to be a socialist party. Only 16 per cent of the members agreed with the statement 'the party will only make an impact if it becomes a truly radical party with a socialist programme' (65.2 per cent disagreed).

Part of the Green outlook involves a *spiritual dimension*. However, very few of the Scottish Greens indicated that this was an important motivation behind their decision to join. Only 15.5 per cent of the members indicated that fulfilment of spiritual needs was important (Table 5.3). Furthermore, only 20.3 per cent agreed with the statement 'the party is becoming too embroiled in traditional politics and neglects the spiritual dimension'. Klapp (1969: 42) referred to the lack of identity in a modern (alienated) society, and he argued that participants in social movements are seeking spiritual identity. There is little evidence of this 'identity quest' in the Scottish Green survey results.

---

[6] 13.7% described themselves as 'mildly right' and 3.8% as 'right'.

**Table 5.5  Position on the Left-Right Spectrum (%)**

|  | (far left) | | | | | | (far right) |
|---|---|---|---|---|---|---|---|
|  | 1 | 2 | 3 | 4 | 5 | 6 | 7 |
| Own position | 5.4 | 30.2 | 34.5 | 26.0 | 3.4 | 0.2 | 0.4 |
| Green Party | 4.4 | 28.2 | 44.6 | 21.3 | 1.6 | 0.0 | 0.0 |
| Conservative Party | 1.1 | 0.2 | 0.6 | 1.1 | 10.5 | 68.9 | 17.6 |
| Labour Party | 4.0 | 21.5 | 37.7 | 24.9 | 9.8 | 1.7 | 0.4 |
| SLD | 0.4 | 1.1 | 13.8 | 52.4 | 28.7 | 3.4 | 0.2 |
| SDP | 1.2 | 1.2 | 8.9 | 36.1 | 40.3 | 11.7 | 0.7 |
| SNP | 3.0 | 23.9 | 37.3 | 18.9 | 11.1 | 3.9 | 2.0 |
| Plaid Cymru | 3.4 | 25.2 | 39.0 | 21.2 | 6.9 | 3.2 | 1.1 |
| National Front | 5.8 | 0.2 | 0.0 | 0.4 | 0.2 | 2.6 | 90.7 |

(*Average N=449*)

*Media Influence*

The clear theme emerging from the data is that these party members wanted to help save the environment. The second most decisive reason for joining the party was that 'ultimately, the Green party can probably do little to save the destruction of the planet, but one has to try to do everything possible to avert such a catastrophe'. Nearly 60 per cent of members described this as decisive or very important, suggesting that members were rather pessimistic about the effectiveness of the party but that they also felt an obligation to do something about threats posed to the environment. The aversion of environmental catastrophe was important to these party members, and this basic concern for the environment is an apparently collective incentive. This explanation would certainly be consistent with many of the other responses. The most popular statement in Table 5.2 was 'learning about a particular event highlighting national or global environmental problems'; 45.6 per cent described this as decisive/very important.

The end of the 1980s saw a massive increase in media coverage of international environmental events (see Bennie and Rüdig 1993; Rüdig *et al.* 1993, 1996). Media influence is evident in the Scottish Green survey results of 1990: 47 per cent said, 'watching a television programme/documentary/film' was an important influence when they were deciding to join. A total of 62 respondents took the opportunity to be specific about these by writing in the space provided.

The largest group amongst these referred to the general high level of television coverage given to environmental matters at that time, in news programmes, documentaries and in chat-shows e.g. 'Various programmes involving green issues, nature, going green', 'Sting and Chief Raoni on various chat-shows'. The next most frequent response was to refer to features on the Green party itself, including interviews with prominent Greens Jonathon Porritt, Sara Parkin and David Icke. Other responses focused on specific environmental issues which were covered by documentaries or television news programmes. The issues included deforestation, threats to the rainforests, pollution of the Rhine, pollution of the North Sea, nuclear threats, the ozone hole, and the Alaskan oil spill. Two respondents mentioned the importance of the film, 'The Emerald Forest'.

The influence of newspapers and journal articles, in their coverage of environmental events, was also important. It is clear that global events and, perhaps more importantly, the media interest in these events, played a significant role in increasing the membership of the Scottish Greens. In many cases, these factors acted as intervening variables between a general concern for the environment and its translation into behaviour in the form of joining the party. Johnson (1995: 13-14) illustrates the importance of media interest in his study of environmental groups in the US. Groups were asked how they made contact with potential members and encouraged them to join. The most widely used method was through the mass media, but this involved the benefits of free media interest, rather than a specific recruitment strategy on the part of the groups. In other words, media reporting of group activities was more effective than specific recruitment techniques like buying media time/space or direct mail campaigns.

## Expressive Environmental Concern

The results of the 1990 survey so far suggest that a basic concern for the environment (collective incentives) dominated the decision to join the Greens. However, it is possible that joining the party involved some element of selective reward, that membership involved satisfaction gained from expressing concern. Parkin (1968: 34) used the distinction between *expressive politics* and *instrumental politics*, the first of which involve psychological reward rather than material and 'tend to revolve around issues which are more moral than economic in content'. The rewards 'are as much in the action itself as in the ends it is directed to'. Parkin (1968: 87) sums up his argument thus:

> The great majority of respondents declared themselves in favour of a style of politics in which the achievement of concrete goals is not the prime consideration. From this point of view, politics is concerned with the strict adherence to principles, and the making of gestures felt to be morally right, even though ineffective in practical terms. The rewards of political activity are derived not so much from a sense of accomplishment, at 'getting things done', as from the satisfaction entailed in being a 'happy few battling against intolerable odds'.

These motivations were also apparent in the survey results of the Scottish Greens. The members were intense in their concern for the environment and seemed to gain some satisfaction from supporting a cause that they perceive to be a difficult, uphill struggle. More than three-quarters said that 'joining like-minded people in the fight for the environment' was at least an important motivation.

It has been suggested that, because commitment can be minimal in the support of some groups, expressive politics is actually about the avoidance of guilt. Moe (1980a: 617) examines the expression of support, and argues that the individual 'receives intangible benefits in return for what he feels he ought to do, and he experiences intangible costs when (for "selfish" economic reasons, say) he fails to do what he believes is right'. This assuaging of guilt has been referred to as the *minimax regret strategy*. Mitchell (1979) suggests that avoidance of bads can be a stronger motivation than the pursuit of improvements i.e. membership can be about minimising maximum regret rather than utility maximisation. Such an approach assumes a rather shallow commitment to the goals of the organisation. As does the suggestion that support for environmental causes is motivated by consumerism or fashion. As Jordan and Maloney (1997: 98) note, membership can be 'a social signal rather than a calculation':

> It may be an expression of self through the conspicuous consumption of membership via stickers and badges which advertise lifestyle orientation. Subscribing to these organisations is a statement, a piece of cultural identification.

Research conducted on young people and their attitudes to the environment provides some evidence that support for the environment can amount to a fashion statement (Bennie and Rüdig 1993; Rüdig *et al.* 1996). For some, acting green at the end of the 1980s *was* fashionable. Furthermore, there is little doubt that attitudes can be influenced by 'equity norms', ideas of fairness which influence the public's behaviour, including fair trade shopping and support for various causes (Walker 1991). Johnson (1995: 29) reveals that leaders of environmental groups are well aware of the importance of 'political events and the temperament of the populace'.

Variations in equity norms and fashion trends make it necessary to consider the context of the decision to join the Scottish Greens. We have to assume that at least some of the members were influenced by such trends, although it could be argued that to view support for environmentalism as a fashion statement is a rather apolitical interpretation of expressive politics. On the whole, the evidence of the survey suggests that fashion and trend-following was not a dominant factor, compared to the motivation provided by political beliefs and a genuine concern for the environment.

The discussion on expressive membership once again illustrates the difficulty of separating selective from collective incentives. While these members would not have joined the party if they did not believe in the party's objectives, we must also recognise that some satisfaction may be gained which is not directly related to collective outcomes. Expressive benefit may take the form of a personal satisfaction gained from donating, 'even if the donation in fact has no impact on the collective interest of the group' (Johnson 1995: 9). However, it is very unlikely that expressive rewards would exist without a basic concern for collective objectives, be they positive or negative.

### Efficacy and Outcomes

Membership of a political party or group is likely to be related in some way to efficacy. Rosenstone and Hansen (1993: 15) distinguish between internal political efficacy and external political efficacy. The first refers to 'a sense of personal competence in one's ability to understand and to participate in politics' and the latter involves the belief that 'one's political activities can influence what the government actually does'.

An explanation for apparently irrational behaviour which stems from the study of efficacy is the idea that movement participants may have *imperfect information* (Rothenberg 1988; Moe 1980b) and this may lead them to have an inflated view of an organisation's effectiveness in its pursuit of certain goals, and indeed an inflated view of the value of their own contribution. Terry Moe (1980a, 1980b), based on a survey of Minnesota interest group members, noted the common tendency of group members to overestimate the significance of their own contribution to collective outcomes. Moe (1980a: 602-603) argues that participants have a distorted view of their own importance because, unlike in an Olsonian world, they are not perfectly informed. Participants find it almost impossible to measure their own influence empirically, which results in an overestimation rather than underestimation of their own effect. This is in part because their perceptions are influenced by leaders. There may therefore be a *tendency* for people to overestimate their own influence in political acts.

The party members in this study were asked a number of questions related to feelings of efficacy. They were presented with a number of statements and asked to indicate to what extent they agreed or disagreed with these statements (Table 5.6). The findings indicate that the respondents did not lack personal efficacy, they strongly believed that they could make a difference within the party, and they rather strongly disagreed with the suggestion that politics is too difficult to understand.

However, when it came to the perceived effectiveness of the party, the members were altogether less efficacious. In fact, the members in 1990 appeared rather fatalistic at times. As has already been noted, there was very strong agreement with the statement 'Ultimately, the Green Party can probably do little to save the destruction of the planet, but one has to try to do everything possible to avert such a catastrophe'. This suggested that they didn't expect the party to achieve a great deal but believed that attempts to save the planet were worthwhile, nevertheless. The members were also rather downbeat about the party's likely performance in forthcoming elections. When asked about the share of the vote the party was likely to poll at the next (1992) General Election, 60 per cent said 5 per cent or less; only 10 per cent of members thought it could achieve 10 per cent or more. Bearing in mind that the survey took place shortly after the 1989 Euro

Elections when the Greens in the UK achieved just under 15 per cent of the vote, these answers seem fairly circumspect.

**Table 5.6  Efficacy (%)**

|  | Strongly agree | Agree | Neither agree nor disagree | Disagree | Strongly disagree |
|---|---|---|---|---|---|
| I generally find it easy to convince others of my views. | 5.6 | 32.2 | 41.0 | 19.8 | 1.4 |
| If I don't organise something myself then normally nobody else will do it. | 7.1 | 20.2 | 33.5 | 30.8 | 8.5 |
| Even if I were to become more active in the party, I doubt whether it would make any difference. | 5.2 | 15.4 | 25.6 | 42.1 | 11.7 |
| Sometimes politics in the party is so complicated that a person like me can't really understand it. | 6.4 | 13.7 | 16.4 | 35.2 | 28.4 |

Moreover, the Scottish Greens in 1990 appeared considerably less efficacious than FoE/Amnesty members who clearly felt that their support could make a difference e.g. more than 70 per cent of FoE members in the Jordan and Maloney (1997: 80) study indicated that their support had an effect on FoE's 'ability to protect the environment' while a very small number (7 per cent) felt that their involvement had no effect, leading the authors to state; 'these responses suggest that group members do not accept the free-riding premise; they believe that their support is an important element in the provision of the collective good'. In contrast, the Scottish Greens did not appear as optimistic about their organisation's effectiveness: 78.9 per cent of members agreed/strongly agreed with the statement, 'Without the introduction of proportional representation, the Green party will never make a major impact in Britain'. The results so far suggest that Moe's analysis is not a very convincing explanation of Green membership. These members display some very realistic, verging on pessimistic, sentiments about the effectiveness of the party and about the future of the planet in general. Moreover, the members were exceptionally well educated and unlikely to be victims of imperfect information.

Nevertheless, the members showed some faith in the party's ability to make a difference, to the extent that they appeared contradictory at times. The members strongly rejected the suggestion that 'The party's success in the 1989 European Elections was just a flash in the pan'; 60.5 per cent disagreed with this statement and only 13.2 per cent agreed with it. Even though they did not envisage direct political power, a large number did see the party having an impact indirectly, on the other parties and on individual lifestyles: 56.3 per cent agreed or strongly agreed with the statement, 'The Party will never gain political power on its own, but it will achieve its aims by pressurising the established parties to adopt a green programme' (only 24 per cent disagreed with this statement); and 68.8 per cent agreed or strongly agreed that 'The Green Party should measure its success not in terms of electoral performance, but in its achievement to convince individuals to adopt a green lifestyle'. Finally, the members rejected a very survivalist suggestion that environmental problems were so severe that it was too late to solve them. 57.2 per cent of the members disagreed with the suggestion that, 'Even if the Green Party had a majority in Parliament tomorrow, the environmental crisis has progressed so far that it is probably too late to avert a major catastrophe'. Only 26.8 per cent agreed with this statement.

Overall, the 1990 Scottish Green Party members appeared to combine high levels of personal effectiveness with low expectations of the party's ability to achieve collective goals, although they were unwilling to concede that the battle to save the environment was entirely a losing battle. Ironically, a lack of success in achieving stated aims may in some ways be beneficial to a cause because it strengthens feelings of moral superiority. Parkin (1968: 39-40) argued that CND was likely to have a 'high survival value' because of a lack of concern amongst its supporters about the movement's concrete political ends. And Byrne (1988: 229) notes, '...the Campaign's supporters were accustomed to thinking of themselves as a battling opposition'. In other words, being an underdog in the pursuit of collective objectives can bring psychological reward. This may explain the contradictory nature of the SGP responses. On the one hand members thought the party had an exceptionally difficult task and was unlikely to make a direct impact, but on the other hand, they valued the party's objectives and wanted to contribute to the cause. As Wilson (1995: 50) argues, purposive goals 'have the virtues of their defects' in that they don't require money or political power.

*Conclusion*

The aim of this chapter was to examine how and why Scottish Green Party members overcame the so-called paradox of participation, described by Finger (1994: 142) as when the individual is unlikely to act to help the environment 'because the individual understands that his or her individual pro-environmental behaviour is not going to make a difference unless a majority of fellow individuals behave similarly'. In Olson's terms, the rational position would have been to *not* join the party and to free-ride on the efforts of others. Indeed, it is possible to question whether Scottish Green Party membership represents a contradiction of the Olson thesis at all. Johnson (1995) suggests that, considering the large amount of concern for the environment and the small number of people involved in membership of environmental organisations, it could be argued that most sympathetic supporters are free-riders. However convincing, this argument does not further our understanding of the people who do choose to join a green organisation. In this instance, why did the 509 respondents to the 1990 survey join the Scottish Green Party?

Explaining membership of the party in 1990 involves consideration of a number of often interrelated factors, but it is possible to identify sets of incentives which are more important than others. Knocke (1988: 315) outlines three main types of incentives by which members of associations can be motivated. Rational choice/utilitarian incentives include membership services in the form of private goods (occupational help, general information). Affective bonding/social incentives involve enjoyment gained through recreational activities with other members. Finally, normative incentives are mainly public goods based on the principles and goals of the organisation. Of the three types, the third dominated the Scottish Green responses in 1990.

The Scottish Greens were unable to offer much in the way of selective incentives (private goods), except for influence within the party, receiving party literature or information, and solidary incentives. In the event these incentives appeared rather unimportant, although it was argued that party literature may be of interest to members because of their concern for collective goods. (Indeed the inter-connectedness of selective and collective goods is a clear theme.) On the whole, the members gave little sign that they had been motivated to participate by self-interest. Furthermore, personal experiences of environmental problems, what were referred to as 'environmental deprivations', were not particularly important. There was little evidence of 'NIMBYism'.

Most of the evidence points to the influence of collective incentives, which may be positive (the pursuit of public goods) or negative (the reduction of a public bad). The political goals of the party were a principal motivation. Many members indicated that the policy objectives of the Greens were of considerable importance to them. Of course, the intensity of commitment to the green vision will vary. Indeed, the motivation for many of the respondents was quite simply, 'concern for environment' and membership of the party was another way of expressing this concern, a concern that had previously been manifested in long-term support for environmental pressure groups. Nevertheless, membership of the Scottish Greens represented a significant challenge to the free-rider argument as participation in this organisation did not appear to serve self interest. The empirical evidence points to public interest and collective incentives as motivations behind membership. Jordan (1998: 15) uses the acronym NAMBI to sum this up: Not Affecting My Best Interests.

A common theme in much of the literature on participation is the existence of 'rational ignorance': 'few citizens know much about politics unless someone else tells them' (Rosenstone and Hansen 1993: 27). In other words, political leaders inform citizens about issues and in this way mobilise them. However, in the case of Scottish Green Party members we cannot assume rational ignorance. Their political background would suggest that the members were in fact knowledgeable about political issues. Indeed they appeared more 'rationally interested' than 'ignorant'.

Examination of the routes, or pathways, to Scottish Green membership revealed a group of members who appeared self-motivated, in that many of them made a conscious decision to contact the party, rather than simply responding to party recruitment strategies. Based on this evidence, it is clearly possible to over-estimate the importance of political leaders/organisational recruitment strategies in attracting party members. Many of the organisational/ resource mobilisation themes outlined in chapter 3 do not appear very relevant in the case of this small, ideologically radical party.

The over-arching theme to emerge is that party members had a long-standing commitment to environmental beliefs and values (the evidence does not suggest short-term trends) and party membership was another manifestation of general concern for the environment. However, it remains to be explained why so many members joined up with the Scottish Greens at the end of the 1980s. The evidence of this chapter suggests that perceptions of environmental threats were probably intensified by the occurrence of a number of environment related incidents and political events, and, perhaps more importantly, the media's willingness to report these events. These contextual factors can act as intervening variables between concern and behaviour, and they are widely under-estimated in studies of participation. Chapter 6 explores the importance of political context and the timing of the decision to join.

Chapter 6

# When the Members Joined: Assessing the 1989/1990 Joiner

In 1990 the Scottish Green Party had more members than at any time in its history. From a base of 300 members in 1988 the party experienced an unprecedented influx of members in 1989 and 1990. While the total number of members involved was small, compared to the membership of major parties and environmental pressure groups in Scotland, this represented a massive upsurge in membership of the party and meant that over 50 per cent of the respondents had joined in the two years prior to the survey in November 1990: 31.1 per cent in 1989, 20.3 per cent in 1990 (Figure 6.1). This chapter attempts to explain why the number of people joining the Scottish Green Party in 1989 and 1990 was exceptionally large.[1] The political *context*, it is argued, is likely to influence the joining decision. An important question underlying the analysis is whether the people joining the party at the end of the 1980s were any different from those with a longer history of party membership. Did they demonstrate different socio-demographic characteristics? Were routes into the party and motivations behind membership any different from those of the established members?

**Why Study the Timing of Joining?**

At the end of the 1980s there was a remarkable rise in the salience of the environment across the UK. While research by Pattie *et al.* (1991: 295) suggests that some regions of the UK, including Scotland, were less 'pro-green' in their attitudes, the trend was nevertheless towards increasing concern. This concern was manifested in a rise in most forms of green behaviour, including a sharp increase in donations to environmental causes and an increase in membership of environmental pressure groups (McCormick 1991: 152; Rüdig *et al.* 1993:16). Another important feature of the period was the rise of green consumerism, with a particularly sharp increase between September 1988 and July 1989 (Frankland

---

[1]Regardless of the year of joining, the most popular months for joining were May and June, an occurrence which must partly be explained by election effects e.g. of 1989 joiners more joined in the month of the Elections to the European parliament (June) than in any other month. However, the Spring/Summer months of May and June are the most popular months for joining the Greens in nearly every year.

1990: 12). There can be little doubt that environmentalism was *fashionable* at the end of the 1980s.

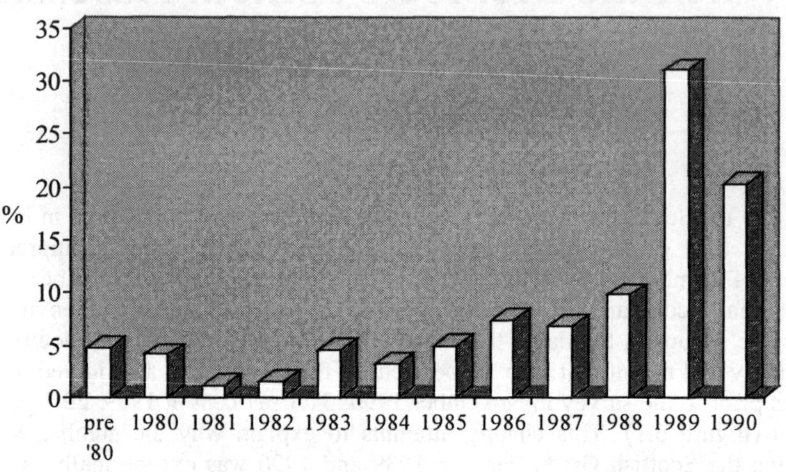


**Figure 6.1  Year Joined Scottish Green Party**

It is also important to note the significance of global environmental issues at this time. Increases in scientific evidence of environmental degradation in the 1980s, combined with extensive media coverage of a number of environmental accidents, contributed to global environmental issues entering the up-swing period of the Downs 'issue attention cycle' (Downs 1972, 1973). Global environmental issues, including the disappearance of the tropical rain forests, the destruction of the ozone layer, and global warming, topped the political agenda.  However, of all the global environmental issues, in Britain the 'greenhouse effect' raised the greatest concerns.  The concern for this issue in Britain was higher than in many other Europe states (see Rüdig *et al.* 1993: 18).  The apparent severity of these global environmental problems, and the seriousness with which they were regarded by the public, is discussed by Beck (1996) and Giddens (1998) in their analyses of 'risk society'. Giddens (1998: 58) points to the prominence of environmental hazard/ecological risk that is global in scale. Beck (1996: 20) demonstrates the importance of understanding heightened *perceptions* of environmental risks; he argues that although the risks are often exaggerated, 'believed dangers have real consequences'.

Another important feature of this time period was the interest shown by the media in environmental issues. The media make an important contribution to political discourse. As Rochon (1988: 22) notes, the media play a key role 'in developing and publicising new ways of thinking about problem areas'. This is particularly true in the case of environmental problems because they are difficult to identify and understand (Anderson 1997).  The end of the 1980s saw a dramatic rise in media interest in the environment, in Scotland as elsewhere in the UK. Global environmental problems were news everywhere. Rochon (1988: 178-9) distinguishes between *acute* issues ('sudden changes in the environment marked by wars, natural disasters, or outbreaks of civil violence') and *chronic* issues ('ongoing problems such as poverty, pollution and crime'). Acute issues are event driven while chronic issues are 'treated as news only if there is some particular peg or angle that makes the issue newsworthy at a particular moment'. In the late 1980s the media responded to environmental issues because they were acute and event driven.[2]

An unprecedented stream of environmental events, not one issue, created a 'critical mass' which fully established the environment's importance on the news agenda. The Chernobyl accident while provoking a rather muted reaction in Britain compared to other European countries (Rüdig *et al.* 1991; 1996) provided a background to other environmental issues about to come to the fore. Seals were dying in the North Sea; the ship Karen B was grounded, releasing toxic waste; food safety, specifically eggs, was a major political issue resulting in Edwina Currie's resignation from the Conservative Government; and the public became concerned about potential environmental hazards of the Sellafield complex, electricity privatisation (including the nuclear component), and plans for privatisation of the water industry (Richardson *et al.* 1992). In the south-east of England the post-1987 economic boom saw increasing pressures on green belts and the countryside. However, of all the environmental issues, in Britain it was the 'greenhouse effect' which appeared to raise the greatest concerns. It was important because it involved the prospect of environmental scandal on a global scale, reinforcing the validity of ecological arguments last prominent in the early 1970s. Slogans like 'Save the Planet' catapulted the standing of environmental issues from apparently local concerns to the national and international levels.

Given the very unique set of circumstances that existed at the end of the 1980s, we might expect the 1989/1990 joiners to display a different set of characteristics, including different motivations behind membership. Literature on participation sometimes suggests a link between contextual factors and motivations behind different forms of behaviour. Of the social movement approaches reviewed in chapter 3, for example, the political opportunity structure/political process approaches most clearly state that participation can be influenced by contextual factors, or broad political opportunities. Gamson and Meyer (1996) highlight the importance of the media. Rootes (1997: 100) points to 'dimensions of context', including social and cultural contexts. From the resource mobilisation perspective,

---

[2]The media is central to the 'issue attention cycle' described by Downs, who clearly illustrates the intense relationship between media reporting and public perceptions. While recognising the importance of 'events', Downs (1973: 63) argues that the media is the key to understanding the waves of public interest in different issues: 'Public perceptions of most crises ... do not reflect changes in real conditions as much as they reflect the operation of a definite and systematic cycle of heightening public interest and then boredom with major issues. The issue attention cycle is rooted in both the nature of certain domestic problems and the way major communications media interact with the public'.

Rosenstone and Hansen (1993) note the importance of 'timing mobilisation', when political leaders decide the time is right to mobilise the public. They speculate about when people are most likely to participate in politics, for example when issues important to them are salient, when they do not have other concerns, such as financial worries, or when 'important decisions are pending', namely elections. These approaches draw attention to the fact that the precise timing of participation is dependent on a vast array of political and individual circumstances. Whiteley and Seyd (1998a, 2002) also illustrate the importance of the time of joining, providing evidence of differences between Labour Party members who joined during different time periods. In a comparison of 'Old' and 'New' Labour members Whiteley and Seyd (1998a: 2-12; 2002: ch. 4) find that new members are younger, a little less educated, and significantly less active (more likely to be 'armchair supporters'). However, these members give more money to the party (Whiteley and Seyd 1998a: 13). This leads Whiteley and Seyd (1998a: 12) to suggest that the Labour Party has been 'recruiting a new type of member'. Furthermore, because these members are more likely to make financial donations to the party and are relatively inactive, Whiteley and Seyd (1998a: 20) argue that this is a group of 'imaginary' participants, who rely on others to participate for them. Moreover, the 'New' Labour members demonstrated some variation in terms of routes into membership and in reasons for joining the party. The new members were, for example, less likely to have joined through social contacts, and less likely to cite expressive motives as reasons for joining (Whiteley and Seyd 2002: 133-137).

The idea of imaginary participation, contracted out to others, was used to explain increasing levels of support for environmental groups (Jordan and Maloney 1997; Maloney 1999). These authors suggest that the increase in support for environmental organisations involved a predominantly passive membership that was happy to financially contribute but preferred others to be active on their behalf. Furthermore, they suggest that these members are likely to be direct mail recruits (have low levels of self-initiative) and have generally low levels of commitment.[3]

Other research points to a *chain of relationships* between contextual factors and environmental behaviour. Finger (1994) for example examines the period of the 1980s and how the Swiss became aware of environmental problems, especially global environmental ones, and he suggests that people who join environmental organisations during a period of high publicity use the media as their main source of information, display a shallow environmental concern and are likely to be

---

[3]Godwin (1988: 51) also makes the link between route into membership and level of commitment. Godwin's research involved a comparison of social network recruits and direct mail recruits and indicated that direct mail recruits tended to have lower levels of political knowledge and/or interest in politics, were more likely to have extreme political positions, and were the most likely to respond positively to extreme and negative messages (1988: 66-67). They were the least likely to be active, or to have remained in membership for a lengthy period of time, and they were generally less committed to their political organisation. And Godwin (1988: 66) suggests that organisations that rely on direct marketing are likely to suffer from 'volatile membership swings and permanent downturns'.

passive. In his study of the Swiss public and the role of environmental information, Finger (1994: 146) distinguishes between 'change learners' and 'awareness learners'. Change learners (activists) mostly belonged to the '1968 generation' and had been 'sensitized to environmental issues and problems via their political engagement during the late 1960s and the early 1970s, mainly through the anti-nuclear and the political ecology movements.' Finger argues that they were seeking environmental information because they 'wanted to change society'. Environmental learning was therefore a continuation of political activism.

Awareness learners, according to Finger (1994: 147), had become aware of environmental issues (mainly global issues) during the 1980s and primarily through the media. Moreover, he argues that 'environmental catastrophes had in fact played a key role in their sensitization process'. These people viewed the environment as 'highly complex and to a certain extent overwhelming'. Gaining information on problems was regarded as 'a goal in and by itself'. And this group revealed a high degree of fear. Learning about information was a way of coping with fear and anxiety. They were not very socially active and did not show any significant change in their everyday behaviour. Finger (1994) argues that awareness learners 'basically considered environmental information and knowledge acquisition as a means to cope with their fears and anxieties, which had been aroused by their negative sensitization experiences during the 1980s'. Therefore, the desire for more information represented a 'substitute for social action'.

Finger (1994: 158) identifies a clear relationship between passive concern, fear, and media as transmitter of information. Awareness learners were most afraid of chemical and nuclear pollution, climate change, and damage to the ozone layer, and they wanted to know more about these issues. They learned about them through the media and so developed a journalistic knowledge. Finger (1994: 158) illustrates that, although this was broad in scope, such knowledge remained rather superficial:

> On the one hand it is mostly the media that have sensitized the majority of the Swiss to global environmental issues and especially environmental catastrophes, which, as has been shown, are highly correlated with fear and anxiety. On the other hand, it is through the same media that these individuals seek answers to their fears and anxieties, generally by continuing to inform themselves about environmental matters. Individuals who have been sensitized and who learn in this way display standard environmental behaviour and do not engage in social environmental action.

**Developing a Set of Hypotheses: The Characteristics of 1989/1990 Joiners**

The task is to determine whether membership of the Scottish Greens at the end of the 1980s was little more than a short-term environmental fad, a response to the publicity surrounding green issues, and indeed the party, during and following the

June 1989 European Elections. A suggestion in much of the literature is that the 'critical mass' of events evident at the time led to support for a number of green organisations, based on financial contributions. It may be that the massive increase in prominence of the environment at this time led some to be swept along by the green wave and led them to join the Greens, along with other green groups. According to this perspective, membership of the party might have involved a rather shallow attachment and have rested on a general, passive support for the environment. If this were the case, we would expect the 'new' membership to appear more like green consumers (more 'symbolic' and 'expressive') than green activists, who are more likely to have a coherent ideological view of the world, 'linking social and environmental problems and solutions' (Witherspoon 1994: 127-8).

If these members were responding to short-term fashion factors we would expect them to be a different type of member. There are a number of possibilities. They may be different in terms of their socio-demographic background, in their experiences of political involvement, in the ways in which they became members of the party, or in terms of their motivations behind membership. Chapter 5 revealed that a minority of members appeared to have responded to party recruitment techniques, such as party advertisements and election broadcasts, but were the new members more or less likely to be 'responders'? Were the new members more or less likely to be involved in party activity? Did the new members display any distinct behavioural patterns at all? For example were they any more or less likely to make financial donations to organisations, including the party?

This chapter will explore the possibility of a relationship between joining the Scottish Greens in 1989 and 1990, and a number of the factors discussed by Finger and others. If such a relationship holds true, we would expect the new members to show signs of 'responsiveness' to party recruitment techniques, as opposed to self-initiative when joining, to have responded to dramatic environmental events reported by the media, and to demonstrate a short-term involvement in environmental causes. Furthermore, these members should be passive rather than active. Finally, we might expect that the new members would display light green attitudes, be pragmatic and expressive, and be rather responsive to selective incentives, not deeply committed to green principles or policies. The hypotheses to be tested are summarised in Table 6.1.

The survey data allow us to compare those members who joined the Scottish Greens in 1989 or 1990 with those respondents who were 'older' in membership terms. The intention was to compare those members who had been members of the party before the general rise in concern for green issues, and those who joined during the period in which interest in the environment was at its peak (the period surrounding the European Elections of 1989 when intense publicity surrounded green issues). The two groups are compared in the following ways: social characteristics and previous political experience; how they joined the party; and why they joined the party. Was the 1989/1990 joiner a *different type* of Scottish Green member?

**Table 6.1  The Hypotheses**

| 1989/1990 joiners | Established members |
| --- | --- |
| Responders | Independents/networkers |
| Media main source of information | Media only one source of information |
| Motivated by fear of global catastrophe | Motivated by range of green issues |
| Shallow/superficial concern | Deep concern |
| Expressive/selective | Purposive/policy oriented |
| Short term commitment | Long term commitment |
| Passive | Active |

*Socio-Demographic Characteristics*

Socio-demographically, the 1989/1990 joiners were not very distinctive. They were a little more likely to be female and they were younger; 85 per cent of new members were between the age of 16 and 44 but only 65 per cent of members who joined prior to 1989 fell into this category. However, the age profile is unsurprising as new members of any organisation are likely to be younger than established members.

A reflection of the younger age profile is the fact that nearly 15 per cent of the 1989/1990 joiners were in full-time higher or further education in 1990, compared to 6.5 per cent of the older members. Therefore, the new members were a little less likely to have been awarded a degree by the time of the survey – 77 per cent of these members 'at one time studied for a degree', 85 per cent of the older members. The main fields of study for both groups were very similar, predominantly arts and social sciences. Long-standing members, however, appeared a little better educated in terms of the number of years spent in school: 33 per cent of the new members had completed their education by the age of 17, 19 per cent of 'older' members. Overall, the educational experiences of the two groups were very similar. All of the members were exceptionally well educated.

Those 1989/1990 joiners in full-time work also had a similarly professional occupational background to the membership as a whole.[4] Just over half of the 1989/1990 joiners described themselves as having a professional or technical occupation, and just fewer than 60 per cent of the established members. So the new members were nearly as professional. However, they were a little more likely to work for a private firm. Nearly one in four (23.1 per cent) of the new members worked for a private firm, compared with 17 per cent of the older members. Conversely, the new members were less likely to work for a local authority.

---

[4] 48% of new members were in full time work, compared with 55% of established members.

Objectively, the 1989/1990 joiners were just as middle class as their more experienced counterparts. They were less likely to own their home but this again is a reflection of age. They were definitely middle class in profile: 62 per cent owned or had mortgaged homes. In fact, the social background of the new wave of members did not appear very distinctive at all. The party was attracting the same sociological types.[5] Nor is there any difference in the type of area in which the two groups lived. New members were just as likely to be country dwellers, no more likely to be city dwellers.

Despite the overwhelming similarities of the two groups, there was a discernible difference in *perceptions* of social class. When asked if they belonged to any social class the 1989/1990 joiners were less likely to say they were middle class and a little less likely to say that they never thought of themselves as belonging to a social class. When 'forced to choose' a class position, 35 per cent of the new members described themselves as working class, but only 20 per cent of the established members. Conversely, 65 per cent of new members and 80 per cent of established members said they were middle class. Consistent with these findings, the newer members were more likely to indicate that they came from working class families. Just over 36 per cent of the new members said that when they were young their family belonged to the working class, but only 29 per cent of the long-term members. However, compared to the Scottish population, even the new members perceived themselves to be very middle-class (see chapter 4).

A comparison of religious background reveals that 33 per cent of the 1989/1990 joiners 'belonged to an organised religious group', only 24 per cent of the older members. Also, to a small extent, the new members who belonged to a religion displayed more of a commitment to 'traditional' religious denominations.

Having examined the social background of the 1989/1990 generation of Scottish Green members, it is clear that, at the end of the 1980s, the party was in fact attracting a very similar kind of person to the more established member. In other words, the party was not very successful at widening its membership base beyond a rather narrow section of the population. However, the party at this time was quite clearly able to mobilise a greater proportion of potential members.

*Political Experience*

If joining the Scottish Greens at the end of the 1980s was simply a question of fashion, we would expect people who joined at the time to be relatively new to politics. However, there is little evidence to suggest that the 1989/1990 joiners were significantly less likely to have had political experience. They appear only a little less involved in membership of other political parties and movements, which is easily explained by the younger age profile: 26 per cent of the new members had been members of another political party, 31 per cent of the older members. The 1989/1990 joiners were also nearly as likely to have been members of

---

[5]These findings are similar to the results of Rothenberg's (1988) study of Common Cause in the US, which showed that although new members were likely to be younger, established and new members were demographically very similar.

environmental pressure groups (Table 6.2). However, they were less likely to have been members of Friends of the Earth, and they were less involved in local level groups, including conservation societies and anti-nuclear campaigns; they were also significantly less likely to be members of CND. Furthermore, the 'new' members were less likely to indicate that they had been members of an environmental type group for a long time. For example, only 20 per cent of the 1989/1990 joiners had been members of Greenpeace for three years or more, compared to 40 per cent of the established members. Once again, however, the age profile of the new generation of members accounts for the fact that they were less likely to have had a long-term commitment to environmental groups. They will have had fewer opportunities to become involved. So far there is little evidence to suggest that the new group of members were very new to politics. In other words, they were not substantially different in terms of their record of membership of parties or groups.

**Table 6.2  Membership of Environmental Groups (%)**

|  | 1989/1990 joiners | Established members |
|---|---|---|
| Friends of the Earth | 42 | 58 |
| Greenpeace | 55 | 62 |
| RSPB | 28 | 37 |
| National Trust | 28 | 40 |
| Ramblers Association | 7 | 7 |
| WWF | 29 | 30 |
| RSPCA | 14 | 15 |
| Local amenity group/conservation society | 24 | 37 |
| Other environmental group | 39 | 54 |
| Anti-nuclear campaign | 10 | 13 |
| Local protest against nuclear energy | 15 | 29 |
| CND | 36 | 59 |
| Amnesty International | 27 | 35 |
| Anti-Apartheid campaign | 17 | 16 |

We would expect the new members to be less active in various social movements over the longer time perspective. 11 per cent of these members and 13 per cent of the older members were active in the student movement in the 1960s, and 8 per cent of the new members and 12 per cent of the older members were active in protests against the Vietnam War. The differences are in fact very small. Moreover, when asked about activism in a number of movements 'over the previous year', the two groups look very alike in their overall level of commitment. As before, the new members appeared to be a little less active in movement activity, particularly in the anti-nuclear movement. Some groups/causes appeared less popular among the new members, for example CND, but because the new members were younger they were less likely to be involved in the peace campaigns of the 1970s and early 1980s, and overall the differences are by no means substantial. Furthermore, the new members were *more* active in the animal rights, and feminist movements. The results so far do not support the suggestion that the new generation of members were distinctly passive supporters of groups.

Although the overall pattern of membership of groups does not vary greatly between new members and long-standing members, it is possible that the new wave of members may have behaved differently as members within organisations. If we were testing for a more shallow level of commitment we might look for signs of different forms of activity, perhaps a tendency to offer financial support rather than active help. However, patterns of contributions from the 1989/1990 party joiner and established members were, once again, very similar. In fact, the new members were a little *less* likely to contribute financially to organisations. New members again appeared a little less committed to the peace and anti-nuclear movements, but in the case of animal rights organisations they were more likely to make a donation. Overall, there appeared to be very few differences in the activity patterns of the new and established members. Both revealed a fairly high level of interest in and commitment to social movements, and both displayed a 'joining' tendency, a proclivity to join. Established members were a little more likely to belong to a sports or social club, voluntary association or trade union but both sets of members were active participants in society.

Although the 1989/1990 joiners were not particularly distinct in terms of their socio-demographic profiles or social movement experiences, it is still possible that the new member was a different type of member. For example, they may have been less active within the party, or they may have had different reasons for joining.

*Activity in the Scottish Green Party*

One area in which differences do emerge between the 1989/1990 joiners and long-term members is involvement with the party itself. When asked to indicate their level of activity within the Scottish Green Party, one in every two of the established members described themselves as active within the party ('fairly', 'very' or 'extremely' active), compared to only 34 per cent of the new members. Furthermore, only 8 per cent of the new joiners described themselves as 'extremely' or 'very' active within the party, compared to 24 per cent of the other members.

These findings may be the result of a new wave of members who were generally less inclined to be active within the party. However, there is another explanation. As Rothenberg (1988: 1140) explains, new members of an organisation are invariably less likely to be active to begin with, and this does not necessarily impact on their long-term patterns of activity. He suggests that only about 10 per cent of all members are activists from the very start and that activism is the result of a number of years as a member. In other words, length of time in an organisation determines the likelihood of being active. This is referred to by Whiteley and Seyd (1998a:10) as the socialisation hypothesis, the idea being that members over time are often socialised into activity. However, Whiteley and Seyd

(1998a: 10) also argue that lower levels of activity amongst a new group of members may indicate the existence of a more passive type of member, chiefly due to the time of joining and the recruitment methods used to secure their membership (the recruitment hypothesis). Unfortunately, it is impossible to assess whether the new wave of members in the study of Scottish Greens did or did not become more active over time.

However, of the two groups of party members, the new members were also the most likely to indicate they were considering leaving the party, suggesting that 1989/1990 joiners were the most volatile. The new members were less likely to declare an intention to renew their membership when next due (Table 6.3).

**Table 6.3  Intention to Renew Membership (%)**

|                  | 1989/1990 joiners | Established members |
| ---------------- | ----------------- | ------------------- |
| Definitely renew | 58.7              | 69.1                |
| Probably renew   | 25.1              | 23.0                |
| Probably not     | 9.7               | 5.2                 |
| Definitely not   | 0.8               | 0.4                 |
| Already left     | 5.7               | 2.2                 |
|                  |                   |                     |
| N                | 248               | 235                 |

At first sight, this suggests that the 1989/1990 joiner may be a more volatile, less committed type of member. However, once again, this is not necessarily the case. Rothenberg (1988: 1144) also illustrates that the longer you have been a member, the less likely you are to leave. He argues that 'there is considerable vacillation among new members about their future intentions, but this uncertainty dissipates over time'. Furthermore, he suggests, 'each year has a positive...impact on the probability that members will remain committed'. Thus, he claims that around 55 per cent of first year Common Cause members continued membership, and around 90 per cent of long-term members. This study supports the claim that the shorter the period of membership, the more likely a member is to leave, and this helps explain why new members reveal signs of greater volatility.

So far, the comparison of 1989/1990 joiners and established members does not suggest the existence of a new 'type' of Scottish Green. The levels of political involvement of the new and old members did not differ to any great extent. New members were less active in the environmental, anti-nuclear and peace movements over the longer time perspective, but there was very little difference between the two groups in the hours of social movement activity per week reported in the year prior to the survey. In terms of financial contributions to groups, the more recent joiners were a little less likely to have donated to groups, except in the case of the animal rights movement. There is no convincing evidence that the new members were less involved in green politics as such or that they were less connected to a green network than the 'old' members. Overall, the backgrounds of 1989/1990 joiners were not very different from the established membership, although they were apparently less keen to become involved in activity in the party. This could be explained by the fact that newer members have simply had fewer opportunities to become active, as Rothenberg (1988) suggests. However, could this be explained by different routes into membership, or by distinct motivations behind membership on the part of the 1989/1990 joiner?

*How the Members Joined*

In fact, an examination of *how* they first became members reveals few differences between the two groups (Table 6.4). However, the 1989/1990 joiners are a little less likely to have joined through a local meeting/stall or rally: 14 per cent of the new members joined in this way, and 21 per cent of the established members. New members were also less likely to have joined through a friend or relative, while they were *more* likely to have contacted a local party independently and to have filled out a form appearing in the national press. The newer members appear to have been a little less integrated into a local green network. They were, if anything, more likely to have been 'self-starters' or 'independents'. The hypotheses outlined at the beginning of the chapter predicted that the new members would be less likely to be self-starters but there is no evidence of such a trend. Overall, the responses on how the members joined are very similar, another sign that 1989/1990 joiner was not a completely different type of member. A large proportion of *all* the members demonstrated high levels of self-initiative. Few looked like direct marketing recruits.

**Table 6.4  How the Members Joined (%)**

|                          | 1989/1990 joiners | Established members |
|--------------------------|-------------------|---------------------|
| Local meeting            | 14.3              | 21.1                |
| Form from friend         | 14.3              | 17.5                |
| Contacted local rep      | 18.0              | 12.3                |
| Form from national press | 14.7              | 12.3                |
| Appeal through post      | 3.3               | 3.5                 |
| Contacted national office| 27.8              | 27.6                |
| Canvasser                | 0.4               | 0.4                 |
| Other                    | 7.3               | 5.3                 |

*Reasons for Joining*

So far, the comparison of 1989/1990 joiners and long-standing members has not revealed many differences. However, some interesting contrasts begin to emerge when we examine those factors that influenced the decision to join the party. When the members were asked to indicate the importance of various factors, 'talking to a party member' was less influential for the new members. Only one out of four said this was decisive/very important, compared to one in three of the older members. Social ties appear even less important for the new member. However, there was no real difference in how often they discussed politics with friends, and there were few differences reported in attitudes towards the Greens amongst friends and family. The friends of the newer members were a little more likely to approve of the party but their families were a little less likely to approve.

Reading a newspaper, magazine or book was significantly more influential for the 1989/1990 joiners: 43 per cent of new members said this was decisive or very important, 33 per cent of established members. The majority of new members (57 per cent) claimed that watching a television programme, documentary or film had an important influence on their decision to join, compared to only 36 per cent of the older generation of members; 32 per cent of new members and 19 per cent of established members claimed this had a decisive or very important influence. These findings suggest that, when they decided to join the party, the new wave of members in 1989/1990 was influenced by the media's coverage of environmental issues to a greater extent than the older generation of members.[6]

The new members were also more likely to identify 'being confronted with a specific environmental problem locally': 44.5 per cent of the new members (32 per cent of the established members) said this was at least an important influence when they were making up their mind about joining. Even more significantly, the 1989/1990 joiners were twice as likely to identify *global problems*, such as Chernobyl, as the problem affecting them, even though the question referred to local problems. This is consistent with the fact that the newer members were influenced to a far greater extent by 'a particular event highlighting national or global environmental problems (for example Chernobyl, Bhopal)'. Over 80 per cent of the new members claimed such an event was important to them when joining, but only 57 per cent of the established members cited this as an important influence; 55 per cent of new members and 34 per cent of established members claimed that this was decisive or very important.

These findings must be related to the increase in incidence of events and disasters that were widely reported by the media in Britain at the time. Nevertheless, the findings imply that the 1989/1990 joiners were, to some extent, influenced by a different set of factors from those members who joined before these events took place. In short, the new members displayed a high level of concern for global environmental problems and were more likely to give this as a reason for joining the party.

Table 6.5 compares new and established members' answers to the question 'A number of reasons why people might join the Green Party are listed below. Please indicate how important a role each reason played in your decision to join'. Again, some small but interesting differences are revealed. On the whole, the new group of members appeared a little more pragmatic in their responses. For example, they placed less of an emphasis on not compromising party principles: 22 per cent of the new members said that a decisive reason for joining was that this

---

[6]They were also 10% more likely to say they watched the news on television every day.

was the only party 'not to compromise its principles' while 31 per cent of 'older' members gave this response.

**Table 6.5  Reason for Joining the Greens (Decisive/Very Important) (%)**

|  | 1989/1990 Joiners | Established Members |
|---|---|---|
| I can join like-minded and interesting people in fighting for the environment. | 46.3 | 42.3 |
| There are many good people in party that I support. | 18.3 | 15.5 |
| It is the only party not to compromise its principles. | 48.9 | 53.3 |
| I don't agree with everything in the party programme but I want to make sure that its point of view is heard. | 61.8 | 54.6 |
| The party provides the best opportunity to achieve the political aims I support. | 63.3 | 65.3 |
| Ultimately, the Green Party can probably do little to save the destruction of the planet, but one has to try to do everything possible to avert such a catastrophe. | 62.3 | 52.4 |
| The party allows its members to play a meaningful, active role within a democratic framework. | 36.4 | 32.0 |
| Fulfilment of spiritual needs. | 15.0 | 16.0 |

The new members were also a little more likely to admit they didn't agree with everything in the party programme, but that they wanted the party's point of view heard. And the new members were most likely to agree that, 'ultimately, the Green Party can probably do little to save the destruction of the planet, but one has to try to do everything possible to avert such a catastrophe'; 41 per cent of new members (34 per cent of established members) claimed this was a decisive reason for joining.

The importance of global environmental problems as a motivation for membership is particularly evident in the responses of the new members. They were concerned about global catastrophe but at the same time they were rather pragmatic about how to avert such a catastrophe. Membership of the party appeared to be a way of expressing their concern but, even more so than the established members, the new members appeared resigned to the fact that the party was unlikely to avert environmental catastrophe.

The survey findings point to an anxiety about global environmental problems that is evocative of theories of risk society (Beck 1992, 1995, 1996, 1997; Giddens 1998). A sense of fatalism is evident in the Scottish Green Party responses, a sense of 'being out of control', particularly in the case of the new joiners. A central plank of Beck's (1997: 29) argument is the significance of large-scale environmental *hazards*. He describes 'the social and political explosiveness of hazards'. It is not always obvious to the public who is responsible for environmental hazards and Beck (1997: 29-30) argues that public perception of risks and hazards 'ignites its own dynamic of cultural and political change'. The legitimacy and authority of governments, bureaucracies, scientists and experts can be challenged as the result of environmental hazards, and Beck (1997: 30) notes the importance of the mass media and social movement organisations (e.g. Greenpeace) in activating and highlighting concerns about ecological destruction.[7]

The respondents in this study appeared genuinely concerned by the ecological risks of modern society identified by Beck and others. They were anxious about global environmental developments reported in the media, were rather fatalistic about the future and may have been seeking information to calm their anxiety. In this respect, the 1989/1990 joiners in particular revealed some similarities with Finger's (1994) description of awareness learners.

*The Role of the Media*

Rochon (1988: 128) argues that environmental campaigns tend to be organised around local sight-specific issues like local nuclear plants. Global environmental issues according to Rochon (1988: 128) are much less likely to be the subject of mobilisation: 'Issues that can be experienced as both personal and group predicaments are most keenly felt and lend themselves most readily to movement mobilization'. Similarly Rüdig (1990b: 3) argues that global environmental problems are abstract, their threats and causes are difficult to identify and therefore 'these types of issues do not offer the environmental movement any targets to mobilise people against'. So we need to provide explanations for the apparent ability of these issues to inspire party membership for many of the Scottish Greens

---

[7]The role of social movements in the creation of a global environmental agenda is further explored by Jamison (1996: 224) who makes the point that very complex scientific information needs to be translated by 'intermediary actors' into issues that concern the public, and the international environmental NGOs perform this task in increasingly sophisticated ways. Jamison (1996: 232) claims that the increasingly professional environmental groups – with sophisticated communication techniques and substantial funds – have been among the most powerful influences in creating the 'global environmental discourse', 'organised strategically and orientated to mass media ... interested in sensational environmental disasters'.

in this study. From a rational choice perspective, was the balance between costs and benefits altered in some way? An answer may lie with the mass media.

At the end of the 1980s, there can be little doubt that stories about environmental issues were news. Moreover, as was noted earlier, the media is central to the 'issue attention cycle' described by Downs (1973) and, as Rochon (1988: 22) has argued, the media play a key role 'in developing and publicising new ways of thinking about problem areas'. In the late 1980s the media highlighted many environmental problems and provided publicity for the environmental movement. In a sense the media pointed up the costs of not acting to save the environment, and the Greens benefited directly from the media exposure of environmental issues.

To recap on the reasons for joining, the 1989/1990 joiners in this study indicated that they were more likely to watch news on television every day and they were more influenced by a Green party political broadcast. One in three of the new members cited television as being a *decisive or very important* influence on their decision to join, compared to only one in five of the established members. Similarly, the recent joiners appeared more receptive to what had been written in newspapers and magazines. The evidence clearly suggests that the more recent joiners were strongly influenced by the media coverage of environmental issues, and certainly more so than the established membership. The dramatic media coverage of the environment clearly had an influence on people joining the party at the time. However, this evidence does not support the conclusions reached by Finger (1994). By and large the party members in this study are not people who only recently became aware of environmental issues. Even the 1989/1990 joiners had a track record of support for the environment. Rather, it seems that media exposure intensified, or increased awareness of, people who were already a part of an environmental constituency.

*Policy Goals and Political Values*

Chapter 5 argued that green political objectives and 'collective rationality' were important to the party members in this study, rather than individual, selective rewards. However, one of the hypotheses outlined at the beginning of this chapter predicted that the 1989/1990 joiner would be less committed to a radical green agenda. We have already established that those members who joined in 1989/1990 were the most likely to be passive within the party. This may be because they had fewer opportunities to become involved but it may also be explained by a lack of interest in radical green policies.

Certainly, as we have already seen, the new members were a little less likely to refer to the party's principles as a reason for joining; over 30 per cent of the established members said that a decisive influence on their decision to join was that the party was the only one not to compromise its principles, compared to only 22 per cent of the new members. And the new members were also more supportive of the statement 'I do not agree with everything in the Green Party programme but I want to make sure that its point of view is heard'. However, the responses of the new members overall are not very distinct. The differences between the two sets of members should not be over-stated.

So can we assume that the new members were less ecological or radical than the established membership? Can we conclude that the new members were likely to be green consumers with little desire for more radical forms of political restructuring? Clearly we cannot. There is no evidence in the survey to suggest that new members were fundamentally different in this respect. Indeed, other research on the policy objectives and ideological beliefs of UK Greens indicated that there was no difference in views between new and old members (Rüdig *et al.* 1993: 42). The overwhelming sense of these findings is that the party members, whether new or established members, were motivated by a combination of collective, purposive incentives. They may or may not have had a clear ideological vision, but the members were committed to the collective goal of protecting the environment.

The limited nature of the data makes it impossible to explore this fully but so far the evidence suggests that differences in findings are explained by natural membership development. As Rothenberg (1988) suggests, new members are rarely motivated by specific issue positions. He suggests that general, purposive beliefs are the motivation at the time of joining. So, the new members may simply be in the early stages of 'experiential search' (Rothenberg 1988) in that they are less aware of policies, joining for rather general, non-specific reasons. Rothenberg's (1988: 1147) comparison of new members and veteran members in Common Cause reveals that they were equally interested in a number of different issues, but crucially the new members were much less aware of the Common Cause policies on these issues:

> While recent members are as opinionated about the public agenda as long-time contributors, they are less well versed in the organization's stances. A substantial portion of new members could not have been motivated to join the group by its overall issue positions, since they did not know them. This finding supports the belief that general, largely purposive benefits, rather than returns from specific collective goods, are at the heart of the initial joining process.

It has already been argued that length of time of membership affects the probability of activism within a group or party, and the relative lack of activity of the 1989/1990 joiners within the party may be explained by their inexperience as members. We should also consider the possibility that activism, or experience of membership, can lead to a set of beliefs and motivations. As Rochon (1988: 144-149) also argues, activism in itself *leads to* information, knowledge and interest. In other words, the experience of activism itself, rather than a difference in original motivations, can result in apparent differences in outlook between active and passive members. Given time, new members may be just as just as likely to develop an activist's view of the world.

*Conclusion*

A number of hypotheses were outlined at the beginning of the chapter. It was suggested that because the political context at the end of the 1980s was so unique, members joining at this time may have had qualities or motivations which were distinct from those members who had joined when environmental ideas were less prominent and less 'fashionable'. The work of Finger (1994) in particular was used to outline the distinction between two categories of green supporter or member. First, those who responded to group mobilisation strategies, gained their information on the environment from the mass media, were motivated by fear of global catastrophe, were rather 'shallow' and 'expressive' in their commitment, and were generally passive in character. The second type included those who joined through networks or self-initiative, used the media as only one source of information, were motivated by a range of green issues, were more deeply committed to purposive green ideals, and were more likely to be active. While recognising that these were two extreme types, these ideas were used as a base from which to compare Scottish Greens who joined in 1989 or 1990, and those who had been members over the longer time-period. It was hypothesised that new members of the Scottish Greens may be more like the first category, as they had joined the party at a time when environmental issues, particularly global issues, were receiving unprecedented publicity and were regarded as 'fashionable'.

While some differences *were* evident in a comparison of 1989/1990 joiners and the more long-standing members, the results overall did not reveal two very different types of party member. For example, in terms of their socio-demographic make-up the new members were almost identical to the 'older' members, except that the new members were younger, as was to be expected. To a very large extent, the differences that did exist between the two groups can be explained by a combination of contextual influence and length of membership. It was illustrated that the new members were more likely to be passive within the party. However, we might regard this as perfectly natural, along with their greater likelihood of leaving, in accordance with the arguments of Rothenberg (1988). The two sets of members were not significantly different in terms of their activity in movement politics, which suggests that they simply had less time to become involved in the party. In fact, all party members, regardless of time of joining, and of activity in party, had a fairly lengthy commitment to green activities. It is very difficult to draw a line between activists and passive members if we consider involvement in the environmental movement overall. Nor is there evidence of a greater tendency to give financial donations amongst the 1989/1990 joiners. Those members who were most likely to be active in the party were also the most likely to be giving money to environmental causes. In other words, activists and those who donated money did not appear to be two different categories of member.

Nor did the mechanisms through which the two groups became members (how they joined) differ significantly. The 1989/1990 joiners were not particularly more responsive to party recruitment techniques. Both sets of members displayed high levels of self initiative in approaching the party (although the new members were a little less likely to have joined through a network or social ties).

However, a comparison of reasons for joining revealed a few interesting differences. While a fundamental concern for the environment was the chief motivation for all members in the study, the new wave of members was more likely to refer to dramatic media coverage of global environmental catastrophes. The new members were clearly concerned about global environmental risks, global warming, resource depletion and so on, which are issues that relate to 'the long-run sustainability of economic systems' (Jacobs 1997: 1). When asked to account for joining the new members were most likely to refer to global-scale environmental problems that were perceived to be 'out of control' (Beck 1992, 1997).

Thus, the membership data suggest that, to a small extent, year of joining *does* influence reasons for joining. Because of the prominence of global environmental issues at the end of the 1980s, widely transmitted through the media, the new wave of members was motivated to join by global environmental concerns to a greater extent than the established members. The political setting is clearly a relevant consideration in analysing these results. The events surrounding the 1989 European Elections represented a unique mix of political and environmental circumstances and it is vital to understand the context of this period in order to understand the party's development. A particular set of factors presented an opportunity for the environmental movement in the late 1980s, a combination of factors which has not occurred since. This particular mix of factors goes a long way in explaining the rise in Scottish Green Party membership at that time. The members in this study demonstrate a gradual realisation that there was a credible political route at the time of joining, but it was the particular combination of events that gave the Greens this credibility.[8]

However, it would be misleading to over-state the differences between the 1989/1990 joiners and the more established members in this study. The 1989/1990 joiners did not appear to be responding to fashion trends. They did not look like awareness learners. They were not completely new to politics. Nor were they significantly less likely to be active in the environmental movement. Overall, the 1989/1990 joiner was not a 'new' type of party member. The evidence strongly suggests that the Scottish Greens were attracting the same type of member at the end of the 1980s as before. The members all came from an environmental constituency, but due to the political setting of the day, potential members of the party had raised expectations of the party.

---

[8]The analysis in this chapter is based on individual level data i.e. asking individuals why they became members. Another approach is to treat the numbers joining at a particular point in time as the dependent variable and conduct a sophisticated time-series analysis of contextual variables including the state of the economy, general levels of concern and so on. Such an analysis was conducted in relation to the membership of the UK Greens (Green Party of England, Wales and Northern Ireland). It was shown that three contextual variables were particularly important in explaining fluctuations in Green membership: the salience of the environment, the rate of unemployment, and election effects (1989 European Election and 1992 General Election) (Rüdig *et al.*. 1993: 44). A lack of appropriate time-series data prevented such an analysis in the Scottish case, but the pattern of membership support was very similar in Scotland, and the findings are consistent with those reported here.

The evidence so far suggests that to fully understand patterns of membership we must consider the political setting, those factors which are situational or contextual. Contextual analysis provides us with another analytical tool, sometimes referred to as contextualisation, or situational analysis. The contextual background and events are important because they may have some bearing on the perceptions, awareness, knowledge, behaviour and actions of members who join an organisation at a particular time, as well as explaining the increase in public knowledge about issues. As Baumgartner and Leech (1998: 177) argue, 'we can ignore the context and hope that our findings will prove robust on average, but the more sophisticated strategy is to build contextual factors into our studies'.

The relationship between context and collective action, however, is a complex one. As Edmondson and Nullmeir (1997: 210) argue, 'settings do not simply supply extra sets of discrete variables whose effects can be calculated when political action occurs. On the contrary, contexts interact with collective action in highly variable ways'. For this reason, it is impossible to 'measure the effects' of contextual influences. Context is not a discrete, dichotomous variable (Edmondson 1997: 5). Nevertheless, we can conclude that collective behaviour and context are fundamentally interdependent. Political actors exist within a political context.

Chapter 7

# The Members in 1997

Following 1990, membership numbers of the Scottish Green Party fell dramatically within a very short space of time. In 1990 the party had more than 1,200 members but by 1993 there were just over 200 members. By 1997 membership levels showed some indication of rising again, but they were not beginning to approach the levels recorded in 1990.[1] So, where did all the 1990 members go? Did they give up on environmental politics? Did they decide to support environmental pressure groups instead because they saw them as more effective? Did they decide to join another political party?

This chapter documents the results of a series of telephone interviews, which took place in 1997, with a number of the original 1990 questionnaire respondents. The interviews explored a number of issues related to joining and leaving the Scottish Greens. What was the membership status of the respondents in 1997? How did they now view their decision to join the party? Even more importantly, why had some left the party by 1997? As Rothenberg 1988: 1129 states '..signing them up in the first place is only half the battle. The conditional joining decisions on whether to stay in the organization are crucial'. Based on the qualitative interview findings, as well as data from the 1990 questionnaire on reasons for leaving, the chapter attempts to assess why so many 1990 members left the party, while others remained as members.

It will be argued that longitudinal analysis of membership dynamics is essential in order to understand why people join and leave. Previous studies have often been undermined by a weak methodological approach. For example, in his study of the retention decision Rothenberg (1988) asked members why they had joined and why they decided to stay or leave *at the same time*. He recognises the problems with this and argues that, 'Future endeavours must employ longitudinal designs, including studies that follow up on individuals who begin, continue, and cease contributing (and perhaps go elsewhere)'. However, the longitudinal approach also has weaknesses. When individuals are interviewed at different points in time, respondents may reconstruct their views in the light of events and experiences that take place between interviews, a process of ex post rationalisation.

---

[1]In 1997 the party estimated that it had approximately 350 members. However, this is a very generous estimate as it includes a number of members who had technically allowed their membership to lapse. For a period of three months or so lapsed members are still treated as members by the party.

## The Political Context in 1997

The political context in 1997 was very different from that of 1989/1990.  At the time of the 1997 British General Election, when Tony Blair's Labour Party swept to power, the environment did not appear to be a very prominent political issue, and certainly significantly less so than in 1989 (see Carter 1992; 1997). Throughout the 1990s there had been a general lack of media interest in the environment, including global environmental issues.  Downs (1973: 67) had argued that events may continue to occur but the media's desire to entertain the public can result in a decline in reporting because the events lack 'intrinsically exciting qualities'. Furthermore, Downs argued, a focus (perhaps over-exposure) of the media on an issue in itself can lead to public boredom with the issue (Downs 1973: 68-69). Rawcliffe (1998: 77) refers to 'doom fatigue', when people become tired of bad news. These patterns were clearly present in the 1990s.  Furthermore, there was little coverage of the party itself in the media, especially in Scotland (see chapter 2).

The British public also appeared to have lost interest in environmental issues (Witherspoon 1994; Worcester 1997).  The MORI monthly polls for example highlighted the dramatic decline between 1989 and 1997 in the numbers who believed the environment was an important issue facing the country (Worcester 1997: 163).  Worcester (1997: 160-161) demonstrates the decline in concern about global ecological issues like global warming and acid rain, precisely those issues which sparked such public interest at the end of the 1980s.[2] The evidence of Scottish attitudes towards the environment is generally more patchy (see chapter 2). However MORI evidence suggests that Scottish public opinion followed a very similar path in the 1990s, with low levels of environmental concern in the run-up to the 1997 General Election.

Another significant feature of the period was the prominence of environmental groups. Despite the media's reduced interest in the environment, a considerable amount of coverage was given to environmental protest.  For example, there were many high profile protests by anti-roads campaigners and animal rights campaigners (see Ridley and Jordan 1998). One of the most widely publicised in Scotland was the protest against the M77 Glasgow to Ayr extension.  These protests, while drawing attention to large-scale environmental problems, were mainly based on local level issues. However, the environmental event that probably attracted the most media coverage in Britain in the 1990s was the Greenpeace Brent Spar campaign. The campaign, which included occupation of the Brent Spar oil platform by Greenpeace activists, appeared to provide evidence that green pressure groups could effectively counter the powerful interests of big business and big government (Bennie 1998).[3]

---

[2]Worcester (1997: 161), however, argues that British level green issues – urban smog, the loss of Green Belt areas – became *increasingly* important.

[3]However, if anything, the Brent Spar episode probably increased public confusion over environmental issues, as Worcester's (1997) data revealed.

Despite the publicity surrounding some environmental issues, and improving economic conditions by 1997,[4] the Scottish Green Party and its sister party South of the border were electorally insignificant during this period, leading observers to refer to the 1989 election result as a 'transient success' (Carter 1997: 157). This was a very difficult time for the Green parties across Britain, but in Scotland in particular membership levels were very low and in some areas the party ceased to exist, with no branch activity whatsoever. However, by the 1997 General Election Labour was promising major constitutional reform, including devolution to Scotland and a review of electoral systems across Britain. The prospect of a Scottish Parliament and of PR provided some impetus for the Greens.

Overall, the political context in 1997 was very different from that of 1990. Public concern for the environment did not appear as intense as the period during and following the 1989 European Elections. However, green issues did not disappear from the public consciousness entirely, nor from the political agenda. The mainstream parties took on board environmental issues to a greater extent than ever before. So much so that Carter (1997: 159) suggests Labour actually 'downplayed' their environmental policies in the 1997 General Election. While the main parties were often criticised for a lack of radicalism in their environmental policies, or for not publicising their policies, they continued to 'green' their policies in a way that could not have been predicted ten years previously (see Robinson 1992).

### The 1997 Telephone Interviews

The interviews were conducted by telephone between April and July 1997. The 1990 questionnaire had asked respondents to give their telephone number if they were willing to discuss some of the points raised in the questionnaire, on an anonymous basis, and of the 509 respondents, 304 (60 per cent) provided a telephone number where they could be contacted. Seven years later, 136 of these numbers were unobtainable (no longer existed). The remaining 168 numbers were called up to four times. 64 of these had moved and were unreachable and another 43 did not reply or were unwilling to be interviewed. In total, therefore, 61 respondents participated in a telephone interview lasting between 10 and 30 minutes.

The fact that so many years separate the original questionnaire and the telephone interviews means that the more mobile 1990 members are inevitably under-represented in the results of the interviews. For example, those respondents who could not be contacted were younger and more likely to have been students in 1990. Table 7.1 compares some of the 1990 social characteristics of the interviewees with those of the entire sample. It is quite clear that the respondents

---

[4]While the whole of Britain experienced economic slump conditions at the beginning of the 1990s, and while the Scottish economy consistently performed less well than areas in the South of England, the trend in 1997 was towards stability (Peat and Boyle 1999).

available for interview in 1997 were much more likely to be male than the whole sample of respondents in 1990; they were considerably older; they were more likely to own their own home; and a smaller proportion classified themselves as single. They were also a little more likely to have a professional occupation, and less likely to be in full-time education. In other words, the telephone interviewees were the most 'stable' of the 1990 respondents. Another question confirms their lack of mobility. When asked in 1990 how often they had moved house 'during the last five years over a distance of more than ten miles', 85 per cent of the interview sample indicated that they had not moved at all, but only 52.5 per cent of the entire sample indicated that they had not been mobile.

**Table 7.1  Social Characteristics Recorded 1990 (%)**

|  | 1997 interviewees | Entire 1990 sample |
|---|---|---|
| Female | 40 | 45 |
| Male | 60 | 55 |
| Age 16-44 | 53 | 75 |
| 45-64 | 34 | 19 |
| 65 and over | 13 | 6 |
| Own house/ mortgage | 77 | 62 |
| Single | 21 | 33 |
| Married/partner etc. | 79 | 67 |
| In full time work | 46 | 51 |
| Professional occupation | 6 | 53 |
| In full-time education | 8 | 11 |
| Studied/ studying for a degree | 77 | 81 |
| N | 61 | 509 |

The difference in characteristics of the interviewees raises some questions about the representativeness of the interview data, in that they appear to be rather atypical members.  However, in other important respects they were not very different.  For example, they were no more or less likely to be active in the party: 39.3 per cent of the interviewees had indicated in 1990 that they were fairly, very or extremely active in the party, compared to 39.9 per cent of the entire sample. Their experience of environmental group membership was also very similar e.g. 49.2 per cent of the interviewees had belonged to Greenpeace, 50.7 per cent of the whole sample.  Furthermore, the group of 61 people interviewed in 1997 were no more likely to be considering leaving the party in 1990 (Table 7.2). Nor did the group of interviewees look at all distinctive in the reasons they gave for joining, or in their attitudes to internal party matters, for example the distribution of power in the party. It appears that the design of the follow-up telephone interviews inevitably resulted in an 'older' sample of members but in terms of their behaviour in the party and basic attitudes, this small group of interviewees actually appear quite typical of all those surveyed in 1990.

**Table 7.2  Intention to Renew, 1990 (%)**

|                  | 1997 interviewees | Entire 1990 sample |
|------------------|:-----------------:|:------------------:|
| Yes, definitely  | 64                | 63                 |
| Yes, probably    | 23                | 25                 |
| Probably not     | 8                 | 7                  |
| Definitely not   | 0                 | 1                  |
| Have already left | 5                | 4                  |
| N                | 61                | 487                |

The interviews followed an informal structure and asked the respondents questions relating to when and why they became members of the Scottish Green Party, why some had left the party, and whether they were currently involved in the environmental movement. The interviews also attempted to investigate perceptions of the impact of the party and how this compared with the perceived effectiveness of environmental pressure groups. Finally, those respondents who had left the party were asked if they would envisage any circumstances in which they would consider rejoining the Greens, and if they had joined another political party. This qualitative exercise had a number of specific objectives:

*1. To establish the interviewees' current membership status.* How many were still members of the Scottish Green Party?

*2. To further assess motivations behind membership.* In 1997 what reasons did respondents give for having joined the party? Did these reasons differ from those given in 1990?

*3. To develop an understanding of leaving.* If respondents were no longer members, why did they leave? For example did leavers move to other parties? Were lapsed members potentially 'remobilisable'?

*4. To explore the relationship between party membership and membership of environmental pressure groups.* Were respondents members of green pressure groups in 1997?  Did they think that pressure groups were more effective than the party in their attempts to protect the environment?

*1997 Membership Status*

The 1997 interviewees were asked to indicate if they still belonged to the party, and if they were members of any other groups.  There were a number of possibilities:

a)  Respondents had remained members.
b)  Respondents had allowed their membership to lapse, but rejoined.
c)  Respondents had given up membership of the Greens and all forms of involvement in the environmental movement.
d)  Respondents had given up membership of the party but remained involved in the environmental movement through membership of green pressure groups.
e)  Respondents had given up membership of the Greens to join another party.

Of the 61 respondents interviewed 27 (44 per cent) were still members of the party.  None of these respondents indicated that they had allowed their membership to lapse and subsequently rejoined.  In other words, they had continuously been members since the 1990 survey. 'Leavers' (N=34) constituted 56 per cent of the sample: 16 respondents (26 per cent) had given up membership of the party and all other forms of involvement in the green movement, while 18 respondents (30 per cent) were no longer members of the party but still involved with environmental pressure groups.  In other words, just over half of the leavers were members of groups.  A total of 7 of the leavers (one in five) indicated that they had gone on to join another party.[5]

Overall, more than four in every ten of the telephone interviewees had remained as members since 1990 (see Figure 7.1). Given the membership attrition rate of the Scottish Green Party at the beginning of the 1990s (declined from 1,200 members in 1990 to 225 in 1993), the proportion of members in the interview sample appears very high.  This may be partly explained by the relative social stability of these individuals, in that mobile members are always the most likely to leave.

---

[5]Three had joined the SNP, two Labour, one the Liberal Democrats (and one n/a).

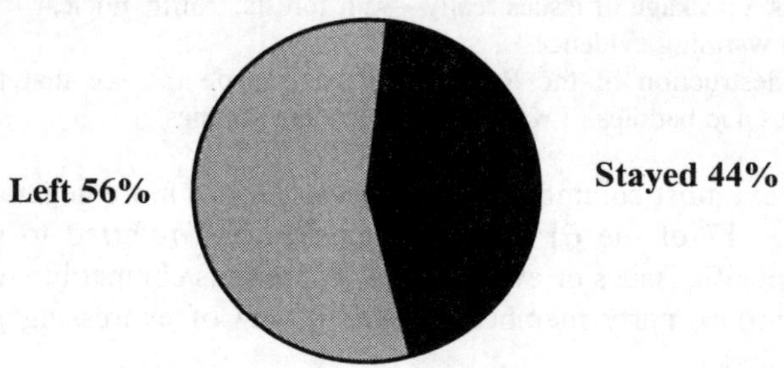


**Figure 7.1  Leavers and Stayers**

## Motivations Behind Membership

One of the central objectives of the telephone interviews in 1997 was to gain an insight into reasons for joining some years after the original joining decision, and irrespective of whether or not the respondents had left the party.  They were asked to think back to when they had first joined the party and recall exactly why they had joined at that time.  A number of different motivations were evident in the responses.  Indeed, respondents often referred to different, yet overlapping, types of motivations, making it very difficult to categorise or quantify the responses.  Nevertheless, some central themes were clear.  In all, there were four main categories of response: concern about a specific environmental problem; a 'general' concern for the environment; commitment to a green philosophy; and a desire to send a message to the main political parties.

The most common type of explanation for having joined the party was reference to a *specific* environmental problem, event or green policy.  Nuclear disarmament, the threats from nuclear power, problems of pollution, global warming, and events such as Chernobyl, Bhopal, and the sinking of the Rainbow Warrior were mentioned frequently.  These issues were generally not experienced first hand.  Rather, the respondents indicated that they had come to learn about these issues through widespread media reports, and they believed that the party had the right policies to deal with these problems.  In total, just over one third of those interviewed pointed to particular issues, policies or events.  Examples include the following extracts from the telephone interviews:

> 'Chernobyl was the final straw for me.'
> 'Environmental problems were becoming more obvious to me, such as pollution and nuclear problems. Nuclear issues were paramount however.'
> 'It was a package of issues really – rain forests, traffic, nuclear issues. And global warming evidence.'
> 'The destruction of the Rainbow Warrior made me see that there were goodies and baddies. I wanted to support the goodies.'

The next most common type of response was a more general concern for the environment. 17 of the 61 telephone interviewees referred to general concern, rather than specific issues or events. This response is compatible with the idea that, for a large group, party membership was a way of expressing general concern. Examples included:

> 'It was a general concern for the environment. Not a particular issue.'
> 'I simply wanted to provide support.'
> 'The environment in general and common sense.'
> 'I hadn't been a member of any party but I felt I should commit myself. It was due to a broad spectrum of issues. It was a general statement'.

The third set of reasons given for joining involved a strong belief in party principles and ideas – the need to promote an ecological society based on green ideals. A total of 13 mentioned the importance of green ideas and philosophy, a number of whom referred to the influence of green writers such as Jonathan Porritt and David Icke.

> 'I read a book – by Jonathan Porritt – and agreed with the community based ideas.'
> 'David Icke. Reading and thinking.'
> 'The green philosophy was tied in with my own thoughts.'
> 'The idealist approach of the Greens. Ideals, not power, are important to the party. Equality. Peace. These things appealed.'
> 'Green principles.'

The other major theme to emerge was 'the need to put pressure on the other parties'. A dozen of the respondents pointed to their dissatisfaction with the policies of the main political parties. Respondents recognised that the party was not about to form a government, but that they could have an influence through pressuring the established parties, not unlike the role performed by pressure groups. Many expressed concern about the other parties' lack of environmental policies:

> 'I was horrified by the non-green policies of the other parties.'
> 'I was very unhappy with the conventional parties, particularly on the question of redistribution/poverty.'
> 'I joined to put pressure on the other parties. I saw this as the party's role.'
> 'To put pressure on the process of government. Pressure groups are not enough.'

'I saw my membership of the party as a logical extension of my pressure group activity – FoE and Greenpeace.'

These four categories of reasons for joining dominated the responses. Only a small number of other reasons for joining were given, including two respondents who had been motivated to join by an occupational experience. They stated: 'I used to teach about pollution/lead. Once retired from teaching, I threw myself into activity'; 'Through my job in scientific research, I came across evidence of ice-cap melting, and the threat this posed to the polar bear. Faced with the evidence I experienced a sudden awakening'. Another three respondents referred to their experiences as parents or grandparents. Examples included: 'My children were at school and I had a baby. It really seemed to matter'; 'To improve the environment for my grandchildren'. One interviewee referred to the German Greens as a source of inspiration: 'I was enthusiastic about the German Greens'.

The 1989 European Elections were mentioned, but by very few of the respondents. Only five respondents in total indicated that the Elections, or the publicity surrounding the Greens at that time, had an influence on their decision to join. One respondent gave the simple answer 'Euros 1989', and another referred to a 'blaze of idealistic naiveté' experienced in 1989. Overall, the events surrounding the 1989 Euros were not identified as having a great influence on the respondents' decisions to join.

Overall, the responses in most cases indicated a mix of motivations behind Scottish Green Party membership. While four central themes were evident, the themes overlap. Indeed, a number of respondents described a combination of many different factors at work. The following examples sum up the complex and multi-dimensional nature of joining:

'I believed in a green society. Organic food production worried me. I had a history of concern for the environment, and joining the party was another way of expressing that concern.'

'It was a combination of lots of different things: Increasing media coverage of global warming problems, and I was fed up with the other parties. These things combined with having a baby.'

These findings, although based on very different research techniques from those reported in chapter 5, are very similar in their conclusions. The responses suggest that the Scottish Greens had joined the party in response to collective, purposive incentives. In short, these people were concerned about the environment, and in particular global environmental problems. The media's reporting of global events and issues is also an important consideration. As with the questionnaire responses, there is little evidence of selective incentives in the shape of solidary rewards, or the desire to be active in the party organisation. Nor do the responses suggest that personal experience of local environmental problems or persuasion by the party were very significant factors in the joining decision.

*Recollection and Reconstruction of Reasons for Joining*

It was possible that, between 1990 and 1997, the respondents had modified their reasons for joining the party, having been influenced by events and experiences during the interim period. The work of C.W. Right Mills (1940: 904) illustrated how vocabularies of motive may be socially constructed. More importantly, reasons for joining (the creation of motive) may be created after membership initiation. Snow *et al.* (1980: 795) describe a form of social reconstruction which often takes place after participants join. They illustrate that participants may be provided with justifications for joining and for remaining members during interaction with the movement organisation. Similarly, Tarrow (1992: 196) refers to the 'construction of meaning in social movements', and Klandermans (1992: 78) refers to the 'social construction of protest'. The key argument is that meaning can be constructed through the interaction of individuals, and it is likely to take place before and *during* collective action. Furthermore, Gamson (1992: 72) suggests that perceptions are constantly revised in the light of different 'encounters', such as encounters with authorities, or with the mass-media. So the very experience of collective involvement shapes and influences individual perceptions, and because the construction of meaning is an ongoing process the rationale for participation may change over time.[6]

The 61 telephone respondents in 1997 were asked to talk about the reasons why they originally became involved as Scottish Green members. The intention was to compare the 1997 responses with those given in the 1990 questionnaires. If the respondents had been influenced by events since 1990, if they were being shaped by contemporary discourse and events, one might have expected a set of more optimistic reasons in 1990, and a stronger sense of disillusionment by 1997. Did the passage of time and events between 1990 and 1997 in any way change their assessment of their own behaviour?

The information gathered in 1990 is of course not directly comparable with the telephone interviews, because of the very different methodological approaches employed. However, in many cases the respondents in 1990 had provided a written explanation for joining, in addition to answering the closed questions i.e. they were given the opportunity to express in their own words why they joined. A comparison of these cases revealed many common, often identical, themes to those offered in 1997. Indeed the similarity of the responses was striking. Many of the respondents identified specific issues – the same issues – in 1990 and in 1997.

A very small number of the telephone interviewees offered a different explanation for joining the party in 1997. These tended to be lapsers who had joined at the end of the 1980s and who now recognised, with the benefit of

---

[6]The precise meaning of social constructionism is widely debated by sociologists. A 'realist' school of thought has criticised these approaches for denying the reality of environmental problems (Burningham and Cooper 1999: 306). For an example of the study of social constructionism in the context of conflict over local planning decisions and the environment see Burningham (1996) and Burningham (1998).

hindsight, that they joined because of the publicity surrounding the Greens and 'partly through curiosity'. The explanations provided by these respondents therefore tend to be different from the ones given in 1990 which were based to a greater extent on 'personal convictions' and general environmental concern. However, it is important to note that less than five of the interview respondents indicated such a change of heart. The vast majority of those talked to in 1997, whether lapsers or members, provided explanations which were in line with their original responses.

Overall, there is very little evidence of a reconstruction of perceptions/reconstruction of reasons for joining over the seven year period. The answers given appear perfectly consistent with those offered in 1990. Furthermore, those people who stayed with the party and those who allowed their membership to lapse did not differ in this respect.

**Reasons for Leaving the Scottish Greens**

*The 1990 Survey Responses*

To develop an understanding of leaving the Scottish Greens we begin by looking back to those members who expressed some doubt about renewing their membership in 1990. In the 1990 survey, respondents were asked if they would renew their party membership when it next became due. Sixty three per cent of the respondents said they would definitely continue their membership (Table 7.2). The questionnaire in 1990 then attempted to explore some of the reasons the party members might be uncertain about renewing their membership. After all, more than one third of the respondents were not completely certain that they would remain as members. The 1990 questionnaire contained two questions on reasons for leaving. One was an open question which gave the respondents the opportunity to express, in their own words, why they had some doubts about renewing their membership. The other question consisted of a battery of items containing reasons for leaving the party. The respondents were asked to indicate how important they were in their own case.

The open question asked 'If you are uncertain whether you will resubscribe, what is the most important reason why you are considering leaving? If you have already left the party what is the most important reason you decided to leave? (N=141). A number of factors appeared completely irrelevant in the written responses. None of the 141 respondents referred to friends leaving the party. Not one of these members suggested that the party was not sufficiently democratic, that ordinary members were not given the opportunity to participate, or that party leaders or spokespersons had too much power. Nor did anyone suggest that they found activities too boring, although some did claim that they 'were not political animals'.

Four themes emerge from the members' 1990 accounts of why they may have been considering leaving: 1) personal circumstances 2) a perception that the party was ineffective 3) disagreement over party objectives or strategy and 4) negative experience of party life, including a poor impression given by other members, activists, or the party organisation. The most common explanation for considering leaving to emerge from the open-ended question in 1990 was the *inability to be active due to personal circumstances.* One third of the 141 respondents (47 in total) pointed to personal factors. Many of these members said that personal circumstances prevented them from offering active support. Indeed many referred to feelings of guilt because they were unable to be active. Rather than stay in the party and be a passive member they thought they should leave. In some cases, the respondents indicated that the local parties had exerted too much pressure on them to be active. Some indicated a *desire* to be non-active, claiming that they were not very political. It is clear that many of these members preferred to be passive or could not be active due to job and family pressures, but the critical point is that they did not feel comfortable in the party as passive members. Examples are noted below:

> 'I was not an active member of the party and felt that it was hypocritical to be a free loader.'
>
> 'I am self employed and our local group was demanding too much of my time at a critical period in our business. Therefore I did not even open up their literature.'
>
> 'I am very much a subscription only member. Due to other causes that I'm actively involved in I am unable to give my time to active party membership. I feel rather guilty about this.'
>
> 'Mainly because I am not very politically minded. I also have a very busy life and never have time to read all the piles of paper that are lying around the kitchen.'
>
> 'I am part of the green movement but do not wish to be active in the Green Party. There should be active and dormant membership of the party. I wish to support it but be a dormant member, focusing my activities elsewhere. Dormant membership is valid (!) and should be encouraged.'

The next most important explanation for considering leaving offered by the members in 1990 was the *perceived ineffectiveness of the party* (38 members gave this type of explanation). Some of these responses suggested that environmental problems were so severe that they could not be solved. However, most of these members argued that the party itself was not effective, and that environmental pressure groups were more likely to successfully confront environmental problems. In many respects, these members appeared to be recognising that the political context did not favour a small green party and, given the circumstances, it would be more effective to support environmental pressure groups.

> 'Regrettably, having studied environmental issues at University, my perception that the environmental issue cannot be solved has been strengthened. Therefore, although there are many individuals in the Green Party and other green organisations whose intentions are good, their ability

to change the attitudes of the world's population is very limited and time is against us.'

'The party requires a minimum amount of media attention for its policies and philosophy to be effectively espoused. If such media coverage is not forthcoming and the party becomes, as a consequence, ineffective, then I may consider supporting another organization.'

'There is little chance that the Green Party will attain substantial representation in Parliament – unless the voting system is changed. Subsequently their ability to influence is limited.'

'I will probably leave because the party seems to be achieving little. I think my time and money would be more worthwhile spent on non-political organisations such as RSPB, Greenpeace, FoE.'

Just over 30 of the members raised *doubts about party policy, aims or strategy*. In these cases, the members appeared to have some fundamental disagreements with what the party stood for. Often, party or group membership involves a process of gradual learning about detailed policies. As Rothenberg (1988) argues, the new member is unlikely to be very knowledgeable about the fine details of organisational goals. Furthermore, Rothenberg (1988: 1144) argues that 'members go from general to specific reasons for staying or leaving as they become more knowledgeable'. The following examples do suggest that these members were not fully aware of party positions before they joined. Other comments suggest that some members were unhappy about short-term party strategy, rather than fundamental policies. Two criticisms which stand out are the party's decision to withdraw from the Scottish Constitutional Convention, and signs of co-operation with the SNP.

'I cannot understand why, to save the world, one must be a very left-wing socialist. Surely it will take all types.'

'I think the party is too middle class and has little to say on issues of social justice e.g. the poll tax. It seems to reflect a class viewpoint which I find alienating. The party as a consequence has little to say to the poor except to offer vague platitudes.'

'Failure of the party to address the most important issue – population. Although an encouraging start was made the issue has been increasingly put to one side over the years.'

'Recent collaboration with the SNP.'

'I am unhappy about the party leaving the Scottish Constitutional Convention.'

Finally, and perhaps most worryingly for the party, 36 of the members who provided a written explanation of why they were considering leaving the Scottish Greens in 1990, referred to their rather *negative perceptions and experiences of other party members and activists*, or to inefficiency in the party. In some cases the members were referring to personal encounters with other members, in other cases they were clearly describing the negative image of the party projected by the media.  The following quotes illustrate the poor image of the party in the eyes of these members:

> 'Living in a rural area, the party (consisting mainly of incomers) is regarded as a bunch of well-intentioned do-gooders who do not really understand issues.'
> 'In my opinion many people active in the Green Party are naive, and present a nice but ineffectual hippy image.'
> 'I am acutely aware of the ridiculous public image that is suffered by the Green Party, who seem to have blown their image once again.  After the Euro Elections they seemed to be a potential fighting force.  Now they need a very good organiser and P.R. worker.'
> 'Some members have no conception of reality and I am inclined to wonder what sort of mushrooms they have for breakfast.'
> 'The party seems so bent on internal democracy that energy which should be used addressing the outside world is wasted on internal bickering.'
> 'A general lack of professionalism in the way the party conducts its affairs e.g. they have not sent me a renewal form.'

Table 7.3 documents the results of the 'closed' question on leaving.[7]  The large N indicates that a number of the respondents who indicated they would definitely be staying with the party also answered this question.  This can be interpreted in two ways. Either there was a rather deep, underlying uncertainty about party membership, even amongst those who thought they would rejoin, or the respondents were simply confused by the question.  Nevertheless, the results reveal some interesting attitudes.

Some of the reasons presented for leaving a political party were clearly not very relevant to the members in this study.  The least relevant reason of all appears to be that of friends leaving the party: only 3 per cent said this was at all important.  This suggests that, while friendship links were a relatively unimportant mechanism through which party members joined, they were even less important in determining whether members stayed or left.  Nor were members at all concerned by 'attention given to national spokespersons'.  The 'boring' nature of party activities, and an inability to 'get support for ideas' were a little more significant in the leaving decision, but still not very important, probably because most of the members were rather inactive and therefore these options did not apply.  Similarly, while over a third of the respondents to this question indicated that they had doubts about their membership because 'ordinary members have no role to play', the majority of respondents – 62 per cent – did not see this as important.  Furthermore, there is little sign of members transferring their membership support to another political party in Scotland.  Of those who were uncertain about their membership, the vast majority – 91.8 per cent – were not considering joining another party.

---

[7]The precise question read: 'Here are a number of reasons why people might consider leaving a party.  Please indicate below the importance of each reason for yourself.'

**Table 7.3  Reasons for Leaving 1990 (%)**

| | Decisive | Very important but not decisive | Important | Not very important | Played no role whatsoever |
|---|---|---|---|---|---|
| I have come to disagree with the party's fundamental aims. | 43 | 5 | 7 | 8 | 37 |
| Most of my friends have left. | 0 | 0 | 3 | 13 | 84 |
| I was not able to get support for my ideas. | 4 | 5 | 20 | 22 | 49 |
| I still agree with the party's aims but there are more effective ways of achieving them. | 21 | 18 | 28 | 11 | 22 |
| Party activities are too boring. | 4 | 8 | 20 | 27 | 4 |
| Ordinary members have no part to play. | 7 | 12 | 19 | 17 | 45 |
| Change in personal circumstances and/or new job duties leave no spare time for political activity. | 12 | 16 | 22 | 16 | 34 |
| I dislike the excessive attention given to national spokespersons. | 2 | 3 | 5 | 26 | 63 |
| I disagree with an important change in party policy. | 15 | 10 | 11 | 9 | 55 |

(Average N 329)

Which factors did appear to explain uncertainty over Scottish Green Party membership in 1990?  A quarter of the respondents to this question indicated that their disagreement with an important change in party policy was either decisive or very important in explaining their uncertainty, although most of the members indicated that this was not important.  Exactly 50 per cent of respondents suggested that personal factors, rather than the party itself, were responsible for their uncertainty.   However, two reasons for leaving stand out.   The first is the importance of 'fundamental aims': 43 per cent claimed that their disagreement with the party's fundamental aims was a *decisive* factor in why they were considering leaving (55 per cent in total said this was important to decisive).  It is very possible that when these members joined they were not fully aware of the party's aims (see Rothenberg 1988: 1144).

However, the statement that appeared most important in the decision to leave was 'I still agree with the party's aims but there are more effective ways of achieving them': 67 per cent of the respondents said this was an important consideration (39 per cent indicated this was decisive or very important).  These results are in some ways rather contradictory.  While most of those Scottish Greens who were considering leaving in 1990 suggested that they still sympathised with party objectives, they had become somewhat disillusioned about the party's ability to achieve these objectives.  However, a notably large group of members at this time pointed to a fundamental disagreement with party aims or policy.

In 1990 the key theme to emerge from the data on leaving was lack of party effectiveness.  The perception of many members in 1990 was that the party was a rather ineffective organisation, partly due to internal party problems, but also because of the unfavourable political circumstances of the time.  The party appeared to be having difficulty convincing its members that it was making an impact.

One possibility is that the party was not communicating effectively with its members.  Most members did not attend party meetings so the only form of contact was party mailings.  Unfortunately for the party, leavers often had a negative view of party publications.  Furthermore, a number of the members had no contact whatsoever with the party.  It is worth noting that the people who intended staying in the party were those most likely to have had direct contact with the party. If we examine the relationship between how the members joined and likelihood of renewing, we find that in 1990, 74 per cent who joined at a local meeting said they would definitely renew, but only 54 per cent who joined after responding to a party advertisement in the press.  Moreover, only 51.6 per cent of members in 1990 who had no local party branch in their area indicated that they would definitely renew their membership, compared to 62.9 per cent of members with a local branch (see Table 7.4).

Greater attempts by the party to maintain contact with its members may have prevented the severe haemorrhaging of members. However, this is not the whole story.  As the open and closed questions indicated, a fairly large proportion of members with doubts about renewing their membership in 1990 claimed to have a fundamental disagreement with party aims or policy.  To explore these contradictions further a multiple regression analysis of leaving the Scottish Greens was conducted in an attempt to identify the relative importance of different variables (Table 7.5).

**Table 7.4  Contact with Party by Intention to Renew (%)[8]**

| | Definitely renew | Probably | Probably not | Definitely not/left |
|---|---|---|---|---|
| No local branch in area | 51.6 | 30.6 | 8.1 | 6.5 |
| No contact with local party | 42.4 | 35.6 | 8.5 | 10.2 |
| Receive local newsletter only | 49.4 | 31.0 | 8.6 | 8.6 |
| Occasionally go to local meetings | 62.8 | 24.1 | 8.0 | 1.5 |
| Regularly attend local meetings | 81.7 | 12.5 | 2.5 | 1.7 |
| Help organise local campaigns | 78.0 | 14.3 | 4.4 | 1.1 |
| Speak in public for local party | 82.0 | 12.0 | 2.0 | 2.0 |
| Convene/ chair local meetings | 82.4 | 11.8 | 2.0 | 2.9 |

**Table 7.5  Regression Analysis of Leaving the Scottish Green Party**

| Independent variables | Regression coefficient with leaving (Beta) |
|---|---|
| Party does not provide the best opportunity to achieve the political aims I support | 0.211* |
| Did not attend an area party meeting in the last year | 0.158* |
| Party should not elect one leader | -0.142 |
| Party's success in 1989 was not just a 'flash in the pan' | -0.194* |
| Member of Friends of the Earth | 0.171* |
| Green Party publications boring | 0.136 |

R2 = 0.24
N = 498                    * Significant at the 0.01 level

---

[8]Figures do not add up to 100% because the table does not include missing values.

The analysis confirms the negative view of party publications amongst members who were considering leaving the party in 1990. It also confirms analysis conducted on the UK Greens (Rüdig *et al.* 1993: 68) which showed that leavers were more likely to support a traditional party structure e.g. more likely to support the election of one party leader. However, other factors are more significant. Lack of activity (not attending an area party meeting) increased the chances of leaving in 1990,[9] as did membership of Friends of the Earth.[10] But the two most important influences were agreement with the statement 'the Green Party's success in 1989 was just a flash in the pan' and *not* joining the party because it offered the best opportunity to achieve political aims. These findings indicate that the Scottish Greens who were considering leaving in 1990 did not view joining the party as a way of pursuing their political aims when they joined; this could either mean that they did not have strong political objectives, or it may mean that they saw other forms of activity, like membership of groups, as more effective. Certainly, they were of the opinion that the party had experienced a short-term period of success that was unlikely to be repeated.[11]

Year of joining was also an important independent predictor of leaving in 1990. Those people who joined the party at the height of the green wave in 1989/1990 were definitely the least likely to have maintained their party membership. The explanation for this is less straightforward. It might be an indication that this group had unrealistic expectations of the party when they joined and were therefore more disappointed. However, this might also be the natural path of membership described by Rothenberg (1988). As has already been argued, new members are always the most likely to leave. The evidence presented in chapter 6 suggests that a combination of the two dynamics was at work.

*Reasons for Leaving: the 1997 Interview Responses*

We turn now to the responses of 1997. The telephone interviews in 1997 also explored reasons for leaving. The 1997 interviewees were asked if they were still members of the party and, if not, why they had decided to leave.[12] A number of

---

[9]Party meetings were also more likely to be viewed negatively by leavers; they are seen as rather boring and badly run.

[10]Overall, however, being a member of an environmental group made the party member *more* likely to renew membership than those who did not belong to a group: 64% of party members who also belonged to a group said they would definitely renew, compared to 57% of members who did not belong to a group.

[11]Previous analysis of the English, Welsh and Northern Irish Greens highlighted a link between demoralisation, lack of leadership and greater effectiveness of supporting groups in the leaving decision (Rüdig *et al.* 1993: 46-47).

[12]The interview data confirm the greater tendency of 1989/1990 joiners to have left the party. When we examined the membership status of 1990 'new members' in 1997 we find that they were noticeably more likely to be lapsed members. Conversely, the long-term members were the most likely to have remained as members: 68% (15 out of 22) of the newcomers had left; only 47% (17 out of 36) of the long-standing members.

pivotal themes emerge, namely factors which involve internal dynamics of the party – party policy and the behaviour of the party members and organisation – as well as external factors which explain the ineffectiveness of the party. The 34 interviewees who had allowed their membership to lapse (56 per cent of the 1997 interview respondents) were asked to explain why they had come to leave the party. Some of the interviewees (N=9) pointed to a combination of different factors, highlighting the complexity of decision-making. However, a number of clear themes emerged. In ascending order of importance, these were personal circumstances; the general lack of progress and difficulties faced by the party in the Scottish/British political system (external factors); and internal party factors (policies, organisation and party members or activists).

A very small number – five of those interviewed – pointed to changing personal circumstances as a reason for leaving. For example, 'I just fell away due to personal circumstances – I was too busy running a business. I never had time to become active and just drifted away'. There will always be a natural wastage of members and it is inevitable that some people will leave a party or group for this type of reason. There is probably very little the party could have done to prevent these people leaving.

A larger group of the lapsers pointed to a 'general disappointment after 1989'. There was a perception that the party had achieved all it could under the circumstances and that it was 'no longer making any progress'. Implicit in these comments was a recognition that the party was functioning in very unfavourable circumstances; the electoral system in particular was seen as unfair and unrepresentative. Many of these people had come to the conclusion that the party was 'facing an uphill struggle' and that pressure groups were a more effective way forward. The factors highlighted by these explanations for leaving were largely outwith the control of the party itself (see examples below). Again, it could be argued that there was very little the party could have done to prevent the kind of disappointment that results from unfavourable political structures. However, less than one third of the lapsers (only nine respondents) offered this type of explanation for lapsing.

> 'The political arena is no use. I have become completely disillusioned with politics – nothing is ever likely to be achieved.'
> 'The party is not going anywhere. Pressure groups are more effective.'
> 'The Green Party would be more effective as a pressure group.'
> 'It was general disappointment after 1989 – the falling away of support at the next General Election. I was disappointed the party couldn't keep up momentum. Nothing happened.'
> 'I was disillusioned. Change in the other parties was some kind of progress, but it was hopeless without PR. The party was fighting a losing battle.'

The more frequent themes related to internal party dynamics – policies, organisation and party members or activists. A total of eight interviewees said they had left the party because they disagreed with party policy. Most of these were concerned about policies that were either too radical or 'wacky', or policies that were not 'left-wing' enough. Two respondents pointed out that Green policies had been subsumed by the debate within the party on Scotland's constitutional future. Examples include;

> 'As an ex-communist, the issues of redistribution and the eradication of poverty were my primary concern. Once I joined the party I felt that it was too right wing on these issues. I felt that the party was only concerned about middle class, prosperous areas and it concentrated its activities there.'
> 'The party concentrated on silly issues and obscure policies e.g. legalisation of cannabis.'
> 'In Scotland, like the SNP, nationalism issues dominated. Green issues were smothered by debate about Scotland's constitutional future. Fed up with fact that party activists obsessed by Scottish nationalism. Lost sight of green issues.'

Another 'internal' party aspect which resulted in respondents leaving the party was the lack of formal party structure or organisation. Nine of the lapsers interviewed suggested they had left the Scottish Greens because of poor party organisation. Some pointed to difficulties of local parties working together, but the more common observation was that the party had failed to send out membership reminders, or a local branch had dissolved. This suggests that, for some of these respondents, leaving the party did not involve a conscious decision to leave. Rather, they 'drifted away' because the party itself ceased contact. The following examples illustrate the point:

> 'I left because the party paid no interest in me. The party fell away.'
> 'There was a lack of local level organisation, and I became disenchanted with the local party experience.'
> 'The local party folded.'

However, the most common explanation offered for leaving the Greens in the 1990s was experience of other party members. Over a third of the lapsers (12 in total) said they had left the party because of negative experiences with party members and activists. A number referred to the 'people in the party' who 'got themselves in a mess'. 'Squabbles', 'bickering', and 'rivalry' were said to be characteristic of relations within the party. These respondents often alluded to the image problem of the party. The examples below reveal the very negative and critical nature of these comments.

> 'It wasn't the ideology or policies. The members of the party were over-concerned with minutiae. There was too much worthiness. I was busy and my experience of the party was rather negative. I wanted to deal with issues, not personalities and internal politics. I had to deal with this every day at work and didn't want to have to deal with it at party meetings.'
> 'They seemed to me to be a bunch of nutters and head-bangers. The image was perhaps media inspired but they seemed ineffective nevertheless.'

'I was not impressed with the internal politics of party. Party members/
activists were too extreme. They had an unrealistic view and weren't
prepared to compromise.'
'It wasn't a particular issue. I left because of my experience in the party.
There were incestuous, localised cliques and an intellectual hierarchy. They
were too consumed by local issues and were rather uninviting.'
'David Icke. I was concerned about the negative image and types of people
in the party. Image one of twee, bohemian types.'
'I was completely disillusioned with the people in the party. They were zany
and obsessed with unimportant and irrelevant issues like the legalisation of
cannabis. I was irritated by squabbles and an inability to execute policies.'

The experience of party membership was clearly not a happy one for many
of these former Scottish Greens. Lapsed members' perceptions are very negative
indeed, although they are probably related to the media's representation of the
Greens, not only personal experience. Nevertheless, these findings should concern
the party. Of the 34 lapsers interviewed, 29 pointed to internal reasons for leaving
(policy, organisation, members), although these were often combined with external
factors. Two thirds (21 out of 34) specified poor party organisation or problems
with Green members or activists. Ineffective party organisation was one problem
that could be rectified but the rather severe image problem was more difficult to
resolve.

In effect many of these members had become aware of the costs of
membership, other than the cost of subscription. In the Scottish Greens they may
have included perceived career costs, family pressures, the difficulties of dealing
with other members, a perceived pressure to be active, feelings of guilt if unable or
unwilling to be active. Rothenberg (1988: 1135) examines the decision to retain
membership, and he argues that the costs of membership only become obvious
when one becomes a member. In other words the member learns about the costs of
participation.[13] In the case of Common Cause, the group's lack of financial
resources meant that members were regarded as an important resource. Members
were solicited for more financial support, and were asked to become politically
active; they were encouraged to 'immerse themselves' (Rothenberg 1988: 1135). A
similar process may have been at work in the Scottish Greens. The party certainly
needed support from members and the members were encouraged to contribute
financially and in other ways. Rothenberg (1988: 1136) argues that high levels of
interaction can help keep contributors in an organisation, but that it may also
frighten naturally passive members away. However, in the case of the Scottish
Greens, the party organisation probably was not active enough; a number of the
members simply drifted away. However, a more deep-rooted problem for the party
in 1997 was its poor image. As some of the interviewees recognised, the media
probably played a role in this. The image was of a small clique of radical party
activists who were rather ineffectual and irrelevant in the political context of the

---

[13]In Bond's (1999) study of Edinburgh Labour party members, respondents were asked what
they 'got out' of membership: 19% replied 'nothing/not very much'.

1990s.  Furthermore, the party's image problem appeared even more acute in the 1997 interview responses than in the 1990 survey.

## Membership of Environmental Groups

One of the key themes to emerge from the data on leaving is the far-reaching perception of party ineffectiveness.  Success is clearly a very potent mobilising agent and continued membership is dependent on the feeling that membership subscriptions are 'well spent' or 'value for money'.  In the 1990s, environmental pressure groups seemed to offer this value for money, the Greenpeace Brent Spar campaign providing a high profile example of how pressure groups can influence policy.

The 1997 interviews explored the relationship between membership of the Greens and membership of environmental pressure groups.  To what extent were Scottish Green Party members committed to environmental pressure groups?  Did members view their party involvement as some kind of extension of pressure group support?  Furthermore, were those people who left the party between 1990 and 1997 more or less likely to be supporters of environmental pressure groups?  Did the leavers transfer their support to pressure groups, or did they reject environmental politics entirely?

In 1997, the interviewees were asked a number of questions about their experiences within the environmental movement.  They were asked if they had been members of an environmental pressure group before they joined the Scottish Greens, whether they had joined up with the party and environmental pressure group(s) at the same time, and whether they were members of a group at the time of the interview.  They were also asked about their perceptions of party and pressure group impact, in an attempt to assess their views of how effective the party had been in relation to environmental pressure groups.

Just over 50 per cent of those people interviewed in 1997 (29 out of 56 who answered the question) indicated that they had been members of an environmental pressure group before they signed up as members of the party.  Of those who could recall, very few remembered joining green pressure groups at the same time as the party (only four respondents in total).  However, 61 per cent of those interviewed belonged to an environmental pressure group in 1997 (36 out of 59 who responded to question). The groups most commonly referred to were Amnesty International, Friends of the Earth, Greenpeace, WWF and the RSPB.  Overall, there is nothing to suggest that they joined the Greens and other environmental groups impulsively at one point in time.  The figures reveal that a large part of the Scottish Green Party membership of 1990 had a historical commitment to environmental groups.  Furthermore, their commitment to environmental groups appears even more secure in 1997.

The evidence so far suggests that a large majority of those interviewed in 1997 were still, in some way, involved in environmental politics.  This leads us to those people who left the party. Some interesting differences are apparent between 'leavers' and 'stayers' when we compare their commitment to green pressure groups. 'Leavers' were *twice* as likely to have been pressure group members before they became members of the party, but they were marginally *less* likely to be members of a group in 1997. So, the former members had a clear historical record of environmental group involvement but in 1997 they were not more likely to be members of environmental groups than those who stayed with the party. In other words, there is little evidence that the former members transferred their support from the party to groups.

Both stayers and leavers were asked to comment on the effectiveness of the party. A large majority were in agreement that the party had in fact had some impact – on public attitudes and policy, but mainly on the behaviour of the main British political parties. However, the tone of these comments suggested that any influence was restricted to a rather short time period, the end of the 1980s. More than half of all the interviewees offered this type of assessment. Examples are listed below:

> 'The party did have an impact – The vote threat was a very powerful tool.'
> 'At one time, the party was more effective than pressure groups. It made other parties notice.'
> 'The party has had an impact. Almost everything it stood for has been adopted by the main parties. But the party has had its day – the late 1980s.'
> 'The party had influence around 1989/ 1990, when it attracted lots of publicity and media interest.'
> 'The impact of the party was clear at the end of the 1980s. Other parties attempted to take on board the trappings of the green movement. And Greens have been elected at the local level in some areas of England. However, the impact was less in Scotland.'

So, the majority of people interviewed in 1997 argued that the party had made a positive contribution. This tended to be an assessment of past achievements and was largely a comment on the environmental policies adopted by the main political parties. However, many of the interviewees pointed to the difficulties created by Britain's 'first-past the post' electoral system. For example, one respondents argued that 'without proportional representation, the Greens were never going to compete'. Most of those interviewed pointed to these external reasons for lack of impact in the 1990s, rather than internal factors. Furthermore, a number picked up on reasons for the relatively poor performance of the Greens in Scotland e.g. 'In Scotland, the Greens find it particularly difficult, due to Labour Party dominance and the SNP challenge for Green support'.

While stayers and leavers don't appear to be very different in how they assess the past achievements of the Greens there were some more significant differences in how they assessed pressure groups and in their views of the party's current role. Leavers stand out in their commitment to the pressure group approach. This group were appreciably more positive about the impact of groups and more likely to state that the party, even if it had enjoyed some influence in the past, had, in effect, 'had its day'. Environmental pressure groups were seen to perform a number of roles. It was argued that pressure groups provided public education and information; and, as one respondent expressed it, this enabled individuals to live in an environmentally friendly way. In addition, many of the lapsed respondents observed that pressure groups were able to influence government in a way that the party could not. For example;

> 'Groups have the ear of political parties. The party has lost its way.'
> 'Groups like Greenpeace and FoE are now most effective. They have captured the imagination of the media and people, the Shell protest being a good example.'
> 'The impact of the party is negligible. Whereas, green groups provide much public information as well as putting pressure on the main parties. I am happy that the parties appear to be taking the issues seriously.'
> 'I am committed to the pressure group approach. They are much more effective. The skills and research of groups is invaluable.'
> 'One policy at a time is much easier to achieve.'
> 'Jonathon Porritt is proof that groups are more effective.'

For many of the lapsed members, joining the Greens had been an extension of their pressure group involvement. Membership of the party had been a way of pressurising the other parties. One person commented; 'In a way the party *was* a pressure group'. Most of the leavers indicated that they were still concerned about environmental issues but that the party was no longer an effective way of pursuing their objectives. As evidence of the fruitlessness of party membership, a number of the leavers pointed to Jonathon Porritt who had turned to the green pressure group arena because it was more influential.

'Stayers', however, tended to defend the role played by the party. In fact, they offered some very sophisticated arguments about the different, although complementary, roles performed by the party and pressure groups. Many argued that environmental pressure groups did appear to be more effective at the time but that, in the final analysis, parties and pressure groups performed different functions. It was argued that pressure groups, by their nature, dealt with single issues, whereas the party offered people an alternative government, based on an *ecological* agenda. Only the party could promote an alternative ideological vision. Groups were seen as a good way of raising public awareness and communicating public concern to government, but the party was required to pressurise for fundamental political change, including reforming undemocratic practices in government and an unfair electoral system. It was argued that political reform could only be achieved by a political party forcing change through electoral pressure:

> 'The party appears to have had a muted impact, but the party and pressure groups work very differently. Green ideas have generally permeated British politics, probably the result of both the party and pressure groups.'
> 'The party has done its bit under a poor system. Pressure groups and party are very different political animals – they play different roles. Pressure groups focus on single issues. The party has to worry about internal party

democracy, and it functions under very unfavourable circumstances. PR under the new Scottish system will help the party re-emerge.'
'Groups are not more effective than the party. Political action is the way forward. It is important that there is a party political arm.'
'Groups are good at raising awareness and communicating public concern to Government. And the public see groups as more effective because of their size. However, when it comes to forcing change, there needs to be electoral pressure. I am convinced that a political movement is required. The party is needed to pressurise for *fundamental* change.'
'Groups are more effective on single issues, but party ideas and philosophy are necessary to reform politics – corruption and the unfair electoral system.'
'Party and groups have different messages. Single issue groups are not offering people alternative government. So, party and pressure groups can't really be compared. Pressure groups deal with single issues. The party has an ecological agenda. The electorate don't want the latter.'

For these members pressure groups were seen as complementary to the party, but membership of the party was definitely not regarded as an extension of pressure group activity. These members were convinced that the party still had a discrete and significant role to play in Scottish politics, despite the special difficulties faced by the Greens in Scotland. One Scottish Green interviewed summed up these concerns when he provided a useful summary of why he was still a member: 'The main parties have taken on board some environmental issues, but this leaves certain core issues yet to be dealt with e.g. the nuclear question. Pressure groups won't pursue this radical green agenda. It needs to be done via Parliament. I am still a member because I still have fundamental green beliefs, which the other parties have not yet taken on board. However, I am rather pessimistic about the future for the party in Scotland'.

In sum, the interviews revealed some differences in the views of people who stayed with the Scottish Greens in the 1990s and those who allowed their membership to lapse. Lapsers appear more moderate in their demands, and more satisfied with pressure group politics. They were still interested in the environment but were happy with the single issue 'one step at a time' approach of groups. Those people who stayed appeared more motivated by deep green ecological concerns.

## Conclusion

The Scottish Greens, indeed all parties, must accept that a general turnover of members is inevitable.[14] To use Salisbury's (1969) expression, membership may be seen as a 'marginal' act and any 'slight change of circumstances' may lead to a failure to renew. Leaving may be a random act, not necessarily a very well

---

[14]It is difficult to calculate the precise yearly turnover rate in the case of the Scottish Greens, because of the lack of detailed membership statistics, but based on party estimates and evidence of the Greens elsewhere in the UK, we can assume that members stayed as members for one or two years on average (Rüdig *et al.* 1993: 57).

thought-out 'decision', bringing into question the basis of rational choice models. Nevertheless, having attracted so many new members at the end of the 1980s, it must be a concern to the Scottish Greens that they were unable to sustain the members' commitment. The investigation of leaving the Scottish Green Party in the 1990s revealed a pungent mix of disappointment and disenchantment. The party had a very poor image amongst leavers; it was seen as divided and ineffective. In many respects, the lapsed members appeared to be part of a pressure group constituency who liked the high profile, single-issue approach of groups like Greenpeace and Friends of the Earth. However, the lapsers were actually a little less likely than the members to belong to these groups in 1997.

The distinctiveness of 'stayers' and 'leavers' should not be over-played. Although 'leavers' were disillusioned with the internal politics of the party, and rather sceptical about what the party could hope to achieve, more than one in three indicated that they would consider rejoining the party. Those respondents who said they might consider rejoining suggested they would do so if the party was able to achieve a higher profile. It was suggested that the creation of a Scottish Parliament might help in this regard. Some of the comments focused on the party itself and the way it was organised; if the party was more professional in its organisation this might persuade some former members to rejoin. Examples included the following comments:

> 'I would consider rejoining if the party was credible again.'
> 'I would join again if the Parliament brought discussion of a green agenda.'
> 'If the party became viable again I would consider rejoining.'
> 'If they decided they wanted to become a mainstream party. Divisions need to be healed. I would consider rejoining if I thought the party was serious about trying to win electoral power.'
> 'I would consider rejoining the party but I wouldn't know how to because I don't hear about or from the party anymore.'
> 'I would rejoin if the party was doing more on the national scene – Having more of an effect.'

The comments made by the leavers reveal a remarkably high level of concern about environmental issues. Nearly all of the leavers claimed that they were still concerned about environmental issues. They may have left the party but the responses suggest that they were still receptive to green arguments. They appeared to have lost faith in the party's ability to achieve purposive objectives, rather than the purpose itself. In this respect these respondents appeared to be 'remobilisable'. However, the party needed to convince them that membership was value for money i.e. that the membership fee was contributing towards the fight to save the environment. The party could also have done more to convince members that, even if they were unable to contribute in the form of time or activity, financial contributions were just as valuable.

On the evidence of the 1990 survey and 1997 interviews, the party is competing with other environmental groups for financial resources. The perception among many of these respondents was that their money was better spent supporting environmental groups such as FoE. While membership of the Scottish Greens in 1990 was not particularly financially costly (ordinary membership rates in 1989 and 1990 were £15 for waged members, £6 for non-waged members) it was not viewed as particularly good value for money, because the party was seen as ineffective. Continued membership requires the member to feel that the party is making a difference and that the membership fee is 'well spent'. Barry (1978: 30) notes the importance of movement effectiveness as an explanation for collective action and, conversely, the difficulty of attracting potential participants to what appears to be a lost cause:

> ... a belief in the efficacy of the process does look as if it is related to participation.... Whatever the reason why a person may attach himself to a cause, more enthusiasm for its pursuit is likely to be elicited if it looks as if it has a chance of succeeding than if it appears to be a forlorn hope. Nobody likes to feel that he is wasting his time, and that feeling may be induced by contributing to a campaign which never looks as if it has a chance.

The findings confirm the importance of considering the political context to fully appreciate what motivates, or indeed demotivates, movement participants. It would appear that the environmentalists in this study tended to choose their tactics according to circumstances, supporting those who argue that movement participants change their tactics over time and according to available opportunities (see Burstein 1995: 10). When the party was given attention by the media and the main political parties, it was viewed as a credible force, worthy of membership support. During the 1990s, pressure groups were viewed as more viable. As participation models based on the concept of 'opportunity' would suggest, members were attracted by better opportunities within other environmental organisations.

Chapter 8

# New Members, Old Motives?
# Comparing Scottish Green Party
# Members 1990 and 2002

The political context in 2002 had changed beyond recognition for the Scottish Green Party.  While the party had been fighting elections in Scotland for over two decades, for much of this time the Scottish Greens had been completely overshadowed by a political system balanced in favour of the major parties (see chapter 2).  Indeed the time spent in the pre-parliamentary stage of politics was lengthy even by green party standards (Muller-Rommell 2002: 4).  The creation of a Scottish Parliament in 1999 and the introduction of a more proportional electoral system changed the political landscape for the Scottish Greens, resulting in the election of one MSP for the party (see chapter 2 and Bennie 2002).  For the first time, Scottish Greens passed the 'threshold of representation' (Muller-Rommell 2002: 3) and were able to participate in parliamentary politics. However, the Scottish Green Party was still a small, marginal party by the standards of many other European green parties.  In no way could it be said, for example, that the Scottish Greens enjoyed 'coalition potential' (Sartori 1976).

As chapter 2 documented, the modest success of the Scottish Greens in 1999 did lead to an increase in party members. However, any increases were very modest compared to the massive influx of members in 1989/1990. During the 1990s membership of the party had fluctuated around the 300 mark but after the 1999 Scottish Parliament Election membership began to climb slowly, reaching approximately 520 by 2002. In the light of these events, this chapter explores the changing membership of the Scottish Green Party.  The surveys of members conducted in 1990 and 2002 allow an analysis of how the characteristics of members may have changed (for survey details see chapter 1).  Chapter 6 revealed that, despite the dramatic increase in membership numbers, the party in 1989/1990 was not in fact very successful at attracting a 'new' kind of member.  This chapter is a first attempt to address whether the profile of Scottish Green members in 2002 was any more distinctive, in terms of social characteristics, political experiences, and motivations for joining the party.

## When Did the Members Join?

Two thirds of the respondents – 68 per cent – joined the party after 1990 i.e. since the original survey, with the average length of membership standing at eight years (8.07). This suggests that we are dealing with a mainly new set of respondents, many of whom joined around the time of the first Scottish Parliament Election in 1999. We find that 8.6 per cent of the respondents had joined the party in 1999, and another 43.4 per cent between 2000 and the time of the survey in 2002. In other words, over half of the respondents had been members of the party for less than four years, with the largest intake in 2001. Compared to the 1990 survey, however, the 2002 sample contained more long-term members. Approximately one third of members – 34.8 per cent – joined in the two years prior to the survey (October 2000-September 2002). In 1990, 51.4 per cent of respondents had joined in the two years leading up to that survey, and the average length of membership was only 3.8 years. The 1990 survey was able to capture a massive upsurge in members at the end of the 1980s, but the 2002 study is likely to be a more accurate reflection of normal membership turnover.

## Social Characteristics

### Sex and Age

In 1990, 45 per cent of the respondents were female. By 2002 this figure had declined quite sharply, to only 36.8 per cent.[1] Moreover, the females in the sample were a little older than the males, suggesting that the party was finding it more difficult to attract young women. As members, however, there were very few differences between males and females. For example, those members who had been in the party for a very long time (maximum 29 years) were more likely to be men, but overall there was little variation between males and females in length of membership, or indeed in activity within the party. 44.4 per cent of men and 45.3 per cent of women were 'not at all active' in the party, although when asked why they joined, men were a little more likely to indicate that they joined in order to be politically active.

In 1990, 75 per cent of all members were below the age of 45, giving the membership a fairly youthful profile. By 2002, only 45 per cent of members belonged in this category, suggesting that the party as a whole was ageing considerably (Table 8.1). The mean age in 2002 was 46.8, compared to only 38.6 in 1990. It is difficult to explain this change in membership profile, but it seems that the Scottish Greens have not been particularly successful at attracting young people into political activity. In 1990 the party looked distinctly youthful compared to other parties. In 2002, however, the age distribution of the Scottish Greens did

---

[1] The Scottish Census of 2001 indicated that females make up 52 per cent of the general population. Seyd and Whiteley's (2002: 35) analysis of Labour members in 1990 and 1997 revealed stability in the proportion of females in the party – 39 per cent in both years.

not look all that different from the other parties. Seyd and Whiteley's (2002: 35-36) analysis of Labour members in 1990 and 1997 points to a general ageing of party members in Britain. One might have expected the Greens to resist this trend somewhat, given their anti-establishment status, but the decline of very young members suggests otherwise.

**Table 8.1  Age of Scottish Green Party Members (%)**

|       |      |      | Age by Sex 2002 | |
|-------|------|------|------|--------|
|       | 2002 | 1990 | Male | Female |
| 16-24 | 2.3  | 11.8 | 3.1  | 1.1    |
| 25-34 | 18.6 | 30.6 | 19.6 | 16.8   |
| 35-44 | 25.6 | 32.4 | 27.6 | 22.1   |
| 45-54 | 27.1 | 12.8 | 28.2 | 25.3   |
| 55-64 | 12.4 | 5.8  | 10.4 | 15.8   |
| 65+   | 14.0 | 6.4  | 11.0 | 18.9   |

*Education*

With a massive expansion in numbers participating in higher education throughout the UK, it is perhaps unsurprising that the 2002 members appear even better educated than those in 1990. For example, less than one quarter of the 2002 respondents had completed continuous full-time education by the age of 20, compared to 43.2 per cent of the 1990 respondents.

**Table 8.2  Educational Profile of Scottish Greens (%)**

|                                                        | 2002 | 1990 |
|--------------------------------------------------------|------|------|
| **Choice of Degree Subject**                           |      |      |
| Business/Management/Economics/Law                      | 7.9  | 7.2  |
| Other Social Sciences (Sociology/Politics/Psychology)  | 28.1 | 20.2 |
| Arts and Humanities                                    | 20.6 | 27.9 |
| Biology/Medicine                                       | 12.3 | 10.0 |
| Other Natural Sciences/Engineering                     | 21.1 | 17.7 |
| None of the above/Other                                | 10.1 | 17.1 |
| **Highest Degree Awarded**                             |      |      |
| Postgraduate/masters degree                            | 23.1 | 25.4 |
| First degree (BA/BSc/Scottish MA)                      | 47.1 | 43.8 |
| Don't have a degree                                    | 21.1 | 23.9 |

Furthermore, a larger proportion of the 2002 respondents were still in full-time education at the time of the survey: 16.8 per cent compared to 10.6 per cent in

1990, and this despite the changing age profile. When asked if they had ever studied for a degree, the responses are almost identical: 82 per cent of the 2002 sample indicated they had attended a university or other higher education institution in order to study for a degree, and in 1990 the figure was 81 per cent.[2] Overall, the educational profile of the members in 1990 and 2002 is almost identical. Table 8.2 illustrates the similarities in choice of degree subject and highest degree awarded.

*Employment*

While the employment status of the two sets of respondents appears quite similar, a few small differences emerge, apart from the greater tendency of 2002 members to be in full-time education. The members in 2002 were less likely to be in part-time work, and they were more likely to be looking after the home full-time (Table 8.3). When we examine this finding more closely, these respondents are, unsurprisingly, disproportionately female: 19.1 per cent of women and 11.1 per cent of men were looking after the home full-time.

**Table 8.3  Employment of Scottish Greens (%)**

|  | 2002 | 1990 |
|---|---|---|
| **Employment Status** | | |
| Employed in full time work/self-employed | 56.6 | 51.6 |
| In full time education | 16.8 | 10.6 |
| Sick/disabled/retired | 5.8 | 6.2 |
| Employed part time | 3.5 | 11.0 |
| Looking after home full time | 14.4 | 6.0 |
| Unemployed | 3.1 | 6.6 |
| Other e.g. on govt scheme | - | 8.2 |
| | | |
| **Description of Work** | | |
| Professional/technical | 59.1 | 53.3 |
| Manager/senior administrator | 8.7 | 4.9 |
| Clerical work | 4.3 | 7.3 |
| Sales/services | 4.7 | 1.8 |
| Small business owner | 6.7 | - |
| Foreman/supervisor | 0.8 | - |
| Skilled manual | 1.6 | 4.9 |
| Semi-skilled/unskilled | 3.1 | 4.7 |
| Other | 9.8 | 22.0 |
| Never had job | 1.2 | - |

---

[2]The 2001 Census indicates that 19 per cent of Scotland's general population had obtained a First Degree, Higher Degree or Professional qualification. Seyd and Whiteley (2002: 37-38) report that 42 per cent of Liberal Democrats in 1999 and 34 per cent of Labour members in 1997 were graduates.

As for the nature of employment, Table 8.3 also reveals the overwhelmingly professional appearance of Scottish Green Party members, in 2002 and 1990. If anything, the members were even more professional in appearance by 2002, with more than two thirds describing their work as professional, technical or managerial. Furthermore, we find that in 2002, 58 per cent of all respondents say they supervise, or are responsible for the work of other people (not asked in 1990). These findings can be compared with 11 per cent of the Scottish population who in 2001 were classified as having higher managerial or professional occupations, with another 25 per cent in lower managerial and professional occupations (Scotland's Census 2001).

The 2002 survey was better able to address which area of the economy party members worked in. We find that education is the most popular area, closely followed by health/social services (Table 8.4). The picture of Greens employed in caring public sector occupations is backed up by a question on type of organisation worked for. In total, only 27.9 per cent worked for a private sector firm or company, compared with 49.8 per cent who were employed in the public sector.[3] Furthermore, 15.5 per cent worked for a charity or voluntary organisation. In 1990, the questions in this area varied somewhat in their format. However, if anything, the members in 2002 appeared even more likely to be working in education or health. We can certainly conclude that, compared to the general population, Scottish Green Party members disproportionately gravitate towards the caring, public-sector professions e.g. in 2001, only 19.7 per cent of Scotland's working population were employed in education, health or social work (Scotland's Census 2001).


**Table 8.4  Sector of Economy 2002 (%)**

| | |
|---|---|
| Agriculture, fishing, forestry etc | 5.5 |
| Industry | 5.1 |
| Education | 24.1 |
| Health, social services | 19.4 |
| Media, culture | 6.3 |
| Security services | 0.8 |
| Other public administration (e.g. local authority/civil service) | 11.5 |
| Banking, finance, insurance, property | 6.3 |
| Other services | 12.6 |
| Other/never had job | 8.3 |

So far, then, the 2002 members do not look very different from the 1990 members. They are a little older, and a little less likely to be female but education and employment trends are almost identical. The predominantly middle-class profile of Scottish Greens in 1990 was documented extensively in chapter 4. The

---

[3] 37 per cent of Labour members in 1997 were working in the private sector (Seyd and Whiteley 2002: 38).

composition of the membership in 2002 was little different in this respect. They were educated to an exceptionally high level and the majority worked in managerial or professional positions. Overall, the socio-demographic profiles of the Scottish Greens in 1990 and in 2002 were very similar and distinctly middle class in character. It is again important to note however that these party members belong to that *section* of the middle class commonly referred to as the 'new' middle class (see Cotgrove 1982). As well as being exceptionally well educated they were likely to have specialised in humanistic degree areas and to be employed in public sector, 'caring', non-commercial based occupations. Based on evidence of social background (education and occupation) these party members did not appear in any way socially or economically excluded.

**Table 8.5  Denomination if Religious (%)**

|  | 2002 | 1990 |
|---|---|---|
| Roman Catholic | 8.6 | 11.3 |
| Church of Scotland | 18.3 | 31.9 |
| Episcopal/Anglican | 15.1 | 13.5 |
| Presbyterian | 2.2 | - |
| Methodist | 3.2 | 3.5 |
| Quaker | 18.3 | 17.0 |
| Baptist | 1.1 | - |
| Other Christian | 8.6 | 7.1 |
| Jewish | 1.1 | 0.7 |
| Buddhist | 6.5 | 8.5 |
| Muslim | 1.1 | - |
| Pagan | 4.3 | - |
| Other | 11.8 | 6.4 |

It has already been suggested that high levels of education may be related to the shedding of religious beliefs (Parkin 1968: 178). Many of the studies reported in chapters 3 and 4 pointed to generally low level of religious belief amongst environmentalists, to an under-representation of traditional denominations, and to the over-representation of non-traditional religions, in particular Quakers (Byrne 1988; Parkin 1968; Taylor and Pritchard 1980).

It is perhaps surprising, then, that Scottish Greens in 2002 were *more* likely than the 1990 members to identify with a religion: 34.1 per cent indicated that they belonged to a religion but in 1990 only 28.6 per cent.[4] The precise religious affiliation of these members can be seen in Table 8.5. Once again, we see a high incidence of Quakers, but a decline in Church of Scotland members. As for attendance at religious services, only 16 per cent of the sample indicated they were

---

[4] 34 per cent of Labour members in 1997 described themselves as 'not at all religious' (Seyd and Whiteley 2002: 39).

regular church-goers i.e. attended a religious service at least once a week. Another 35 per cent attended very infrequently.[5]

Finally, the two surveys were able to assess the area in which members resided. In 1990, the survey found that Scottish Green members were more likely than the general population to live in rural areas and small communities, with 40 per cent describing their area as 'rural' (chapter 4). Is there any evidence to suggest that the Scottish Greens have recently been any more successful at attracting city dwellers? While the question varied a little in 2002, an even smaller proportion – 49 per cent – of the 2002 members indicated that they lived in a big city or in the suburbs/outskirts of a big city (as compared with 60 per cent in 1990 who lived in an inner-city or suburban area). We can safely conclude that the Scottish Greens in 2002 were no more likely to be living in Scotland's big cities.


**Political Background**

Having identified the types of individuals who participate as members in the Scottish Green Party, we turn now to the political experiences of the members. Based on the results of 1990, we would expect the members in 2002 to be seasoned political animals. In 1990 the members were exceptionally well connected to other individuals and groups. They had a history of involvement in a number of causes, including political party membership, and support for social movements, either through direct activity or financial support. In short, the party members were by no means inexperienced politically, and there appeared to be evidence of an environmental network at work. Table 8.6 compares membership of environmental groups in 2002 and 1990. It should be noted that in 1990 respondents were asked of they had *ever* been members of these groups, while the 2002 figures relate to current membership, thus explaining the generally higher figures of 1990. Nevertheless, the level of commitment to environmental groups is impressive, for both sets of respondents.

Moreover, the members displayed a lengthy history of involvement in a range of social movements. More than a third of the members in 2002 claimed to have been active in the anti-nuclear movement during the 1980s, 31 per cent were active in the peace movement in the same decade, and nearly half were active in the environmental movement in the 1990s. In 1990, respondents were asked to look back over the entire period of their involvement in political campaigning, and to describe their own level of activity in social movements (see chapter 4). The overall pattern is similar but the 1990 members were in fact more likely to have been completely *inactive* in comparable social movements. For example, 33.2 per cent of the 1990 members said they had never been active in the environmental

---

[5]According to the 2001 Scottish Census, only 27.5 per cent of Scots categorise themselves as having 'no religion'. Those with a religion are as follows: 42.4 per cent Church of Scotland; 15.9 per cent RC; 6.8 per cent Other Christian; 0.1 per cent Buddhist; 0.1 per cent Hindu; 0.1 per cent Jewish; 0.8 per cent Muslim: 0.1 per cent Sikh; 0.5 per cent Other religion; 5.5. per cent NA.

movement, compared to 26.9 per cent of the 2002 members. Similarly 46.5 per cent of the 1990 survey respondents indicated they had not been active in the anti-nuclear movement, compared to only 37.7 per cent of the 2002 members.

**Table 8.6  Membership of Groups (%)**

|  | 2002 | 1990 |
|---|---|---|
| Friends of the Earth | 38.5 | 41.3 |
| Greenpeace | 32.3 | 50.7 |
| WWF | 12.7 | 22.8 |
| National Trust | 15.4 | 24.5 |
| RSPB | 14.6 | 25.5 |
| Civic Trust or affiliated group | 1.9 | - |
| Wildlife Trusts | 9.2 | - |
| Woodland Trust | 12.3 | - |
| Assoc. for Protection of Rural Scotland | 1.2 | - |
| Ramblers' Association | 5.8 | 5.0 |
| John Muir Trust | 10.4 | - |
| Other environmental group | 40.0 | 32.2 |
| CND | 20.0 | 39.1 |
| Amnesty International | 23.1 | 24.2 |

The Scottish Green Party members of 2002 also participated in a range of other political activities. For example, during the four years prior to the survey, 40.5 per cent had frequently worked in a voluntary organisation/association (another 18.6 per cent did so occasionally); 68.1 per cent frequently boycotted certain products (25.7 per cent occasionally); and 26.4 per cent had frequently participated in public demonstration (with another 24.4 per cent occasionally). 85.9 per cent frequently voted in elections. (These findings are consistent with their views on effectiveness of these activities.)

The 2002 survey also examined some of the lifestyle choices of the Scottish Greens. The lifestyles of these members look very green indeed: 90.7 per cent claimed to always or often make a special effort to sort glass, tins, plastic or newspapers and so on for recycling; 73.3 per cent always or often bought organic fruits and vegetables; 56.8 per cent always/often refused to eat meat for moral or environmental reasons; and 40.6 per cent always/often used alternative medicine, such as homeopathy. Perhaps surprisingly, 70.2 per cent indicated that they or someone in their household ran a car. However, more than half of these car-owning respondents (53.3 per cent) said they always or often cut back on driving the car for environmental reasons. Of those who did not have a car, 55.4 per cent said this was due to environmental reasons, 22.7 per cent for economic reasons. (There was also strong agreement with the statement 'Petrol taxes should be increased substantially to help combat global warming' – three in every four members agreed.)

Just over one third of the 2002 respondents (35 per cent) belonged to a Trade Union or Staff Association, a significant reduction from the figure of 47 per cent in 1990.  However, this is probably explained by the overall decline in trade union membership across the UK. Indeed, Seyd and Whiteley's (2002: 37) study of Labour members also documents a decline in trade union membership, from 64 per cent in 1990 to only 34 per cent in 1997. As for membership of other political parties, nearly one third of the Scottish Greens – 32.2 per cent – had been members of another party; in 1990 this figure was 28 per cent.  The profile is once again very similar to that of 1990, with the largest numbers coming from the Labour Party, although in the more recent survey former Labour members were even more prominent (Table 8.7).  In total, just over 15.5 per cent of the 2002 Scottish Greens had previously been members of the Labour Party.

**Table 8.7  Membership of Other Political Parties (%)**

|  | 2002 | 1990 |
|---|---|---|
| Labour | 15.5 | 11.8 |
| Conservative | 3.8 | 2.2 |
| Liberal Democrat | 3.5 | 0.8 |
| Liberal | 6.2 | 6.7 |
| SDP | 0.4 | 0.6 |
| SNP | 5.8 | 5.7 |
| SSP | 0.4 | - |
| Other | 5.4 | 4.3 |
| Total | 32.2 | 28.0 |

Overall levels of commitment to social movements and general political activities of the two groups are very alike.  When examining the routes into membership of the Scottish Green Party we must conclude that the 2002 members are just as 'integrated' as their 1990 predecessors.  This form of collective action does not look like 'irrational outburst' (Smelser 1962). Rather, we appear to be looking at a socially confident group of people who enjoy participation in many different fields.  We can therefore conclude that the 2002 members we just as likely to be 'joiners' as their 1990 counterparts.

**Activity in the Scottish Green Party**

While the two sets of members demonstrate very similar political backgrounds, is there anything distinctive about the 2002 members in their levels of commitment to the party itself?  When asked to indicate the strtength of their support for the Scottish Green Party, 30.2 per cent of the 2002 respondents said 'very strong', 45.3 per cent 'fairly strong', 20.2 per cent 'not very strong' and 4.3 per cent 'not at all strong'. Compared to Labour members, strength of party support appears rather weak: 50 per cent of Seyd and Whiteley's (2002: 35) Labour respondents in 1997 described themselves as strong supporters, and another 43 per cent as fairly strong supporters (6 per cent not very strong and 1 per cent not at all strong). Unfortunately, this question was not put to the Scottish Greens in 1990, but there are other indicators of party commitment we can examine.

In 2002, 52.8 per cent of the respondents had not attended a local SGP meeting in the last year (16.1 per cent rarely; 16.9 per cent occasionally; 14.2 per cent frequently). In addition, 53.5 per cent claimed to devote no time at all to party activities in the average month. Furthermore, when asked how active they were in the party at the time, only 5.4 per cent said very active; 17.1 per cent were fairly active; 32.7 per cent were not very active; and 44.7 per cent were not at all active. And a question on party conferences reveals that 63.6 per cent of members had *not* attended a national conference in the previous four years. Members were also asked if they had participated in any of the party's big campaigns and we find that a minority had participated in this way: 44.3 per cent had occasionally or frequently participated in the campaign for the Organic Food and Farming Targets Bill (OFFTB); 20.9 per cent were involved in Scotland Against Nuclear Expansion (SANE); and 27.3 per cent claimed to have participated in other campaigns. Nor are members interacting with each other socially. When asked how often they met party members socially 42.6 per cent said 'never', 23.4 per cent 'rarely, 20.7 per cent 'sometimes' 11.3 per cent 'quire often', and only 2 per cent 'very regularly'.

Overall, we find that the majority of 2002 party members were rather inactive. However, this pattern of (in)activity is not so different from that reported in 1990. In that year, members were asked to assess their own level of activity in the party over the entire period of their political involvement: 62 per cent indicated that they had been 'not very active' (38.9 per cent) or 'not at all active' (23.0 per cent). 60.5 per cent of the members in 1990 indicated that they had devoted no time at all to the party in the average week, 48.2 per cent had not attended a local meeting in the last year, and 88.7 per cent had never attended a national conference.

While there is some variation in the questions and responses, the overall pattern of activities reported is much more similar than dissimilar. In both surveys, between 50 and 60 per cent of the members were passive, around 30 per cent were occasionally active, and 20 per cent were more regular activists. While party activism requires more analysis, these early comparisons do not suggest that activism has either increased or decreased. Certainly, there is little evidence of a decline in party activism on the scale of that occurring within the Labour Party. Seyd and Whiteley (2002: 79-80) report that between 1990 and 1999, the numbers *not* attending a party meeting rose from 36 per cent to 61 per cent.


**Reasons for Joining**

We turn now to the decision to join the Scottish Green Party. As can be seen in Table 8.8, when asked to assess their reasons for first joining the Scottish Green Party, the 2002 respondents clearly pointed to political aims as a motivation behind membership: 92 per cent of the respondents indicated that 'helping in the realisation of the political aims that I supported' was very important or important in their decision to join. Above all other options, this reason stands out as 'very important', and it clearly suggests a collective or purposive motivation. The next most important motivation was a desire to 'learn more about green politics'; more than 70 per cent point to the importance of such a motivation. This response can be viewed as selective process incentives in the sense that the respondents expect to learn about green politics through their membership. Reasons for joining which appear least important are the belief that membership can be good for one's career (2.4 per cent said this was at all important) and, secondly, the desire to 'pursue a career in green politics' (8.7 per cent at all important). In other words, the selective outcome incentives prove the least powerful as an explanation for joining. 'Wanting to meet politically like-minded people' is a relatively popular choice and this could be regarded as a solidary type incentive, although this might simply indicate a desire to be part of a collective grouping with similar political objectives.

**Table 8.8  Reason for First Joining the Scottish Green Party 2002 (%)**

| | Very important | Important | Neither | Not important | Not at all important |
|---|---|---|---|---|---|
| To meet politically like-minded. | 15.0 | 37.0 | 25.6 | 13.0 | 9.4 |
| To be politically active. | 15.5 | 40.9 | 23.0 | 12.3 | 8.3 |
| Political aims. | 51.0 | 42.0 | 4.7 | 0.8 | 1.6 |
| Selection of candidates. | 7.1 | 18.1 | 31.1 | 26.8 | 16.9 |
| Career in green politics. | 3.2 | 5.5 | 13.4 | 25.3 | 52.6 |
| To support party financially. | 9.2 | 41.4 | 28.7 | 11.6 | 9.2 |
| Good for career. | 0.8 | 1.6 | 7.1 | 13.0 | 77.6 |
| To learn about green politics. | 21.2 | 51.8 | 18.0 | 5.5 | 3.5 |

To further explore incentives behind membership we can compare some of the responses of the 2002 and 1990 members (Tables 8.9 and 8.10). Is there any evidence to suggest that reasons for joining have changed over the years? For example, did the 2002 members have a greater sense of group efficacy, following the party's breakthrough into parliamentary politics? The questions vary slightly (the first relates to reasons for joining and the second to reasons for joining or remaining a member) and the value categories are also different, but the comparison is nevertheless useful.

**Table 8.9  Reasons for Joining and Remaining a Member 2002 (%)**

| | Very important | Important | Neither | Not Important | Not at all important |
|---|---|---|---|---|---|
| Enjoy working with like-minded & interesting people. | 12.1 | 47.2 | 20.2 | 10.9 | 9.7 |
| Many good people in the party I support. | 12.0 | 57.4 | 20.5 | 4.8 | 5.2 |
| Only party not to compromise on principle. | 23.8 | 54.1 | 18.0 | 2.0 | 2.0 |
| Best opportunity to achieve political aims. | 48.0 | 46.8 | 3.6 | 1.2 | 0.4 |
| Can do little to save planet but have to try. | 27.5 | 46.3 | 15.2 | 8.2 | 2.9 |
| Party allows members meaningful role. | 13.2 | 56.6 | 22.3 | 6.6 | 1.2 |
| Party helps to fulfil spiritual needs. | 5.8 | 21.1 | 24.0 | 18.2 | 31.0 |

Once again, the importance of party objectives and principles is very clear. In both years, the statement that receives most approval is 'The party provides the best opportunity to achieve the political aims I support', and there is strong support for the view that the party does not compromise on principles. The least popular response was to indicate that the party helped fulfil spiritual needs. As for changes over time, by 2002, support for 'good people in the party' had risen, perhaps reflecting the relatively high-profile position of the Scottish Green MSP Robin Harper, and members were a little more likely to claim that the party's democratic framework was attractive to them.

**Table 8.10  Role Played in the Decision to Join 1990 (%)**

| | Decisive | Very important | Important | Not very important | No role whatsoever |
|---|---|---|---|---|---|
| Can join like-minded people in fight for the environment. | 22.2 | 21.6 | 33.8 | 13.4 | 9.0 |
| Many good people in the party I support. | 5.4 | 11.4 | 32.0 | 26.8 | 24.5 |
| Only party not to compromise on principle. | 26.6 | 24.7 | 23.3 | 13.2 | 12.2 |
| Want party's point of view heard. | 25.5 | 31.8 | 22.4 | 11.3 | 9.0 |
| Best opportunity to achieve political aims. | 46.3 | 17.1 | 18.8 | 10.8 | 6.9 |
| Can do little to save planet but have to try. | 37.5 | 18.4 | 18.4 | 12.3 | 13.3 |
| Party allows members meaningful role. | 13.2 | 20.5 | 31.2 | 16.7 | 18.4 |
| Helps to fulfil spiritual needs. | 7.2 | 8.3 | 14.9 | 19.6 | 50.0 |

The importance of working with like-minded people appears to have declined, but this may be the result of a change to the question wording. In 1990 the statement read 'As a member I can join like-minded and interesting people *in the fight for the environment*', providing a more purposive meaning.  Overall, the responses are overwhelmingly similar.

Particularly intriguing is the continuing high level of agreement with the statement, 'Ultimately, the party can probably do little to save the planet but one has to try to do everything possible to avert such a catastrophe'.  In 1990, 74.3 per cent indicated this was at least important and in 2002 the figure was 73.8 per cent. This appears to provide evidence of negative collective incentives in that concern about environmental degradation appears to be an important motive.  However, it also suggests that the members are rather pessimistic about the party's ability to make a difference to environmental problems i.e. there is doubt over the party's efficacy.  Furthermore, the 2002 respondents do not show any signs of being less pessimistic in this regard.

**Looking to the Future: Party Strategy**

Scottish politics has seen fundamental change in recent years. Devolution, involving the setting-up of the new Parliament and the use of a semi-proportional electoral system to elect MSPs, has created a new set of opportunities for the Greens in Scotland, not least the opportunity to participate in parliamentary politics. On the question of party strategy (Table 8.11), there is some evidence to suggest that the views of the 2002 membership reflect these changing political circumstances.

**Table 8.11  Party Strategy (% agree or strongly agree)**

|  | 2002 | 1990 |
| --- | --- | --- |
| Concentrate on grassroots campaigning. | 91.7 | 87.2 |
| Elect one leader. | 44.0 | 41.6 |
| Explore pre-election pacts. | 42.9 | 16.6 |
| Improve media image. | 85.3 | 84.5 |
| More emphasis on social issues. | 63.3 | 69.8 |
| Employ non-violent direct action/civil disobedience. | 52.0 | 43.7 |
| Adopt a more decentralised structure. | 19.8 | 25.8 |
| Reverse concentration on electoral campaigning and more emphasis on individual life-style change. | 22.7 | 43.2 |
| Devise more detailed policies. | 74.2 | 75.5 |
| Without PR for UK general elections, the party will never make a major impact. | 80.5 | 78.9 |
| Will achieve aims not on its own but by pressuring other parties. | 57.4 | 56.3 |
| Party should always stand by principles, even if this loses votes. | 85.5 | 86.3 |
| Success should be defined by changes to individual lifestyle. | 64.1 | 68.8 |

The 2002 members were considerably less supportive of a scaling down of electoral campaigning to put more emphasis on individual life-style change, and they were much *more* positive about exploring the possibilities of pre-election pacts with other parties. It seems likely that the new electoral context in which the party operates has influenced attitudes on these issues. The rewards of electoral campaigning are increasingly apparent under a more proportional electoral system, and one of the unavoidable realities of the new system is that parties must work together (see Bennie and Clark 2003).

On all other issues, however, this comparison reveals, once again, a remarkable stability of attitudes. In fact, the consistency of responses between 1990 and 2002 suggests that Scottish Greens are very united on what their priorities should and should not be. The strategic options which meet with least approval are related to internal party organisation. There is minority support for decentralising party structures and the election of one party leader. By contrast, those strategies most strongly supported by the members relate to grassroots campaigning, party principles and the development of policy.

'Concentrating on grassroots campaigning' is supported most strongly by the members, and there is similar consensus that 'the party should always stand by its principles, even if this loses votes'. The pragmatism of the members is also revealed by the view that the party will never make an impact in Westminster general elections without the introduction of PR, and by recognising the importance of 'improving the party's media image'. The other priority identified by at least three quarters of the members is the desire to devise a more detailed set of policies. And the responses to other questions in the 2002 survey reveal that the policies most important to these members are, in order of importance, 'stopping global warming' (a 'top or high priority' for 99 per cent of members), 'opposing globalisation', 'phasing out of nuclear energy', 'creating a more democratic society', and 'promoting nuclear disarmament'. These policies are given a much higher priority by the members than, for example, 'reforming the welfare state', 'fighting unemployment', or 'improving the status of women'. In short, the 2002 members appeared strongly motivated by traditional green policies.

*Conclusion*

According to the evidence presented in this chapter, devolution has had little impact on the type of member joining the Scottish Greens. The comparison of members in 1990 and 2002 reveals overwhelming similarities in social characteristics, former political experiences, and in party activism. There is little evidence here of the party being able to expand their membership base to new social types. In fact, the differences that do exist (age and sex) suggest that the members are being drawn from a narrower group of social types, and suggest some difficulties in recruitment for the party.

Motivations for joining the party also appear very similar. Most of the evidence points to the influence of collective incentives, which may be positive (the pursuit of public goods) or negative (the reduction of a public bad). Many members indicated that the policy objectives of the Scottish Greens were of considerable importance to them. In this respect, membership of the Scottish Greens represents a significant challenge to the free-rider argument as participation does not appear to serve self-interest. Nevertheless, it also appears that the members in this study gain some sense of expressive satisfaction from their association with the party. The activists in particular are likely to experience more obvious selective rewards, but these incentives are less applicable to passive members and the majority of members are in fact rather inactive. Furthermore, the lack of social contact between members suggests that solidary incentives are relatively unimportant.

The central theme to emerge from this analysis is that party members had a long-standing commitment to environmental politics and party membership was another manifestation of this concern. In these key respects the members of 2002 cannot be separated from the 1990 respondents. Overall, the comparison of the two sets of members revealed very little differences. It seems that the changing political environment in Scotland had, by 2002, had very little impact on the composition of the party's membership.

# Chapter 9

# Conclusion

<blockquote>There is an urgent need for systematic empirical accounts of the contextual dynamics of fluid, developing political journeys (Edmondson 1997: 8).</blockquote>

The objective of this study of the Scottish Greens has been to develop an understanding of why individuals become members of the party.  This has also involved examining who joins the party, how they join, and why some leave. This chapter reviews the most important findings and considers their theoretical implications.  In addition, the chapter explores the implications for the Scottish Green Party itself, and sets out a future research agenda.

The historical account of the party's development revealed that, for most of their existence, the Scottish Greens have struggled to attract both voters and members. Chapter 2 outlined those features of Scottish politics which worked against the Scottish Greens, including a rather 'working class' and materialistic political culture, and a very competitive party system. These factors, combined with the first-past-the-post electoral system, meant that the party organisation could do little to attract support.  However, the Greens managed to remain in existence and at the end of the 1980s they were rewarded with an unprecedented increase in members. The party's long-term survival and up-turn in fortunes at this time were quite remarkable, considering the traditionally hostile political environment in Scotland.  The success of the Scottish Greens since the arrival of constitutional reform is in a sense less surprising.  It was in fact predictable that the new Parliament and electoral system would create new electoral opportunities for small parties like the Scottish Greens.  However, these new openings have not led to the kind of rise in membership numbers experienced in 1989/1990.

The membership success of the Scottish Greens at the end of the 1980s was a quite exceptional political event.  At first sight, membership of such a party appears to be an example of paradoxical participation. The Scottish Green Party exists to 'promote a clean environment, a healthy way of life and a peaceful world'.[1]  The achievement of these objectives is a formidable task.  Global warming, the hole in the ozone layer, increasing levels of pollution and constant reminders of international conflict suggest that the party is fighting an exceptionally difficult collective cause. So why would anyone have taken the trouble to join a party which appeared to have little chance of realising its stated objectives?

---

[1]Scottish Green Party election leaflet.

In an attempt to explain these developments, the book reported on the results of a 1990 survey of Scottish Greens while assessing the relevance of different explanations of participation (reviewed in chapter 3). A number of theorists have commented on *who* is likely to participate. The classical social movement approaches highlighted the socially isolated individual who feels frustrated and rejected and seeks comfort in a movement setting. Collective action was viewed as a kind of irrational outburst and a result of structural strain. Others pointed to those who felt relatively deprived. The more contemporary approaches in the study of participation (the civic voluntarism approach, resource mobilisation theories, theories which focus on interaction, and new politics approaches) argued that, rather than being marginal, alienated or deprived, the people most likely to participate were of a high socio-economic status and integrated into social and movement networks. The evidence presented in chapter 4 on who joined the Scottish Greens clearly pointed to the existence of economically 'well off' individuals who had many connections with other organisations. To reiterate, more than half of these 1990 members had a professional or technical occupation, and only one tenth had *never* belonged to another environmental or peace group. These party members were clearly 'joiners' as opposed to the socially marginalised and deprived. This evidence strongly pointed to the existence of an environmental network which involved interaction between different sets of members and drew the 'joiner' into other organisations. The existence of multiple and overlapping memberships was very clear, suggesting that party membership had evolved from involvement in other groups. However, just as clear was the lack of involvement in traditional political parties. The rise of the Scottish Green membership at this time was not the result of a major shift from other parties.

Although chapter 4 pointed to a high level of membership in other organisations, it was also revealed that the members were not necessarily very active. Around 40 per cent of the respondents appeared to have been somewhat active social movement participants, in a number of different movements. However, the majority appeared more like passive supporters than activists. This was also true of their involvement in the Scottish Green Party itself. Between 50 and 60 per cent were classified as passive members. This finding raises some questions about the nature of interaction between members. If passivity is the key feature of these members, we would not in fact expect there to have been a great deal of interaction between members, for example in the form of social relations.

Another way of exploring the importance of interaction is to assess *how* members become involved. Chapter 5 explored routes into membership of the 1990 Scottish Greens. The evidence indeed indicated that social interaction was not very important. Few members got a membership form from a friend or relative when joining, few had friends as members before they joined, and few met other members socially outside of party activities. It was estimated that only around 15 per cent of the members joined the party through social networks. Lack of social interaction between members at the time may have been a sign that the party would have a problem mobilising more members. Social networks provide information and induce members to join. They can be a useful form of indirect mobilisation for political organisations, where 'leaders get the word out, and citizens get the word' (Rosenstone and Hansen 1993: 28).

Movement networks appeared a little more important as a pathway into membership of the Scottish Greens, as were party recruitment appeals. Overall, however, these party members displayed remarkably high levels of self-initiative when joining. The largest group contacted the party independently and appeared to be 'self-starters'. The level of self-initiative displayed by these members challenges those theories which emphasise the importance of organisational persuasion. Most observers of party or group membership emphasise the importance of active recruitment strategies on the part of the organisation, either face-to-face or mediated, so much so that they appear to under-estimate other membership motivations at work, such as agreement with the organisation's stated objectives. Johnson for example (1995: 31) refers to a 'proclivity to join', which is unrelated to a person's collective or personal interests. Snow *et al.* (1980: 794-795) argue that 'it is important to emphasise that people seldom initially join movements *per se*. Rather they typically are asked to participate in movement activities'. The emphasis appears to be on the opportunities to join that are created by the organisation, a kind of 'exposure effect', rather than the collective goals pursued by that organisation. It should be noted that the Scottish Green Party did not have a very clear recruitment strategy at the time of the study, which must partly explain why the proportion of members responding to the party was small. However, the fact remains that too much emphasis on how organisational leaders 'persuade' individuals to join often neglects the under-lying motivations behind membership. Some highly motivated individuals don't need to be asked. The Scottish Greens in this study don't appear to have been actively recruited as such.

The analysis of why members joined revealed that the party's collective goals provided the key motivation. Selective rewards for membership, such as solidary incentives, and the satisfaction of participating in the party organisation did not appear very important. Nor was there much evidence of 'environmental deprivation', being personally confronted with a specific environmental problem. While a significant proportion of the respondents suggested that they had suffered negative effects from an environmental problem, the majority of members indicated that personal experiences of this nature were not very influential in their decision to join. It was argued, however, that this group of members probably had heightened *perceptions* of environmental problems. Particularly influential on the decision to join the Scottish Greens was 'learning about a national or global environmental event'. These members were concerned about environmental issues. Thus, concern for public goods provided the key to membership, although with environmental issues this partly involves a desire to see the reduction of a public bad.

One of the weaknesses of the 1990 survey was its lack of detailed information on the political views of the members, making conclusions about their ideological belief structures and political values rather tentative. It is impossible to tell how many of these members had a radical ecological vision, as opposed to a more moderate 'environmental' set of demands (see Dobson 1994). However, of all the reasons for joining, the members were most likely to agree with the statement, 'The party provides the best opportunity to achieve the political aims I support'. Such high levels of support for this proposition point to the existence of an ideological precondition for mobilisation. However, we should also be aware that their motivations may have been goal-oriented (based on particular issues), rather than ideological. Nevertheless, the evidence available suggests a mix of 'purpose, principle and ideology' (Wilson 1995: 96) behind membership of the Scottish Greens, rather than selective reward. The members showed every sign of being *committed to the collective cause.*

However, this does not necessarily mean commitment to one organisation only. The Scottish Greens demonstrated an impressively high level of membership involvement in environmental and other social movement organisations. They were a little less likely to belong to FoE than their UK counterparts but they were a little more likely to belong to an environmental group overall (see Rüdig *et al.* 1991: 34). The evidence points to the existence of a green membership network, suggesting that we should not discount the importance of interaction between organisations and between individuals in different organisations, even if social interaction with other party members does not appear very important. Most of these members were completely new to party political membership but they had considerable experience as members of other groups. Even if, as has just been argued, their experience was of passive membership in these organisations, they are likely to have been exposed to information on issues which interested them as well as information on other organisations promoting similar themes. The relevant point, however, is that a belief in the collective cause binds this network.

This study illustrates that incentives for membership are exceptionally difficult to identify and measure, largely because incentives intertwine. It was argued in chapter 5 that selective rewards can act as symbols of collective goods. In addition, the pursuit of a collective objective can involve an element of selective reward. Membership may involve some perception of what is good for the individual. For example, concern about the environment can involve a concern for one's family. Also, the individual may 'feel good about themselves' because they are contributing towards the common good, or through a sense of civic duty. Some studies consider 'civic gratification', 'doing your bit' for the welfare of the community, to be a selective reward for participation. For example Verba *et al.* (1995: 109-110) separate this sense of civic duty from collective incentives, which involve influencing government policy.[2] However, can we practically separate a sense of civic duty from collective incentives? The sense of civic duty is unlikely to be 'felt' if the participant does not agree with the policy goals of the organisation. The study of the Scottish Greens does not suggest that these motivations are separated in the minds of members. The members express themselves in collective terms. They consider themselves to be motivated by the collective good.

---

[2]Verba *et al.* (1995: 109-110) outline four types of motivation: selective material benefits, selective social gratifications, selective civic gratifications and collective outcomes (influencing government policy).

This study began by adopting a rather cautious approach to rational choice theory. It was argued (chapter 3) that political scientists had been preoccupied with rational choice approaches, to the exclusion of other relevant theories. It was also assumed that it is possible to over-estimate the rationality of members. For example, the cost of membership may have been so small and so marginal that joining didn't involve a great deal of thought or deliberation, and it may have involved a very shallow commitment to the organisation. Indeed, as has been seen in this study, party membership does not always involve an intense, high-cost form of participation. However, rational choice *has* been useful in this analysis. As Wilson (1995: 25) has argued, '...it is useful to the extent that it prompts us to search for rational explanations for what heretofore had seemed instinctual, paradoxical, neurotic, habitual, or unconventional behavior'. While recognising the weaknesses of this approach – namely that rationality is difficult to measure – this study has concluded, like Wilson, that people behave in a *more or less* rational way. As Wilson (1995: 26) argues, people 'join associations for a variety of reasons and that they are more or less rational about action taken on behalf of these reasons'.

The Scottish Green Party members were concerned about environmental issues, with global issues appearing most important. Given their commitment to the issues, membership was rational behaviour. Many studies of participation under-estimate the importance of issues, choosing to concentrate on the socio-economic background of members, or the recruitment strategies of organisations. These approaches often neglect the role played by specific issues, the issues that arise spontaneously and get people excited – the passion of politics. Verba *et al.* (1995: 391) comment that many accounts of participation are 'devoid of substantive issue content'. In fact, individuals have concerns and policy preferences. They engage with issues. Verba *et al.* (1995: 392) refer to 'issue engagements' which are 'policy commitments that might serve on their own to stimulate participation'. These can take on two manifestations; when the individual has a 'personal stake' in the policy, or 'caring deeply about a particular political issue'. So, strong views on particular subjects can act as short-term boosts to levels of participation in a party or group. Issue-engagements can perform the role of unpredictable 'wild card' in participation (Verba *et al.* 1995: 522). 'Thus', argue Verba *et al.* (1995: 414) 'political participation is deeply enmeshed with the substance of politics'.

As for *when* people engage with issues, a number of the theories reviewed in chapter 3 pointed to the relevance of political context, or political opportunities. Aarts (1997: 104) points to a neglect of politics in the study of collective action and suggests that studies often concentrate on the individual's decision to contribute, 'instead of exploring the links between collective action and elements of the political context'. This study recognises that the decision to join and the political context are inter-related. It has attempted to address questions of mobilisation within a contextual setting. As Klandermans (1988: 174) argues, we can identify periods of 'insurgency' when the political environment dictates it. The context-sensitive approach recognises that time, place and cultural setting have some relevance.

Chapter 6 explored the relationship between context of joining and reasons for joining. Members who joined at the height of media and general interest in the environment were compared with those members who had a more long-standing membership of the party. The influence of the general political context of the day was clear. The media, critical environmental events and the rise of global issues were more influential in the decision to join the party in 1989 and 1990. However, a comparison of the socio-demographic background and political experiences of the two sets of members suggested that the Scottish Greens had in fact attracted a virtually identical type of member. While activity levels and retention rates were lower amongst the new members, this is probably explained away by the shorter term of membership (see Rothenberg 1988). The party had clearly attracted members from the same potential pool of supporters as before. Nor is there evidence to suggest that these members saw membership of the party as a fashionable act. Nevertheless, the particular set of circumstances that existed at the end of the 1980s did shine through in the responses of the new members. New members had been influenced by the media's coverage of environmental issues to a greater extent than the established membership, and they were significantly more likely to point to 'a particular event highlighting national or global environmental problems (for example Chernobyl, Bhopal)'. These findings illustrate the importance of exploring contextual details surrounding the decision to join. The perceptions of the potential party member will inevitably be influenced by a vast range of external factors which cannot be controlled by the party. One cannot fully understand the development of the Scottish Greens without reference to these types of factors. Indeed, a central theme to emerge from this study is the importance of contextual analysis. The book has argued that it is important to recreate the contextual background in which the decision to join is taken. Such an approach considers a wider set of variables than most approaches (see Foweraker 1997: 66-67).

However, the rise of Scottish Green Party membership at this time also illustrates the importance of organisational effectiveness. At the end of the 1980s, the survey respondents viewed the Scottish Greens as a credible membership option. However, as was revealed in chapter 5, the members in 1990 had their doubts about the party's ability to affect change. In fact, they appeared to have rather low expectations of what the party might achieve. Six in every ten thought the party's 1989 success was 'just a flash in the pan'. This theme re-emerged in the analysis of why many of the members left the party (chapter 7). While some of the members left the party because of a change in their personal circumstances, or because they had come to disagree with what the party stood for, the most common explanation for leaving was the party's failure to make an impact. This was true of the questionnaire respondents in 1990 who were considering leaving as well as ex-members interviewed in 1997. This lack of effectiveness was seen to be the result of a combination of poor party organisation and unfavourable political circumstances, including the difficulties of the first-past-the-post electoral system.[3] Considering these perceptions, it is hardly surprising that environmental pressure groups were viewed as significantly more effective by many of those respondents who had left the party by 1997. Groups like Greenpeace provide a media-communicated demonstration of effectiveness.

Parkin (1968) and Wilson (1995) argue that the position of underdog breeds a sense of moral superiority and this can sustain membership commitment, but is this enough to motivate a party's membership when there appears to be little hope of achieving collective goals?  To an extent purposive goals *were* sufficient to motivate the Scottish Greens when they joined.  However, some evidence of organisational effectiveness and concrete political outcomes is necessary to maintain commitment.  In the case of the Scottish Greens, demoralisation set in during the 1990s precisely because the specific aims (collective goals) of the organisation were not achieved.

By the year 2002 however the Scottish Green Party was operating within a very different political setting and could argue that it was, for the first time, making an electoral impact (see Bennie 2002).  Having entered the new Parliament in 1999 the party could point to concrete evidence of success as well as highlighting improved prospects for future elections.  However, as the 2002 survey of Scottish Greens revealed (chapter 8) these developments had very little impact on the membership profile of the party.  The Scottish Greens in 2002 looked very like their 1990 counterparts, in terms of social and political background, as well as motivations for joining the party.  This suggests that the party has been rather unsuccessful at expanding its membership base beyond the typical green supporter. However, the steady rise in membership at this time does suggest that the party can attract more of these people during periods of relative electoral success. Furthermore, the commitment of members in 2002 to green policies and principles confirms the importance of collective, purpose incentives.

This study of the Scottish Greens has considered a number of different approaches to participation.  While these approaches have weaknesses, each has something to offer in an explanation of why people join the Scottish Green Party. As was argued in chapter 3, they can be combined to offer a more complete understanding. Human beings can be motivated by different identities and values, while at the same time evaluating the consequences (costs and benefits) of different courses of action which may change according to their assessment of the political environment.

*Implications for the Scottish Green Party*

The findings of this study also have implications for the Scottish Green Party itself. To a large extent, the party cannot be held responsible for fluctuations in

---

[3]As noted in chapter 2, the English Greens suffered from internal arguments to a greater extent than the Scottish party.  Therefore, the English party members were more likely to blame lack of effectiveness on internal party problems (Rüdig *et al.* 1993: 63).

membership. It has been argued that the rise in membership at the end of the 1980s appeared to be due to a series of events outside the control of the party. As for the numbers leaving so soon after they joined, it could be argued that there was nothing very exceptional about this. There is a natural turnover effect in any organisation and in many groups and parties length of membership tends to be short. As Rothenberg (1988) demonstrates, members of organisations come and go. Furthermore, new members are always the most likely to leave. Given the direction of political events and the natural dynamics of party membership, the fact that most of the 1990 members left the party is not particularly surprising.

However, the party probably should take some responsibility for members leaving. The party had failed to convince these members that their subscription was contributing to a greater good. It is worth noting that the members in this study did not necessarily define party success as electoral achievements. They were as likely to consider putting pressure on the other parties, or changing individual lifestyles as indications of party success. However, the party had failed to convince many of these members that it was having such an impact. It is clear that a small party that relies so heavily on members' financial contributions needs to communicate with its members and convince them of its effectiveness. This is even more important during those periods when the media are not interested in party activities. The party must maintain contact with its members, the majority of whom are passive, and provide them with reasons for staying. Furthermore, the party probably needs to accept that some members will never be active. Party literature could do more to make the passive member feel valued within the organisation. As has previously been argued the party might consider developing a more sophisticated 'membership care' programme which would involve party literature designed specifically for the passive member (Rüdig *et al.* 1991: 82).

The party cannot offer its members many tangible benefits in return for membership. It must therefore find a way to convince members that they are part of an important movement that is trying to do something to 'save the planet'. Unfortunately for the party, motivation provided by collective goods is not often enough to sustain membership. Rothenberg's work is again useful, illustrating that the decision to stay is not always the same as the decision to join in the first place. 'Broad motivations are replaced by more specific ones', Rothenberg (1988: 1143) argues. A similar process appears to be at work in the Scottish Green Party. While the decision to join appeared to be motivated by general points of principle (a desire to protect the environment) specific issues were much more important in the retention decision, including assessment of organisational effectiveness. In other words, collective incentives may explain the decision to join but the decision to stay is dependent on more specific assessments of the party.

Cause for concern for the party was that many leavers interviewed in 1997 had a very negative view of their membership experience. The party had a severe image problem amongst the lapsed members. Quite possibly, these members were simply not party animals, and they didn't like the culture of debate in the party. Very few came to the Scottish Greens from membership of another political party. Very few left the Greens to join up with another party. In other words, there may not have been much the party could have done to prevent these people leaving. Nor could they do anything about those people who fundamentally disagreed with an aspect of party policy. However, an important feature of leaving highlighted by the study was the inefficient party organisation that failed to keep track of members and allowed them to drift away. A small party that relies on its members cannot afford to lose members who might stay if encouraged to do so. Some members will inevitably leave, but others will stay if they are sent a reminder and new membership form.

However, the Scottish Greens in the year 2004 have a number of reasons to be more optimistic. Most obviously, the political backdrop of party activity is now much less hostile. The 2003 Scottish Parliamentary Election result provides tangible evidence of the party's ability to make an impact. The presence of seven Green MSPs in the Parliament acts as a constant reminder of party effectiveness (see chapter 2).

Just as important, this study suggests that the Greens in Scotland have a core of activists and members who sustain the party through good times and bad. The 1997 interviews pointed to a small group of members who were completely committed to the party. They were very ideologically motivated and insisted that the party was the only way to promote a vision of an alternative, ecological society. These kinds of activists are an absolutely necessity for any party. Furthermore, the 2002 survey provides more detailed evidence that the new wave of ordinary members is also highly committed to green politics. The overall impression is that the 2002 Scottish Greens have a long-standing attachment to green ideas and they are united on policy priorities.

The organisation of the Scottish Greens has also received an enormous boost in recent years, partly due to the financial rewards of parliamentary status but also due to the party's more energetic attempts to organise internal structures more effectively. Moreover, the party now accepts the need to actively recruit new members, and to make efforts to retain the commitment of members. In previous years the party was not good at keeping in touch with its membership base, but it would appear to have learned from these experiences.

These factors make the party look like a more attractive membership option. As has been stated, the members in this study did not join because of a high-profile party membership drive. They were fairly self-motivated. However, this is not to say that more serious attempts to recruit members cannot be successful. There is a large environmental constituency that can be tapped by the party. People who are committed to the environmental movement may be encouraged to change their tactics to take advantage of a new set of political opportunities.

*Implications for Future Research*

The central theme to emerge from the theoretical review was the fragmentation of research on political participation and social movements. For example, there is definitely scope for increased co-operation between political scientists and sociologists in this area. As Burstein (1995: 13) has argued, 'Unfortunately, tradition, vocabulary, and, perhaps, assumptions about the nature of democratic politics have served to divide political scientists and sociologists'. It has also been shown that studies of participation and social movement often reside in one of a number of 'camps', for example those that emphasise the resources of participants, those that look to organisational recruitment methods, and those that examine individual motivations. Too much emphasis on one approach can neglect the value of others.

Furthermore, there is a need to combine theoretical understanding of participation with empirical evidence. To date, there are remarkably few examples of studies of environmental participants. It is very difficult to reach any clear conclusions on the nature of participation in the environmental movement based on the limited range of information that currently exists, in Britain as a whole but especially in Scotland. More empirical evidence needs to be gathered on who joins green groups and parties, and why. At the moment, we know very little about how organisations overlap and what the implications are for membership. Indeed, the extensive range of green groups and networks that exists suggests endless possibilities for empirical research. However, these studies ought to be theoretically informed. Empirical case studies in the British social sciences can lack such a theoretical framework.[4]

Future research might also address the gap in our knowledge of Scottish party members more generally. This study did not reveal any fundamental differences between Greens in Scotland and the rest of the UK, but there is a need for more research to assess the 'uniqueness' of the party membership experience in Scotland. The large studies of the UK parties in recent years included only a small sample of Scottish members, and detailed assessments of these members were not possible (Bennie *et al.* 1996; Curtice *et al.* 1993; Seyd and Whiteley 1992, 2002; Whiteley *et al.* 1994; Whiteley and Seyd 2002). In particular, very little is known about the nationalist party membership, and motivations behind membership of the other small parties remains a mystery. The creation of the new Scottish Parliament changes the political landscape and may have implications in terms of how potential political participants behave. Now would be an appropriate time to extend our knowledge of party membership in Scotland. These arguments also apply to the membership of environmental groups. Is there anything distinctive about the decision to join an environmental organisation in Scotland? Has the setting-up of the Parliament increased mobilisation potential? At the moment, these questions cannot be answered.

---

[4]Over a decade ago Rüdig *et al.* (1991) noted the 'atheoretical inclination of much of British social sciences'.

# Bibliography


Aarts, K. (1997) 'Soil pollution, community action and political opportunities', in R. Edmondson (ed) (1997) *The Political Context of Collective Action: Power, Argumentation and Democracy*, Routledge, London and New York, pp.105-125.

Aberle, D. F. (1966) *The Peyote Religion Among the Navaho*, Aldine Publishing, Chicago.

Abrams, P. and Little, A. (1965) 'The Young Activist in British Politics', *British Journal of Sociology*, Vol.16, pp.315-333.

Abrams, P. and McCulloch, A. (1976) *Communes, Sociology and Society*, Cambridge UP, Cambridge.

Alber, J. (1989) 'Modernization, cleavage structures, and the rise of green parties and lists in Europe', in F. Muller-Rommel (ed) *New Politics in Western Europe: The Rise and Success of Green Parties and Alternative Lists*, Westview Press: Boulder CO, pp. 195-210.

Aldrich, J.H. (1993) 'Rational Choice and Turnout', *American Journal of Political Science*, Vol.37, pp.246-78.

Almond, G.A. (1954) *The Appeals of Communism*, Princeton UP, Princeton New Jersey.

Almond, G.A. and Verba, S. (1963) *The Civic Culture*, Princeton UP, Princeton New Jersey.

Anderson, A. (1997) *Media, Culture and the Environment*, UCL Press, London.

Arendt, H. (1951) *The Origins of Totalitarianism*, Harcourt, Brace, New York.

Bahro, R. (1982) *Socialism and Survival*, Heretic Books, London.

Bahro, R. (1986) *Building the Green Movement*, GMP, London.

Barber, B. (1984) *Strong Democracy: Participatory Politics for a New Age*, University of California Press, Berkeley, California.

Barker, C., Johnson, A. and Lavalette, M. (2001) (eds) *Leadership and Social Movements*, Manchester University Press, Manchester.

Barnes, S. and Kasse, M. (1979) *Political Action: Mass Participation in Five Western Democracies*, Sage, London.

Barry, B. (1978) *Sociologists, Economists and Democracy*, University of Chicago Press, Chicago.

Barton, T. and Doring, H. (1986) 'The Social and Attitudinal Profile of Social Democratic Party Activists', *Political Studies*, Vol.34, pp.296-305.

Baumgartner, F. R., and Leech, B. L. (1998) *Basic Interests: The Importance of Groups in Politics and in Political Science*, Princeton University Press, Princeton, New Jersey.

Beck, U. (1992) *Risk Society: Towards a New Modernity*, Sage, London.

Beck, U. (1995) *Ecological Politics in an Age of Risk*, Polity, Cambridge.

Beck, U. (1996) 'Environment, Knowledge and Indeterminacy: Beyond Modernist Ecology?' in S. Lash, B. Szerszynski and B. Wynne (eds) *Risk, Environment and Modernity: Towards a New Ecology*, pp.27-43.

Beck, U. (1997) 'Global Risk Politics' in M. Jacobs (ed) *Greening the Millennium? The New Politics of the Environment*, Blackwell, Oxford, pp.18-33.

Beckford, J.A. (1975) *The Trumpet of Prophecy: A Sociological Study of Jehovah's Witnesses*, Blackwell, London.

Bell, D. (1999) *The Coming of Post-Industrial Society: A Venture in Social Forecasting*, Basic Books, New York.

Bennie, L. (1998) 'Greenpeace and the Oil Companies: Beyond Brent Spar', *Parliamentary Affairs,* Vol. 51, No.3. pp.397-410. Reprinted in G. Jordan and F.F. Ridley (eds) *Protest Politics: Cause Groups and Campaigns*, Oxford University Press, Oxford, pp.89-102.

Bennie, L. (2002) 'Exploiting New Electoral Opportunities: The Small Parties in Scotland', in G. Hassan and C. Warhurst (eds) *Tomorrow's Scotland* (London: Lawrence and Wishart), pp. 98-115.

Bennie, L. (2003) 'Social Movements' in R. Axtmann (ed) *Understanding Democratic Politics: An Introduction*, Sage, London, pp.164-173.

Bennie, L., Brand, J. and Mitchell, J. (1997) *How Scotland Votes: Scottish Parties and Elections*, Manchester University Press, Manchester.

Bennie, L. and Clark, A. (2003) 'Towards Moderate Pluralism: Scotland's Post-Devolution Party System 1999-2002', *British Elections and Parties Review 13,* Frank Cass, London, pp.134-158.

Bennie, L., Curtice, J. and Rüdig, W. (1996) 'Party Members' in D. McIver (ed) *The Liberal Democrats*, Prentice Hall/Harvester Wheatsheaf, Hemel Hempstead, pp.135-154.

Bennie, L.G., Franklin, M.N. and Rüdig, W. (1993) 'The Mixed Fortunes of the British Green Party: 1989-1992' in J. Holder (ed) *Perspectives on the Environment: Research and Action in the 1990's,* Edward Elgar, Cheltenham.

Bennie, L.G., Franklin, M.N. and Rüdig, W. (1995) 'Green Dimensions: The Ideology of the British Greens', in W. Rüdig (ed) *Green Politics Three*, Edinburgh Univerity Press, Edinburgh.

Bennie, L. and Rüdig, W. (1993) 'Youth and the Environment' *Youth and Policy,* Issue no.42, Autumn 1993.

Berrington, H. (1989) 'The literature on parties and pressure groups', *Contemporary Record*, Vol.2, pp.18-25.

Berry, D. (1970) *The Sociology of Grass Roots Politics: A Study of Party Membership,* MacMillan, London.

Berry, J. M. (1984) *The Interest Group Society,* Little Brown, Boston and Toronto.

Blondel, J. (1973) *Voters, Parties and Leaders*, Penguin Harmondsworth.

Blumer, H. (1960) 'Social Movements', in A. McClung Lee (ed) *Principles of Sociology,* Barnes and Noble: New York, pp.199-220.

Bochel, J. and Denver, D. (1983) 'The 1983 General Election in Scotland', in D. McCrone, (ed) *The Scottish Government Yearbook 1984*, Unit for the Study of Government in Scotland, Edinburgh, pp. 4-18.

Bochel, J. and Denver, D. (1988) 'The 1987 General Election in Scotland', in D. McCrone, and A. Brown (eds) *The Scottish Government Yearbook 1988*, Unit for the Study of Government in Scotland, Edinburgh, pp. 36-45.

Bochel, J. and Denver, D. (1989) 'The Scottish District Elections of 1988', in A. Brown, and D. McCrone (eds) *The Scottish Government Yearbook 1989*, Unit for the Study of Government in Scotland, Edinburgh, pp. 20-31.

Bochel, J. and Denver, D. (1990) 'The 1989 European Elections in Scotland', in A. Brown, and R. Parry (eds) *The Scottish Government Yearbook 1990*, Unit for the Study of Government in Scotland: Edinburgh, pp. 90-99.

Bochel, J. and Denver, D. (1992) 'The 1992 General Election in Scotland', *Scottish Affairs*, no.1, pp.14-26.

Bomberg, E. (2002) 'The Europeanisation of Green Parties', *West European Politics*, Vol.25, No.3, pp.29-50.

Bond, R. (1999) 'Situating the Blair Membership Boom Within its Social and Political Context', *Scottish Affairs*, No.26, pp.47-72.

Boon, M. and Curtice, J. (2003) 'Scottish Elections Research May-June 2003', Report for the *Electoral Commission*, 2003.

Bosso, C. J. (1991) 'Adaptation and Change in the Environmental Movement', in A. Cigler and B. Loomis (eds) *Interest Group Politics*, 3rd edition, CQ Press, Washington DC, pp.51-176.

Bosso, C. J. (1994) 'The Color of Money: Environmental Groups and the Pathologies of Fund-Raising', in A. Cigler and B. Loomis (eds) *Interest Group Politics*, 4th edition, CQ Press, Washington DC, pp.101-130.

Bosso, C.J. (2003) 'Rethinking the Concept of Membership in Nature Advocacy Orgnaizations', *The Policy Studies Journal*, Vol.13, No.3, pp.397-411.

Bosso, C. J. and Guber, D. L. (2002) 'New Challenges for US Environmental Organization' in N. Vig and M. Kraft (eds) *Environmental Policy: New Directions for the 21st Century*, 5th edition, CQ Press: Washington DC, pp.79-101.

Brand, J. (1973) 'Party Organization and the Recruitment of Councillors', *British Journal of Political Science*, Vol.3, pp.473-486.

Brand, J., Mitchell, J. and Surridge, P. (1993) 'Identity and the Vote: Class and Nationality in Scotland', in Norris, P. *et al.* (eds) *British Elections and Parties Yearbook 1993*, Harverster Wheatsheaf, Hemel Hemstead pp.143-157.

Brand, J., Mitchell, J. and Surridge, P. (1995) 'Will Scotland Come to the Aid of the Party?', in Heath, A., Jowell, R. and Curtice, J. (eds) *Labour's Last Chance?: The 1992 Election and Beyond*, Dartmouth, Aldershot.

Bromley, C., Curtice, J., Hinds, K. and Park, A. (eds) (2003) *Devolution – Scottish Answers to Scottish Questions?*, Edinburgh University Press, Edinburgh.

Brown, A., McCrone, D. and Paterson, L. (1998) *Politics and Society in Scotland*, 2nd Edition, MacMillan, London.

Brown, A., McCrone, D., Paterson, L. and Surridge, P. (1999) *The Scottish Electorate: The 1997 General Election and Beyond*, MacMillan, London.

Browne, W. P. (1998) *Groups, Interests and U.S. Public Policy*, Georgetown University Press, Washington D.C.

Bryner, G. C. (2001) *Gaia's Wager: Environmental Movements and the Challenge of Sustainability*, Rowman and Littlefield, Lanham, Maryland.

Budge, I. and Farlie, D. (1975) 'Political Recruitment and Dropout', *British Journal of Political Science*, Vol.5, pp.33-68.

Burchell, J. (2001) 'Evolving or Reforming? Assessing Organisational Reform Within European Green Parties', *West European Politics*, Vol.24, No.3, pp.113-134.

Burchell, J. (2002) *The Evolution of Green Politics: Development and Change Within European Green Parties*, Earthscan, London.

Burgess, M. and Lee, A. (1990) 'The United Kingdom' in J. Lodge (ed.) *The 1989 Election of the European Parliament*, MacMillan, Houndmills.

Burningham, K. (1996) 'Us and Them: The Construction and Maintenance of Divisions in a Planning Dispute', in C. Samson and N. South (eds) *The Social Construction of Social Policy: Methodologies, Racism, Citizenship and the Environment*, MacMillan Press, London, pp.193-209.

Burningham, K. (1998) 'A noisy road or noisy resident? A demonstration of the utility of social constructionism for analysing environmental problems', *Sociological Review*, Vol. 46 No.3, pp.536-563.

Burstein, P. (1995) 'What Do Interest Groups, Social Movements, and Political Parties Do? A Synthesis', Paper presented to American Political Science Association, Chicago, September 2, 1995.

Butler, D. and Kavangh, D. (1997) *The British General Election of 1997*, MacMillan, London.

Butler, D. and Stokes, D. (1969) *Political Change in Britain*, St.Martin's Press, New York.

Byrne, P. (1988) *The Campaign for Nuclear Disarmament*, Croom Helm, London.

Byrne, P. (1989) 'Great Britain: The Green Party', in F. Muller-Rommel (ed.) *New Politics in Western Europe*, Westview Press, Boulder, San Francisco and London, pp. 101-111.

Byrne, P. (1997) *Social Movements in Britain*, Routledge, London and New York.

Carter, N. (1992) 'Whatever Happened to the Environment? The British General Election of 1992', *Environmental Politics*, Vol.1 No.3.

Carter, N. (1997) 'The 1997 British General Election', *Environmental Politics*, Vol. 6, No. 3, pp.156-161.

Carter, N. (2002) *The Politics of the Environment: Ideas, Activism, Policy*, Cambridge University Press, Cambridge.

Central Statistical Office (1992), *Regional Trends 27*, HMSO, London.

Central Statistical Office (1993), *Regional Trends 28*, HMSO, London.

Cigler, A. J. and Loomis, B. A. (2002) (eds) *Interest Group Politics*, 6th edition, CQ Press, Washington DC.

Clarke, P.B. and Wilson, J.Q. (1961) 'Incentive systems: a theory of organisations', *Administrative Science Quarterly*, Vol.6, pp.129-166.

Corbett, G. (2003a) 'Getting into the winning habit', *GreenPrint: The Journal of the Scottish Green Party*, April, p.4.

Corbett, G. (2003b) 'A job well done and now more to do', *GreenPrint: The Journal of the Scottish Green Party*, May 2003.

Corbett, R. (1994) 'The European Election Results and the Composition of the New European Parliament', *Representation*, Vol.32, No.120.

Cotgrove, S. (1982) *Catastrophe or Cornucopia*, John Wiley and Sons, New York.

Cotgrove, S. and Duff, A. (1980) 'Environmentalism, Middle-Class Radicalism, and Politics', *British Journal of Sociology*, Vol.32, pp.92-110.

Cowley, P. (2000) 'Voting in the Scottish Parliament: The First Year', in J. Tonge *et al.* (eds) *British Elections and Parties Review 11: The 2001 General Election*, Frank Cass, London, pp.84-103.

Cramb, A. (1992) 'Shades of Radicalism as Greens Call for Civil Disobedience', *The Scotsman*, 21st March.

Crewe, I. (1984) 'The Electorate: Partisan Dealignment Ten Years On', in Berrington, H. (ed.) *Change in British Politics*, Frank Cass.

Curtice, J. (1989) 'The 1989 European Elections: Protest or Green Tide?', *Electoral Studies*, Vol.8, pp.217-30.

Curtice, J. (1992) 'The North-South Divide', *British Social Attitudes Survey*, No. 9, pp.71-88.

Curtice, J. (2002) 'Devolution and Democracy: Old Trust or New Cynicism?' in J. Curtice *et al.* (eds) *New Scotland: New Society?*, Polygon, Edinburgh.

Curtice, J. (2003a) 'Devolution Meets the Voters: Lessons from the Second Scottish Parliament Election', paper prepared for *Elections, Public Opinion and Parties* conference, Cardiff, 12-14 September 2003.

Curtice, J. (2003b) 'Turnout, Electoral Behaviour and Fragmentation of the Party System', in R. Burnside, S. Herbert and S. Curtis 'Election 2003', Scottish Parliament Information Centre, Research Report, The Scottish Parliament, Edinburgh, pp.12-13.

Curtice, J., D. McCrone, A. Park and L. Paterson (2002) *New Scotland: New Society?*, Polygon, Edinburgh.

Curtice, J., Rüdig, W. and Bennie, L.G. (1993) 'Liberal Democrats Reveal All', *Strathclyde Papers on Government and Politics*, no.96.

Dahl, R. (1961) *Who Governs?* Yale University Press, New Haven, CT.

Dahl, R. (1982) *Dilemmas of Pluralist Democracy,* Yale University Press, New Haven, CT.

Dalton, R. J. (1996) *Citizen Politics: Public Opinion and Political Parties in Advanced Industrial Democracies*, Chatham House, Chatham, N.J.

Dalton, R. J. (1998) *Citizen Politics: Public Opinion and Political Parties in Advanced Industrial Democracies,* 2nd edition, Chatham House, Chatham, N.J.

Dalton, R. J., and Keuchler, M. (1990) (eds) *Challenging the Political Order: New Social and Political Movements in Western Democracy*, Polity Press, Cambridge.

Dalton, R. J. and Wattenberg, M. P. (2002) *Parties Without Partisans: Political Change in Advanced Industrial Democracies*, Oxford University Press, Oxford.

Davies, J.A. (1959) 'A formal interpretation of the theory of relative deprivation', *Sociometry*, Vol.22, pp.280-296.

Della Porta, D. and Diani, M. (1999) *Social Movements: An Introduction*, Blackwell, Oxford.

Denver, D. (1994) 'The 1994 European Elections in Scotland', *Scottish Affairs*, No.9, pp.59-67.

Denver, D. (2003) 'A Wake Up! Call to the Parties? The Results of the Scottish Parliament Elections 2003', *Scottish Affairs*, No.44, pp.31-53.

Denver, D. and Bochel, H. (1973) 'The Political Socialization of Activists in the British Communist Party', *British Journal of Political Science*, Vol. 3, pp.53-71.

Denver, D. and Bochel, H. (1994) 'The Last Act: The Regional Elections of 1994', *Scottish Affairs*, No.9, pp. 68-79.

Denver, D. and I. MacAllister (1999) 'The Scottish Parliament Elections 1999', *Scottish Affairs*, No.28, pp.10-31.

Diani, M. (1992) 'The Concept of Social Movement', *Sociological Review*, Vol.40, pp.1-25.

Diani, M. (2003a) 'Introduction: Social Movements, Contentious Actions, and Social Networks: From Metaphor to Substance?' in M. Diani and D. McAdam (eds) *Social Movements and Networks: Relational Approaches to Collective Action*, Oxford University Press, New York, pp.1-18.

Diani, M. (2003b) 'Networks and Social Movements: A Research Programme', in M. Diani, and D. McAdam, (eds) *Social Movements and Networks: Relational Approaches to Collective Action*, Oxford University Press, New York, pp.299-319.

Diani, M. and Eyerman, R. (1992) *Studying Collective Action*, Sage, London.

Diani, M. and McAdam, D. (2003) (eds) *Social Movements and Networks: Relational Approaches to Collective Action*, Oxford University Press, New York.

Dobson, A. (1990) *Green Political Thought*, Routledge, London.

Dobson, A. (1995) *Green Political Thought,* 2nd edition, Unwin Hyman, London.

Dobson, A. (2000) *Green Political Thought*, 3rd edition, Routledge, London.

Doherty, B. (1992a) 'The Fundi-Realo Controversy: An Analysis of Four European Green Parties', *Environmental Politics* Vol.1, No.1, pp.95-120.

Doherty, B. (1992b) 'The Autumn 1991 Conference of the UK Green Party', *Environmental Politics* Vol.1, No.2, pp.292-8.

Doherty, B. (2002) *Ideas and Actions in the Green Movement*, Routledge, London.

Doherty, B., Paterson, M., Plows A. and Wall, D. (2003) 'Explaining the Fuel Protests', *British Journal of Politics and International Relations*, Vol.5, No.1, pp.1-23.

Downs, A. (1957) *An Economic Theory of Democracy*, Harper, New York.

Downs, A. (1972) 'Up and down with ecology – the issue-attention cycle', *The Public Interest*, No.28, pp.38-50.

Downs, A. (1973) 'The Political Economy of Improving Our Environment', in J. S. Bain, *Environmental Decay: Economic Causes and Remedies*, Little, Brown and Company, Boston, pp.59-81.

Dryzek, J.S., D. Downes, C. Hunold, D. Schlosberg, and H.K. Hernes (2003) *Green States and Social Movements: Environmentalism in the United States, United Kingdom, Germany and Norway*, Oxford University Press, Oxford/New York.

Dunleavy, P. (1991) *Democracy, Bureaucracy and Public Choice*, Harvester Wheatsheaf, London.

Duverger, M. (1954, 1964) *Political Parties*, Methuen: London.

Eckstein, H. (1992) 'Rationality and Frustration', in H. Eckstein (ed) *Regarding Politics: Essays on Political Theory, Stability and Change*, University of California Press, Berkeley.

Edmondson, R. (1997) (ed) *The Political Context of Collective Action: Power, Argumentation and Democracy*, Routledge, London and New York.

Edmondson, R., and Nullmeier, F. (1997) 'Knowledge, rhetoric and political action in context', in R. Edmondson (ed) (1997) *The Political Context of Collective Action: Power, Argumentation and Democracy*, Routledge, London and New York, pp. 210-238.

Ehrlich, P. (1968) *The Population Bomb*, Ballantine, New York.

Ehrlich, P. and Ehrlich, A. (1972) *Population, Resources, Environment*, Freeman, San Francisco.

Eyerman, R. and Jamison, A. (1991) *Social Movements: A Cognitive Approach*, Polity Press, Cambridge.

Finger, M. (1994) 'From Knowledge to Action? Exploring the Relationship Between Environmental Experiences, Learning, and Behaviour', *Journal of Social Issues*, Vol.50, No.3, pp.141-160.

Fisher, S.L. (1980) 'The Decline of Parties Thesis and the Role of Minor Parties', in P. Merkl (ed) *Western European Party Systems*, Free Press, New York, pp.609-13.

Flynn. A. and Lowe, P. (1992) 'The Greening of the Tories: The Conservative Party and the Environment', in W. Rüdig (ed) *Green Politics Two*, Edinburgh University Press, Edinburgh, pp.9-36.

Foster, K, Wilmot, A. and Dobbs, J. (1990) *General Household Survey 1988*, HMSO, London.

Foweraker, J. (1997) 'Social movement theory and the political context of collective action', in R. Edmondson (ed) *The Political Context of Collective Action: Power, Argumentation and Democracy*, Routledge, London and New York, pp.64-77.

Frankland, E.G. (1990) 'Does Green Politics have a Future in Britain? An American Perspective' in W. Rüdig (ed) *Green Politics One 1990*, Edinburgh University Press, Edinburgh pp.7-28.

Frankland, E.G. and Schoonmaker, D. (1992) *Between Protest and Power: The Green Party in Germany*, Westview Press, Bolder, Colo. and Oxford.

Franklin, M. and Rüdig, W. (1992) 'The green voter in the 1989 European Elections', *Environmental Politics*, Vol.1, No.4, pp.129-159.

Franklin, M. and Rüdig, W. (1995) 'On the Durability of Green Politics: Evidence From the 1989 European Election Study', *Comparative Political Studies*, Vol. 28, No.3, pp.409-439.

Fraser, D. (2003) 'The Media Campaign', in Burnside, R., Herbert, S. and Curtis, S. 'Election 2003', *Scottish Parliament Information Centre*, Research Report, The Scottish

Parliament, Edinburgh, pp.28-29.

Freeman, J. (1983) (ed) *Social Movements of the Sixties and Seventies*, Longman, New York.

Friends of the Earth Scotland (2003) 'How Green Was My Party? FoE Comparison of Manifesto Commitments', http://www.foe-scotland.org.uk/press.

Gamson, W. (1975) *The Strategy of Social Protest*, Dorsey, Homewood, Ill.

Gamson, W.A (1992) 'The Social Psychology of Collective Action', in A.D Morris and C.M. Mueller (eds) *Frontiers in Social Movement Theory*, Yale UP, New Haven/London, pp.53-76.

Gamson, W. A. and Meyer, D. S. (1996) 'Framing political opportunity' in D. McAdam, J.D. McCarthy and M.N. Zald. (eds) *Comparative Perspectives on Social Movements: Political Opportunitites, Mobilizing Structures, and Cultural Framings*, Cambridge University Press, Cambridge, New York, pp.275-290.

Garner, R. (1996) *Contemporary Movements and Ideologies*, McGraw Hill, New York.

Garner, R. (1996) *Environmental Politics*, Prentice Hall/Harvester Wheatsheaf, Hemel Hempstead.

Garner, R. (2000) *Environmental Politics*, Palgrave, Basingstoke.

Garner, R., and Kelly, R. (1998) *British Political Parties Today*, 2nd edition, MUP Manchester.

Giddens, A. (1998) *The Third Way: The Renewal of Social Democracy*, Polity Press, Cambridge.

Giugni, M.G., McAdam, D. and Tilly, C. (1998) (eds) *From Contention to Democracy*, Rowman and Littlefield, Latham, Maryland.

Godwin, J., J. M. Jasper and F. Polletta (2001) *Passionate Politics: Emotions and Social Movements*, University of Chicago Press, Chicago.

Godwin, R.K. (1988) *One Billion Dollars of Influence*, Chatham House, Chatham House, NJ.

Goldsmith, E. (1971) (ed.) *Can Britain Survive?*, Tom Stacey, London.

Goldsmith, E. (1978) *The Stable Society: Its Structure and Control*, Wadebridge Press, Wadebridge.

Gorz, A. (1985) *Paths to Paradise*, Pluto, London.

Green, D.P. and Shapiro, I. (1994) *Pathologies of Rational Choice Theory*, Yale UP, New Haven and London.

Hallman, W. K. and Wandersman, A. (1992) 'Attribution of Responsibility and Individual and Collective Coping with Environmental Threats', *Journal of Social Issues*, Vol.48., No., 4, 1992, pp.102-118.

Hallsworth, S. (1994) 'Understanding New Social Movements', *Sociological Review*, Vol.51.

Hanson, A. (1993) (ed.) *The Mass Media and Environmental Issues*, Leicester University Press, Leicester.

Harper, R. (2003) 'Let's be winners out there', *Greenprint: The Journal of the Scottish Green Party*, April 2003.

Heath, A., McLean, I. and Taylor, B. (1997) 'How Much is at Stake? Electoral Behaviour in Second-Order Elections', *Centre for Research into Elections and Social Trends*, Working Paper, no.59., SCPR, London.

Held, D. (1987) *Models of Democracy*, Stanford University Press, Stanford CA.

*The Herald* 23 April 1999.

*The Herald* 8 February 2003.

*The Herald* 7 March 2003.

*The Herald* 18 April 2003.

*The Herald* 29 April 2003.

*The Herald* 5 June 2003.

Hetherington, P. (1979) 'The 1979 General Election Campaign in Scotland', in M.N. Drucker and N.L. Drucker *The Scottish Government Yearbook 1980*, Paul Harris Publishing, Edinburgh, pp. 91-100.

Hindess, B. (1988) *Choice, Rationality and Social Theory,* Unwin Hyman, London.

Hoffer, E. (1951) *The True Believer: Thoughts on the Nature of Mass Movements,* Harper and Row, New York.

Hyvarinen, M. (1997) 'The merging of context into political action', in Edmondson, R. (ed) (1997) *The Political Context of Collective Action: Power, Argumentation and Democracy,* Routledge, London and New York, pp.33-46.

Inglehart, R. (1977) *The Silent Revolution: Changing Values and Political Styles among Western Publics,* Princeton UP, Princeton, NJ.

Inglehart, R. (1990) 'Values, Ideology and Cognitive Mobilization in New Social Movements', in R. J. Dalton and M. Kuechler (eds) *Challenging the Political Order,* Polity Press, Cambridge.

Inglehart, R. (1997) *Modernization and Postmodernization,* Princeton University Press, Princeton, NJ.

Jackman, R. (1987) 'Political Institutions and Voter Turnout in Industrialized Democracies', *American Political Science Review,* Vol. 81, pp.405-423.

Jackman, R. (1993) 'Response to Aldrich's Rational Choice and Turnout: Rationality and Political Participation', *American Journal of Political Science,* Vol. 37, pp.279-90.

Jacobs, M. (1997) 'The Politics of the Environment', in M. Jacobs (ed) *Greening the Millennium? The New Politics of the Environment,* Blackwell, Oxford, pp. 1-17.

Jacobs, M. (1999) 'Environmental Modernisation: The New Labour Agenda', *Fabian Society Pamphlet,* No.591.

Jacobs, E. and Worcester, R. (1990) *We British: Britain Under the MORIscope,* Weidenfeld and Nicolson, London.

Jamieson, B. (1999) (ed) *An Illustrated Guide to the Scottish Economy,* Duckworth, London.

Jamison, A. (1996) 'The Shaping of the Global Environmental Agenda: The Role of Non-Governmental Organisations', in S. Lash, B. Szerszynski, and B. Wynne (eds) *Risk, Environment and Modernity: Towards a New Ecology,* pp.224-245.

Jenkins, J.C. (1983) 'Resource Mobilisation Theory and the Study of Social Movements', *Annual Review of Sociology,* Vol.9, pp.527-553.

Jenkins, J. Craig, and C. Perrow (1977) 'Insurgency of the Powerless: Farm Worker Movements (1946-1972)' *American Sociological Review,* Vol. 42, pp.249-68.

Johnson, P.E. (1995) 'How Environmental Groups Recruit Members: Does the Logic Still Hold Up?', Paper presented at the 1995 American Political Science Association Meeting, Chicago, USA.

Johnson, P. (1998) 'Interest Group Recruiting: Finding Members and Keeping Them', in A.J. Cigler and B.A. Loomis (eds) *Interest Group Politics,* Congressional Quarterly, Washington D.C.

Johnston, H. and Klandermans, B. (1995) (eds) *Social Movements and Culture,* University of Minnesota Press, Minneapolis.

Jordan, G. (1998) 'Introduction' in F.F. Ridley and G. Jordan,. *Protest Politics: Cause Groups and Campaigns,* Oxford University Press, Oxford.

Jordan, G. and Maloney, W. (1997) *The Protest Business? Mobilising Campaign Groups,* Manchester University Press, Manchester and New York.

Jordan, G. and Richardson, J. (1987) *British Politics and the Policy Process*, Allen and Unwin, London.

Katz, R.S. and Mair, P. (1992) (eds) *Party Organization: A Data Handbook*, Sage, London.

Kartz, R.S. and Mair, P. (1994) (eds) *How Parties Organise*, Sage, London.

Kavanagh, D. (1983) *Political Science and Political Behaviour*, Unwin Hyman, London.

Keck, M.E., and Sikkink, K. (1998) *Activists Beyond Borders: Advocacy Networks in International Politics*, Cornell University Press, Ithaca, New York.

Kellas, J. (1989) *The Scottish Political System* 4th edition, Cambridge University Press, Cambridge.

Kellas, J. (1990) *The Scottish Political System* 5th edition, Cambridge University Press, Cambridge.

Kellner, P. (1989) 'Decoding the Green Message', *The Independent*, 7 July.

Kemp, P. and Wall, D. (1990) *A Green Manifesto for the 1990s*, Penguin, London.

Kitschelt, H. (1986) 'Political opportunity structures and political protest: anti-nuclear movements in four democracies', *British Journal of Political Science*, Vol.16, pp.57-85.

Kitschelt, H. (1988) 'Left-libertarian Parties: Explaining Innovation in Competitive Party Systems', *World Politics*, Vol.40, pp.194-234.

Kitschelt, H. (1989) *The Logics of Party Formation: Ecological Parties in Belgium and West Germany*, Cornell University Press, Ithaca, NY.

Kitschelt, H. and Hellemans, S. (1990) *Beyond the European Left: Ideology and Political Action in the Belgian Ecology Parties*, Duke University Press, Durham, N.C.

Klandermans, B. (1988) 'The Formation and Mobilization of Consensus', in B.K. Klandermans, H. Kreisi, and S. Tarrow (eds) *From Structure to Action*, JAI Press Greenwich, pp. 173-96.

Klandermans, B. (1992) 'The Social Construction of Protest and Multiorganizational Fields' in A.D. Morris, and C.M. Mueller, (eds) *Frontiers in Social Movement Theory*, Yale UP, New Haven/ London, pp.77-103.

Klapp, O.E. (1969) *Collective Search for Identity*, Rinehart and Winston.

Knocke, D. (1988) 'Incentives in Collective Action Organizations', *American Sociological Review*, 1988, Vol.53, pp.311-329.

Knocke, D and Wisely, N. (1990) 'Social Movements', in D. Knocke (ed) *Political Networks*, Cambridge University Press, Cambridge, New York, pp.57-84.

Kornberg, A., Smith, S. and Clarke, H.D. (1979) *Citizen Politicians – Canada*, Carolina Academic Press, Durham, North Carolina.

Kornhauser, W. (1959) *The Politics of Mass Society*, Routledge, London.

Kreisi, H. (1995) 'The Political Opportunity Structure of New Social Movements', in J.C. Jenkins, and B. Klandermans (eds) *The Politics of Social Protest: Comparative Perspectives on States and Social Movements*, UCL Press, London, pp.167-198.

Labour Party (1997) *Because Britain Deserves Better*, General Election Manifesto, Labour Party, London.

Lawson, A. (1988) 'Mair Nor a Rouch Wind Blawin', in D. McCrone and A. Brown (eds) *The Scottish Government Yearbook 1988*, Unit for the Study of Government in Scotland, Edinburgh, pp. 36-45.

LeDuc, L., Niemi, R. G. and Norris, P. (1996) (eds) *Comparing Democracies: Elections and Voting in Global Perspective*, Sage, Thousand Oaks, California.

LeDuc, L., Niemi, R.. G. and Norris, P. (2002) (eds) *Comparing Democracies 2: New Challenges in the Study of Elections and Voting*, Sage, London.

Liberal Democrats (1991) *Policy and Information Briefings, October 1991*, Liberal Democrat Policy Unit, London.

Liberal Party (1979) *Liberal Party Manifesto* (Liberal Party).

Lipset, S.M. (1960) *Political Man: The Social Bases of Politics*, Doubleday, New York.

Lowe, P. and Goyder, S. (1983) *Environmental Groups in Politics,* Allen & Unwin, London.

Lynch, P. (1994) 'The 1994 European Elections in Scotland: Campaigns and Strategies', *Scottish Affairs*, no.9, pp.45-58.

Lynch, P. (1996) 'The Scottish Constitutional Convention 1992-5' *Scottish Affairs*, no.15, pp.1-16.

MacWhirter, I. (1990) 'After Doomsday. The Convention and Scotland's Constitutional Crisis', in A. Brown and R. Parry (eds) *The Scottish Government Yearbook 1990*, Unit for the Study of Government in Scotland, Edinburgh, pp.21-34.

MacWhirter, I. (1992) 'The Disaster that Never Was – The Failure of Scottish Opposition After the 1992 General Election', *Scottish Affairs*, no.1, pp.3-8.

MacWhirter, I. (2003) 'Who ate all the policies?' *Sunday Herald*, 13 April.

MacWhirter, I. (2004) 'Why It's Time for the Lib Dems to Break Free', *Sunday Herald*, 14 March.

Mair, P. (2001) 'The Green Challenge and Political Competition: How Typical is the German Experience?' *German Politics*, Vol.10, No.2, pp.99-134.

Maloney, W. (1999) 'Contracting Out the Participation Function: Social Capital and Checkbook Participation', in J.W. Van Deth, M. Maraffi, K. Newton, and P. Whiteley (eds) *Social Capital and European Democracy*, Routledge, London, pp.108-119.

Marquand, D. and Seldon, A. (1996) *The Ideas That Shaped Post-War Britain*, Fontana.

Marsh, D. (1976) 'On Joining Interest Groups: An Empirical Consideration of the Works of Mancur Olson' *British Journal of Political Science*, Vol.6, pp.257-271.

Marsh, D. and Rhodes, R. (1992) *Implementing Thatcherite Policies: Audit of an Era,* Open University Press.

Martin, S. (1988) 'Power Politics' in McCrone, D. and Brown, A. (eds) *The Scottish Government Yearbook 1988,* Unit for the Study of Government in Scotland, Edinburgh, pp. 200-215.

Maslow, A. (1954) *Motivations and Personality*, Harper and Row, New York.

May, J. D. (1973) 'Opinion Structure of Political Parties: The Special Law of Curvilinear Disparity', *Political Studies*, Vol. 21, pp.135-51.

McAdam, D. (1988) 'Micromobilisation contexts and recruitment to activism', *International Social Movement Research*, Vol. 1, pp. 125-154.

McAdam, D. (1996) 'Conceptual origins, current problems, future directions' in D. McAdam, J.D. McCarthy, and M.N. Zald (eds) *Comparative Perspectives on Social Movements: Political Opportunitites, Mobilizing Structures, and Cultural Framings*, Cambridge University Press, Cambridge, pp.23-40.

McAdam, D. (2003) 'Beyond Structural Analysis: Toward a More Dynamic Understanding of Social Movements' in M. Diani and D. McAdam (eds) *Social Movements and Networks: Relational Approaches to Collective Action*, Oxford University Press, New York, pp.281-298.

McAdam, D., McCarthy, J.D., and Zald, M.N. (1988) in N.J. Smelser, *Handbook of Sociology*, Sage, London, pp.695-739.

McAdam, D., McCarthy, J.D., and Zald, M.N. (1996) (eds) *Comparative Perspectives on Social Movements: Political Opportunities, Mobilizing Structures and Cultural Framing*, Cambridge University Press, Cambridge, New York.

McCabe, D. (1994) *Scottish Green Print*, June 1994.

McCarthy, J.D. and Zald, M.N. (1973) *The Trends of Social Movements in America: Professionalization and Resource Mobilization*, General Learning Press, Morristown, N.J.

McCarthy, J.D. and Zald, M.N. (1977) 'Resource Mobilization Theory and Social Movements: A Partial Theory', *American Journal of Sociology*, Vol.82, pp.1212-1241.

McCormick, J. (1991) *British Politics and the Environment*, Earthscan, London.

McCormick, J. and McDowell, E. (1999) 'Environmental Beliefs and Behaviour in Scotland', in E. McDowell and J. McCormick (eds) *Environment Scotland: Prospects for Sustainability,* Ashgate, Aldershot, pp.42-64.

McCrone, D. (1980) 'The Social Structure of Modern Scotland', in H. M. Drucker, and N. L. Drucker (eds) *The Scottish Government Yearbook 1981*, Paul Harris, Edinburgh, pp.39-59.

McCrone, D. (1989) 'Opinion Polls in Scotland: July 1987-September 1988', in Brown, A., and McCrone, D. (eds) *The Scottish Government Yearbook 1989*, Unit for the Study of Government in Scotland, Edinburgh, pp. 338-343.

McCrone, D. (1990) 'Opinion Polls in Scotland: August 1988-July 1989', in A. Brown and R. Parry (eds) *The Scottish Government Yearbook 1990*, Unit for the Study of Government in Scotland, Edinburgh, pp.281-286.

McCrone, D. (1992) *Understanding Scotland: The Sociology of a Stateless Nation,* Routledge, London.

McCulloch, A. (1988) 'Shades of Green: Ideas in the British Green Movement', *Teaching Politics*, Vol.17, pp. 186-207.

McCulloch, A. (1990) 'Joining a political party: a reassessment of the economic approach to membership', *British Journal of Sociology*, Vol. 41, no.4, pp.497-516.

McCulloch, A. (1992) 'The Green Party in England and Wales: Structure and Development. The Early Years', *Environmental Politics* Vol. 1, pp.417-435.

McCulloch, A. (1993) 'The Ecology Party in England and Wales: Branch Organisation and Activity', *Environmental Politics* Vol. 2, pp.20-39.

McDowell, E. (1993) 'Green Politics in Scotland: An Analysis of Historical and Contemporary Aspects of the Scottish Environmental Movement', Ph.D. thesis, University of Strathclyde.

McEwen, N. (2003) 'Is Devolution At Risk? Examining Attitudes Towards the Scottish Parliament in Light of the 2003 Election', *Scottish Affairs*, No.44, pp.54-73.

McKenzie, R. (1964) *British Political Parties*, Heinemann.

McKitterick, T. E. (1960) 'The Membership of the Party', *Political Quarterly*, Vol.31, pp.312-23.

Meadows, D., Meadows, D. and Randers, J. and Behrens III, W. (1972) *The Limits to Growth*, Pan, London.

Melucci, A. (1989) *Nomads of the Present*, Hutchison Radius, London.

Melucci, A. (1996) *Challenging Codes*, Cambridge University Press, Cambridge/New York.

Meyer, D. (1999) 'Tending the Vineyard: Cultivating Political Process Research', *Sociological Forum* Vol.14, no.1, pp.79-92.

Meyer, D. S. (2002) 'Opportunities and Identities: Bridge-Building in the Study of Social Movements', in D. S. Meyer, N. Whittier and B. Robnett *Social Movements: Identity, Culture, and the State*, Oxford University Press, New York, pp.3-21.

Meyer, D. S. and Tarrow, S. (1998) (eds) *The Social Movement Society: Contentious Politics for a New Century*, Rowman and Littlefield, Lanham, Maryland.

Meyer, D. S., Whittier, N., and Robnett, B. (2002) *Social Movements: Identity, Culture, and the State*, Oxford University Press, New York.

Michels, R. (1962) *Political Parties: A Sociological Study of the Oligarchical Tendencies of Modern Democracy,* Free Press, New York.

Milbrath, L. (1965) *Political Participation: How and Why Do People Get Involved in Politics*, Rand McNally, Chicago.

Miller, W., Timpson, A. M. and Lessnoff, M. (1996) *Political Culture in Contemporary Britain: People and Politicians, Principles and Practice*, Clarendon Press, Oxford.

Mills, C. Right (1940) 'Situated Actions and Vocabularies of Motive', *American Sociological Review*, Vol.5, pp.904-13.

Minkin, L. (1978) The Labour Party Conference, Allen Lane, London.

Mitchell, J. (1991) 'Constitutional Conventions and the Scottish National Movement: Origins, Agendas and Outcomes' *Strathclyde Papers in Government and Politics*, No.78, University of Strathclyde, Glasgow.

Mitchell, J. (1996) *Strategies for Self-Government: The Campaigns for a Scottish Parliament*, Polygon, Edinburgh.

Mitchell, R.C. (1979) 'National Environmental Lobbies and the Apparent Illogic of Collective Action', in Russell, C. (ed) *Collective Decision-Making*, John Hopkins UP, Baltimore.

Mitchell, R.C. (1980) 'How "soft", "deep", or "left"?: Present Constituencies in the Environmental Movement for Certain World Views', *Natural Resources Journal*, Vol.20, pp.345-58.

Moe, T. M. (1980a) 'A Calculus of Group Membership', *American Journal of Political Science*, Vol.24, No.4, November 1980, pp.593-632.

Moe, T. M. (1980b*) The Organisation of Interests: Incentives and the Internal Dynamics of Poiltical Interest Groups*, Chicago University Press, Chicago and London.

Moe, T. M. (1981) 'Toward a Broader View of Interest Groups', *Journal of Politics*, Vol.43, pp.531-543.

Müller-Rommell, F. (1982) 'Ecology Parties in Western Europe', *West European Politics*, Vol.5, pp.68-74.

Müller-Rommell, F. (1989) (ed.) *New Politics in Western Europe: The Rise and Success of New Parties and Alternative Lists*, Westview, Boulder.

Müller-Rommell, F. (1998) 'Explaining the Electoral Success of Green Parties: A Cross-National Analysis', *Environmental Politics*, Vol.7, No.4, pp.145-154.

Muller-Rommell, F. (2002) 'The Lifespan and the Political Performance of Green Parties in Western Europe', *Enironmental Politics*, Vol. 11, No.1, pp.1-16.

Müller-Rommell, F. and Poguntke, T. (1995) *New Politics*, Dartmouth, Aldershot.

Müller-Rommell, F. and Poguntke, T. (2002) (eds) *Green Parties in National Governments*, Frank Cass, London.

Norris, P. (1999) (ed.) *Critical Citizens: Global Support for Democratic Government*, Oxford University Press, Oxford.

Norris, P. (2002) *Democratic Phoenix: Reinventing Political Activism*, Cambridge University Press, Cambridge.

O'Connell, Sanjida (1997) 'That Caring Sharing Feeling', *The Guardian*, 12 August.

Offe, C (1985) 'New Social Movements: Changing Boundaries of the Political', *Social Research*, Vol.52, pp.817-868.

Office of National Statistics (1999), *Regional Trends 34*, The Stationery Office, London.

Olson, M. (1965) *The Logic of Collective Action: Public Goods and the Theory of Groups*, Harvard University Press, Cambridge, MA.

Olson, M. (1971) *The Logic of Collective Action: Public Goods and the Theory of Groups*, revised edition, Schocken Books, New York.

O'Neill, M. (1997) *Green Parties and Political Change in Contemporary Europe: New Politics, Old Predicaments*, Ashgate, Aldershot.

Opp, K. (1986) 'Soft incentives and collective action: participation in the anti-nuclear movement', *British Journal of Political Science*, Vol.16, pp.87-112.

Opp, K. (1988) 'Grievances and Participation in Social Movements', *American Sociological Review*, December 1988, Vol.53, pp.853-864.

Opp, K. (1989) *The Rationality of Political Protest*, Westview Press, Boulder, CO.

Panebianco, A. (1988) *Political Parties: Organisation and Power*, Cambridge University Press, Cambridge.

Parkin, F. (1968) *Middle Class Radicalism*, Manchester University Press, Manchester.

Parkin, S. (1989) *Green Parties: An International Guide*, Heretic Books, London.

Parry, G., Moyser, G. and Day, N. (1992) *Political Participation and Democracy in Britain*, Cambridge University Press, Cambridge.

Paterson, L., Brown, A., Curtice, J., Hinds, K,., McCrone, D., Park, A., Sproston, K. and Surridge, P. (2001) *New Scotland, New Politics*, Polygon, Edinburgh.

Pattie, C.J., Russell, A.T. and Johnston, R.J. (1991) 'Going Green in Britain? Votes for the Green Party and Attitudes to Green Issues in the Late 1980s', *Journal of Rural Studies*, Vol.7, No.3, pp.285-297.

Peat, J. and Boyle, S. (1999) 'Scotland in Overview', in Jamieson, B. (ed) *An Illustrated Guide to the Scottish Economy*, Duckworth, London, pp.8-37.

Piven, F. F. (1976) 'The Social Structuring of Political Protest', *Politics and Society*, Vol 6, part 3, pp.297-326.

Poguntke, T. (1990) 'Party activists versus voters: Are the German Green losing touch with the electorate?' in Rüdig, W. (ed) *Green Politics One*, Edinburgh University Press, Edinburgh, pp.29-46.

Poguntke, T. (1993) *Alternative Politics*, Edinburgh University Press, Edinburgh.

Porritt, J. (1984) *Seeing Green*, Basil Blackwell, Cambridge.

Porritt, J. and Winner, D. (1988) *The Coming of the Greens*, Fontana, London.

Prendiville, B. and Chafer, T. (1990) 'Activists and ideas in the Green Movement in France', in Rüdig, W. (ed.) *Green Politics One*, Edinburgh University Press, Edinburgh, pp.177-209.

Putnam, R. (1995) *Making Democracy Work*, Princeton University Press, Princeton, NJ.

Putnam, R. (2000) *Bowling Alone: The Collapse and Revival of American Community*, Simon and Schuster, New York.

Putnam, R. (2002) (ed.) *Democracies in Flux: The Evolution of Social Capital in Contemporary Societies*, Oxford University Press, New York.

Rawcliffe, P. (1998) *Environmental Pressure Groups in Transition*, Manchester University Press, Manchester.

Reif, K. (1984) 'National Electoral Cycles and European Elections 1979 and 1984', *Electoral Studies*, Vol.3, pp.244-255.

Richardson, D. and Rootes, C. (1995) (eds) *The Green Challenge: The Development of Green parties in Europe*, Routledge, London.

Richardson, J.J., Maloney, W.A., and Rüdig, W. (1992) 'The dynamics of policy change: Lobbying and water privatisation', *Public Administration*, Vol.70, pp.157-175.

Ridley, F. and Jordan, G. (1998) (eds) *Protest Politics: Cause Groups and Campaigns*, Oxford University Press, Oxford.

Rigby, A. (1974) *Alternative Realities: A Study of Communes and Their Members*, RKP.

Robinson, M. (1992) *The Greening of British Party Politics*, Manchester University Press, Manchester.

Rochon, T. R. (1988) *Culture Moves: Ideas, Activism, and Changing Values*, Princeton University Press, Princeton, New Jersey.

Rokkan, S. and Urwin, D. W. (1983) *Economy, Territory, Identity: Politics of West European Peripheries*, Sage, London.

Rokkan, S., Urwin, D., Aarebrot, F.H., Malaba, P. and Sande, T. (1987) *Centre-Periphery Structures in Europe*, Campus Verlag, Franfurt.

Rootes, C. A. (1991) 'Environmentalism and Political Competition: The British Greens in the 1989 Elections to the European Parliament', *Politics* Vol.11, no.2, pp.39-44.

Rootes, C. (1995a) 'Britain: Greens in a Cold Climate', in Richardson, D. and Rootes, C. (eds) *The Green Challenge: The Development of Green Parties in Europe*, Routledge, London, pp. 66-90.

Rootes, C. (1995b) 'Environmental consciousness, institutional stuctures and political competition in the formation and development of Green parties', in D. Richardson and C. Rootes, C. (eds) *The Green Challenge: The Development of Green Parties in Europe*, Routledge, London, pp. 232-252.

Rootes, C. (1997) Shaping collective action: structure, contingency and knowledge' in R. Edmondson (ed) (1997) *The Political Context of Collective Action: Power, Argumentation and Democracy*, Routledge, London and New York, pp.81-104.

Rosenstone, S.J. and Hansen, J.M. (1993) *Mobilization, Participation, and Democracy in America*, MacMillan, New York.

Rosie, M. and Bond, R. (2003) 'Identity Matters: The Personal and Political Significance of Feeling Scottish', in C. Bromley *et al.* (eds) *Devolution – Scottish Answers to Scottish Questions*? Edinburgh University Press, Edinburgh, pp.116-136.

Rothenberg, Lawrence S. (1988) 'Organizational Maintenance and the Retention Decision in Groups', *American Political Science Review*, Vol.82, No.4. pp.1129-52.

Rucht, D. and Neidhardt, F. (2002) 'Towards a Movement Society? On the Possibilities of Institutionalizing Social Movements', *Social Movement Studies*, Vol.1, No.1, pp7-30.

Rüdig, W. (1985) 'The Greens in Europe: Ecological Parties and the European Elections of 1984', *Parliamentary Affairs*, Vol.38, pp.56-72.

Rüdig, W. (1990a) *Anti-Nuclear Movements: A World Survey of Opposition to Nuclear Energy*, Longman, Harlow, Essex.

Rüdig, W. (1990b) 'Explaining Green Party Development: Reflections on a Theoretical Framework', *Strathclyde Papers on Government and Politics*, No.71, Department of Government, University of Strathclyde, Glasgow.

Rüdig, W. (1992) 'Comparing Green Parties', in W. Rüdig (ed.) *Green Politics Two*, Edinburgh University Press, Edinburgh, pp.185-198.

Rüdig, W. (1993) 'Wilted Greenery', *The Times Higher Education Supplement*, 17 September.

Rüdig, W. (1994) 'Between Moderation and Marginalisation: Environmental Radicalism in Britain' in B. Taylor (ed) *Ecological Resistance Movements: The Global Emergence of Radical and Popular Environmentalism*, State University of New York Press, Albany, N.Y.

Rüdig, W. (1995) 'Public Opinion and Global Warming' *Strathclyde Papers on Government and Politics*, No.101, Department of Government, University of Strathclyde, Glasgow.

Rüdig, W. (1996) 'Green Parties and the European Union', in J. Gaffney *Political Parties and the European Union*, Routledge, London.

Rüdig, W. (2002) 'Between Ecotopia and Disillusionment: Green Parties in European Government', *Environment*, Vol.44, No.3, April 2002, pp.20-33.

Rüdig, W., Bennie, L. and Franklin, M. (1991) *Green Party Members: A Profile*, Delta Publications, Glasgow.

Rüdig, W. and Franklin, M. (1992) 'Green Prospects: The Future of Green Parties in Britain, France and Germany' in Rüdig, W. (ed) *Green Politics Two*, Edinburgh University Press, Edinburgh, pp.37-58.

Rüdig, W., Franklin, M.N. and Bennie, L.G. (1993) 'Green Blues: The Rise and Decline of the British Green Party' *Strathclyde Papers on Government and Politics, No.95,* Department of Government, University of Strathclyde, Glasgow.

Rüdig, W., Franklin, M.N. and Bennie, L.G. (1996) 'Up and down with the Greens: Ecology and Politics in Britain, 1989-1992', *Electoral Studies,* Vol.15, No.1, pp. 1-20.

Rüdig, W. and Lowe, P. (1986) 'The withered "greening" of British politics: the case of the Ecology Party', *Political Studies,* Vol.34, pp.262-284.

Rüdig, W., Mitchell, J., Chapman, J. and Lowe, P. (1991) 'Social Movements and the Social Sciences in Britain', in Rucht, D. (ed) *Research on Social Movements* Westview Press, Bolder, Colerado.

Rule, J.B. (1988) *Theories of Civil Violence,* University of California Press, Berkely.

Runciman, W.G. (1966) *Relative Deprivation and Social Justice,* Routledge and Kegan Paul, London.

Sabatier, P. (1992) 'Interest Group Membership and Organization: Multiple Theories, in M. Petracca (ed.) *The Politics of Interests,* Westview Press, Boulder.

Salisbury, R.H. (1969) 'An Exchange Theory of Interest Groups', *Midwest Journal of Political Science,* Vol. 13, pp.1-32.

Sanders, D. (1995) 'Behavioural Analysis' in D. Marsh and G. Stoker, G. (eds) *Theory and Methods in Political Science,* MacMillan, London, pp.58-75.

Sartori, G. (1976) *Parties and Party Systems: A Framework for Analysis,* Cambridge University Press, Cambridge.

Saville, R. (1990) 'Power Politics: The Implications for Nuclear Policy and Electricity in Scotland 1973-89', in A. Brown and R. Parry (eds) *The Scottish Government Yearbook 1990,* Unit for the Study of Government in Scotland, Edinburgh, pp.243-266.

Scarrow, S. (1996) *Parties and their Members: Organizing for Victory in Britain and Germany,* Oxford University Press, Oxford.

Schlozman, K.L., Verba, S. and Brady, H.E. (1999) 'Civic Engagement and the Equality Problem' in T. Skocpol, T. and M.P. Fiorina (eds) *Civic Engagement in American Democracy,* Brookings/Russell Sage Foundation, Washington D.C. and New York, pp. 427-459.

Schumpeter, J. (1943) *Capitalism, Socialism and Democracy,* Allen and Unwin, London.

Scotland's Census 2001 http://www.gro-scotland.gov.uk.

*The Scotsman* 1 May 2003.

*The Scotsman* 5 May 2003.

*The Scotsman* 16 August 2002.

Scott, A. (1990) *Ideology and the New Social Movements,* Unwyn Hyman, London.

Scottish Conservative and Unionist Party (1997) *Fighting for Scotland,* General Election Manifesto, Scottish Conservative and Unionist Party, Edinburgh.

Scottish Conservative and Unionist Party (1999) *Scotland First,* Scottish Parliamentary Election Manifesto, Scottish Conservative and Unionist Party, Edinburgh.

Scottish Conservative and Unionist Party (2003) *Time To Do Something About It,* Scottish Parliamentary Election Manifesto, Scottish Conservative and Unionist Party, Edinburgh.

Scottish Green Party (1999) *Caring for Scotland,* Scottish Parliamentary Election Manifesto, Scottish Green Party, Edinburgh.

Scottish Green Party (2003) *Reach for the Future: 2nd Vote Green,* Scottish Parliamentary Election Manifesto, Scottish Green Party, Edinburgh.

Scottish Labour Party (1992) *It's Time to Get Scotland Moving Again,* General Election Manifesto, Scottish Labour Party, Glasgow.

Scottish Labour Party (1997) *New Labour Because Britain Deserves Better,* General Election Manifesto, Scottish Labour Party, Glasgow.

Scottish Labour Party (2003) *On Your Side*, Scottish Parliamentary Election Manifesto, Scottish Labour Party, Glasgow.

Scottish Liberal Democrats (2003) *Make the Difference*, Scottish Parliamentary Election Manifesto, Scottish Liberal Democrats, Edinburgh.

Scottish National Party (1997) *Yes We Can Win the Best for Scotland*, General Election Manifesto, SNP, Edinburgh.

Scottish National Party (2003) *The Case for a Better Scotland*, Scottish Parliamentary Election Manifesto Scottish National Party, Edinburgh.

Scottish Office (1990) *Scottish Abstract of Statistics* no. 19, Government Statistical Service, Edinburgh.

Scottish Office (1991) *Scottish Abstract of Statistics* no. 20, Government Statistical Service, Edinburgh.

Seyd, P. and Whiteley, P. (1992) *Labour's Grass Roots: The Politics of Party Membership*, Clarendon Press, Oxford.

Seyd, P. and Whiteley, P. (1995) 'Labour and Conservative Party Members: Change Over Time', *Parliamentary Affairs*, Vol.48, No. 3, pp. 456-71.

Seyd, P. and Whiteley, P. (1999) 'Liberal Democrats at the Grass Roots: Who Are They?', Paper presented at the annual conference of the Elections, Public Opinion, and Parties (EPOP) group, University College, Northampton.

Seyd, P. and Whiteley, P. (2002) *New Labour's Grassroots: The Transformation of the Labour Party Membership*, Palgrave MacMillan, Basingstoke.

Shaiko, R.G. (1999) *Voices and Echoes for the Environment: Public Interest Representation in the 1990s and Beyond*, Columbia University Press, New York.

Skocpol, T. and Fiorina, M.P. (1999) 'Making Sense of the Civic Engagement Debate' in T. Skocpol, and M. P. Fiorina (eds) *Civic Engagement in American Democracy*, Brookings/ Russell Sage Foundation, Washington D.C. and New York, pp. 1-23.

Smelser, N. J. (1962) *Theory of Collective Behaviour*, Routledge & Kegan Paul, London.

Snow, D.A., Zurcher, L.A., and Sheldon E. (1980) 'Social Networks and Social Movements', *American Sociological Review*, Vol.45, pp.787-801.

Starkey, P. (1997) 'Using Science' in M. Jacobs (ed) *Greening the Millennium? The New Politics of the Environment*, Blackwell, Oxford, pp.123-129.

Stern, P.C. and Dietz, T. (1994) 'The Value Basis of Environmental Concern', *Journal of Social Issues*, Vol.50, No.3, pp.65-84.

Stoker, G. (1995) 'Introduction' to D. Marsh, D. and G. Stoker (eds) *Theory and Methods in Political Science*, MacMillan, London, pp.1-18.

*The Sunday Herald* 4 May 2003.

*The Sunday Herald* 1 June 2003.

Surridge, P. (2003) 'A Classless Society? Social Attitudes and Social Class' in C. Bromley *et al.* (eds) *Devolution – Scottish Answers to Scottish Questions?* Edinburgh University Press, Edinburgh pp.137-160.

Talshir, G. (2002) *The Political Ideology of Green Parties*, Palgrave MacMillan, London.

Tarrow, S. (1989) *Democracy and Disorder: Protest and Politics in Italy 1965-1975*, Clarendon Press, Oxford.

Tarrow, S. (1992) 'Mentalities, Political Cultures and Collective Action Frames' in A.D. Morris, and C.M. Mueller (eds.) *Frontiers in Social Movement Theory*, Yale UP, New Haven/ London, pp.174-202.

Tarrow, S. (1994) *Power in Movement: Social Movements, Collective Action and Politics*, Cambridge University Press, Cambridge.

Tarrow, S. (1996) 'States and opportunities: The political structuring of social movements' in D. McAdam, J. D. McCarthy, and M.N Zald, (eds) *Comparative Perspectives on*

*Social Movements: Political Opportunitites, Mobilizing Structures, and Cultural Framings*, Cambridge, University Press, Cambridge, pp.41-61.

Taylor, B. (1999) *The Scottish Parliament*, Polygon, Edinburgh.

Taylor, B. (2002) *Scotland's Parliament: Triumph and Disaster*, Edinburgh University Press, Edinburgh.

Taylor, R. and Pritchard, C. (1980) *The Protest Makers*, Pergamon Press, Oxford.

Tocqueville, Alexis de (1988) *Democracy in America,* edited by J.P.Mayer, Harper Perennial.

Truman, D. B. (1951) *The Governmental Process*, Knopf, New York.

Turner, R.H. and Killian, L. (1972) *Collective Behaviour*, 2nd edition, Prentice Hall, Englewood Cliffs, N.J.

Van Dyke, V. (1995) *Ideology and Political Choice*, Chatham House, Chatham, N.J.

Verba, S. and Nie, N. (1972) *Participation in America: Political Democracy and Social Equality*, Harper and Row, New York.

Verba, S., Nie, N. and Kim, J.O. (1978) *Participation and Political Equality* Cambridge University Press, Cambridge.

Verba, S., Schlozman, K.L., and Brady, H. E. (1995) *Voice and Equality: Civic Voluntarism in American Politics*, Harvard University Press, Cambridge, Massachusetts and London, England.

Vig, N. and Kraft, M. (2002) (eds.) *Environmental Policy: New Directions for the 21$^{st}$ Century*, 5$^{th}$ edition, CQ Press, Washington DC, pp.79-101.

Walker, J. (1991) *Mobilising Interest Groups in America*, University of Michigan Press, Ann Arbor.

Wall, D. (2003) '30 Years of the Greens: A Brief History of the Green Party', *Green World*, Vol. 41, pp.32-33.

Walsh, E.J. (1981) 'Resource Mobilisation and Citizen Protest in Communities Around Three Mile Island', *Social Problems* Vol.29, pp.1-21.

Walsh, E.J. and Warland, R.H. (1983) 'Social Movement Involvement in the Wake of a Nuclear Accident: activists and free riders in the TNI area', *American Sociological Review*, Vol.48, pp.764-780.

Ward, H. (1995) 'Rational Choice Theory', in D. Marsh and G. Stoker (eds) *Theory and Methods in Political Science*, MacMillan, London, pp.76-93.

Webb, P. (1996) 'Are British Political Parties in decline?' *Party Politics*, Vol.2, pp.299-322.

Webb, P. (2000) *The Modern British Party System*, Sage, London.

Whiteley, P. (1981) 'Who are the Labour Activists?' *Political Quarterly*, Vol.52, pp.160-170.

Whiteley, P. F. (1995) 'Rational Choice and Political Participation, Evaluating the Debate', *Political Research Quarterly*, Vol.48, No.1, pp.211-233.

Whiteley, P. and Seyd, P. (1998a) 'New Labour - New Grass Roots Party?', Paper presented at the annual meeting of the Political Studies Association, University of Keele, April 1998.

Whiteley, P. and Seyd, P. (1998b) 'The Dynamics of Party Activism in Britain – A Spiral of Demobilisation?' *British Journal of Political Science*, Vol.28, No.1.

Whiteley, P. and Seyd, P. (2002) *High-Intensity Participation: The Dynamics of Party Activism in Britain*, University of Michigan Press, Ann Arbor.

Whiteley, P., Seyd. P. and Richardson, J. (1994) *True Blues: The Politics of Conservative Party Membership*, Clarendon Press, Oxford.

Whiteley, P, Seyd, P, Richardson, J. and Bissell, P. (1994) 'Explaining Party Activism: The Case of the British Conservative Party', *British Journal of Political Science*, Vol.24, pp.79-94.

Whittier, N. (2002) 'Meaning and Structure in Social Movements', in D. Meyer, N. Whittier, and B. Robnett (2002) *Social Movements: Identity, Culture, and the State*, Oxford University Press, New York, pp. 289-307.

Widfeldt, A. (1997) *Linking Parties with People? Party Membership in Sweden 1960-1994*, Gothenburg University Studies in Politics, No.46, Gothenberg.

Widfeldt, A. (1999) *Linking Parties with People? Party Membership in Sweden 1960-1997*, Ashgate, Aldershot.

Wilkinson, P. (1971) *Social Movements*, Pall Mall, London.

Wilkinson, D. and Waterton, J. (1991) 'Public Attitudes to the Environment in Scotland', *Central Research Unit Paper*, Scottish Office, Edinburgh.

Wilson, J.Q. (1995) *Political Organizations*, Princeton University Press, Princeton, New Jersey.

Witherspoon, S. (1994) 'The Greening of Britain: romance and rationality', in R. Jowell, J. Curtice, L. Brook, and D. Ahrendt, (eds) *British Social Attitudes: the 11th Report*, Dartmouth, Aldershot, pp.107-139.

Witherspoon, S. and Martin, J. (1993) 'What do we mean by green?', *British Social Attitudes, 7th Report*, Dartmouth, Aldershot.

Worcester, R. (1997) 'Public Opinion and the Environment', in M. Jacobs (ed) *Greening the Millennium? The New Politics of the Environment*, Blackwell, Oxford, pp.160-173.

Young, K. (1991) 'Shades of Green', in J. Roger B. Lindsay and T. Bridget (eds), *British Social Attitudes: the 8th Report*, Dartmouth, Aldershot, pp.107-129.

Young, S. (1993) *The Politics of the Environment*, Baseline Books, Manchester.

Young, S. (2000) 'New Labour and the Environment', in D. Coates and P. Lawler, *New Labour in Power*, Manchester University Press, Manchester.

Zirakzadeh, C.E. (1997) *Social Movements in Politics: A Comparative Study*, Addison Wesley Longman, Harlow, Essex.

# Index

Note: Page numbers in italics refer to tables and graphs; *n* in brackets indicates footnotes.